PRAISE FOR
ENHANCED PHYSICIAN E[...]

Enhanced Physician Engagement is the book I wish I had when I was a chief medical officer. It clearly identifies what physician engagement is and is not (it's not physician satisfaction), and it clearly outlines a framework for doing more than just getting through the complexity of physician culture and moving past ineffective but tightly held beliefs. Most important, it goes beyond theory, providing practical guidance for addressing the biggest challenges in physician engagement—burnout, electronic health records, supply chains, physician leadership pipelines, and more. Succinctly put, this book should be mandatory reading for every healthcare leader.

Halee Fischer-Wright, MD, FAAP, FACMPE
President and CEO
Medical Group Management Association

Carson Dye brings his decades of experience in working with physicians to address one of the new critical issues facing healthcare. He and his coauthors help us understand the complexity of physician engagement and offer new perspectives on how to address the challenges. As the role of the physician changes with rapid healthcare consolidation, advances in technology, and a post-pandemic environment, physician engagement should become a new vital sign in assessing the health of any patient care organization. Working effectively with physicians must be a core competency of every healthcare leader, and this book is an essential part of the tool kit.

The Honorable David Shulkin, MD
Ninth Secretary
US Department of Veterans Affairs

I highly recommend *Enhanced Physician Engagement* by Carson Dye and colleagues. It's an easy read and jam-packed with many applicable, proven tactics. And the eight-factor model of physician engagement is a great tool for healthcare leaders to have in their toolbox.

Michele K. Sutton, FACHE
President/CEO
North Oaks Health System

PRAISE FOR
ENHANCED PHYSICIAN ENGAGEMENT

In years past, tension commonly existed between hospital administrators and physicians. Different training, perspectives, and goals contributed to the misalignment, and we all could have done better. External forces are now pushing us together. Success in the future will require much-improved attitudes and relationships built on mutual respect between executives and physicians. The authors of this book are all experts in physician engagement, and their advice is valuable to any hospital executive or physician leader seeking to optimize their organization's performance in a radically changing paradigm.

Mark Laney, MD
President and CEO
Mosaic Life Care

As the healthcare landscape continues to rapidly evolve from a transactional fee-for-service world to a transformational value-based future, physician engagement is absolutely essential. If you are committed to meaningful and effective relationships with physicians to improve quality and your organization's bottom line, *Enhanced Physician Engagement* should be on your nightstand rather than your bookshelf. Read, study, and implement the sage advice from Carson Dye and physician leaders across the healthcare industry . . . and repeat!

Saria Saccocio, MD, FAAFP
Ambulatory Chief Medical Officer
Prisma Health

A thought-provoking book, and a must read! Finally, a practical and achievable approach to addressing physician engagement. Clearly one of this year's best books.

Rodney Stout, MD
Chief Medical Officer
Holzer Health System

Enhanced Physician Engagement

CARSON F. DYE, EDITOR

Enhanced Physician Engagement

VOLUME 1

What It Is,
Why You Need It,
and Where to Begin

ACHE Management Series

26   25   24   23   22   5   4   3   2

Library of Congress Cataloging-in-Publication Data
Names: Dye, Carson F., editor.
Title: Enhanced physician engagement / Carson F. Dye, editor.
Other titles: Management series (Ann Arbor, Mich.)
Description: Chicago, IL : Health Administration Press, [2022] | Series: HAP/ACHE
    management series | Includes bibliographical references and index. | Contents: v. 1.
    What it is, why you need it, and where to begin—v. 2. Tools and tactics for success. |
    Summary: "This book examines physician engagement as a strategic and tactical priority.
    Recognized physician leaders share personal views on what successful physician engagement is,
    approaches to developing strategy, and practical methods for addressing issues such as burnout,
    the burden of electronic health records, and accountability"—Provided by publisher.
Identifiers: LCCN 2021013743 (print) | LCCN 2021013744 (ebook) | ISBN 9781640552678
    (v. 1 ; paperback : alk. paper) | ISBN 9781640552722 (v. 2 ; paperback : alk. paper) |
    ISBN 9781640552647 (v. 1 ; epub) | ISBN 9781640552654 (v. 1 ; mobi) |
    ISBN 9781640552692 (v. 2 ; epub) | ISBN 9781640552708 (v. 2 ; mobi)
Subjects: MESH: Hospital-Physician Relations | Hospital Administration | Leadership
Classification: LCC RA971 (print) | LCC RA971 (ebook) | NLM WX 160 | DDC
    362.11068—dc23
LC record available at https://lccn.loc.gov/2021013743
LC ebook record available at https://lccn.loc.gov/2021013744

The paper used in this publication meets the minimum requirements of American National Standard for Information Sciences—Permanence of Paper for Printed Library Materials, ANSI Z39.48-1984.♾™

Acquisitions editor: Jennette McClain; Manuscript editor: Patricia Boyd; Project manager: Andrew Baumann; Cover design: James Slate; Layout: Integra

Found an error or a typo? We want to know! Please e-mail it to hapbooks@ache.org, mentioning the book's title and putting "Book Error" in the subject line.

For photocopying and copyright information, please contact Copyright Clearance Center at www.copyright.com or at (978) 750-8400.

Health Administration Press
A division of the Foundation of the American
    College of Healthcare Executives
300 S. Riverside Plaza, Suite 1900
Chicago, IL 60606-6698
(312) 424-2800

To my family, for whose support I am so grateful—C.F.D.

Contents

Foreword

OF THE SEVEN habits that Stephen R. Covey talks about in his book *The 7 Habits of Highly Effective People*, the fifth is "Seek first to understand, then to be understood."

I don't know that anyone chooses to attend medical school, do clinical rotations at multiple sites, work at the bottom of the totem pole with many different faculty and residents, go through subinternships, and graduate from medical school only to start all over again at the bottom, dragging oneself through a minimum of three years of residency (and sometimes as many as nine) without a mission in life to help one's fellow human beings. How could that be true? This is what we physicians set out to do—to improve the human condition by dedicating ourselves completely to learning and understanding the patient's every word, move, and gesture and then applying rigorous algorithms to reach the right diagnoses so that we can problem-solve and create lasting solutions to heal or alleviate our patients' pain and suffering.

If that is what physicians train to do, then why is every group, hospital, and health system breaking its back trying to figure out how to better communicate, understand, and engage with its physicians? Most days it feels like an enigma, an unsolvable mystery, a bridge too far. Some days the dialogue between administrators and their physician counterparts are signals lost in space, proverbial ships crossing in the night, or whatever other metaphor you can think of. As Covey said, "The biggest communication problem is we do not listen to understand. We listen to reply."

Over the past year, COVID-19 has confirmed what all the signals in healthcare have been pointing to for a very long time—that without an engaged and aligned workforce, and an engaged physician group in particular, there is no way we can be successful, irrespective of the current state of healthcare or its transformation to a value-based model. In fact, the need for physician leadership, alignment, engagement, and integration is greater than ever. From thinking "They are employed, so they are aligned" to "Why can't they just understand?" to "All they want is to make more money" to "They don't care about the patients, it's all about them"—we have heard it all.

Carson Dye is a brilliant leader, a consummate educator, and a master at talent acquisition and development. He is someone I have had the distinct pleasure of knowing personally and professionally for more than 20 years. I have seen him completely immerse himself in bringing leaders together, creating opportunities to learn from and with them, and developing them to be more effective at what they do. He has a passion for engaging physicians, aligning them, and developing them to lead organizations. The difference between Carson and others who try to do what he does is that he has spent hours upon hours walking with leaders to learn by being curious; watching them do their work; being there in the room; having crucial conversations; and creating transparency, clarity, and a higher level of trust. Even though he is not a physician, he gets it.

In this book, Carson and his star lineup of contributing authors have done an incredible job with a very important and complex subject. With ease and fluidity, they approach physician engagement from many different perspectives not only to define what it is but also how to understand it, know it, and address it each and every day to create a high-performing team and organization.

As a physician CEO who has spent a lifetime taking care of patients in one-on-one interactions as a clinician and the past three decades in leadership roles, I know that this is a topic each and every one in healthcare—physician leader or not—must know about, think about, and do something about to create a high-value offering in their respective community.

I highly recommend this book, as well as Carson's other titles, to be a part of your leadership library so that you can be enlightened and transformed in your head, heart, and hands to accomplish what we all set out to achieve as leaders in the first place.

Congratulations, Carson and team, for the collective wisdom shared.

Imran A. Andrabi, MD, FAAFP
President and CEO
ThedaCare

Preface

Historically, the focus has always been less on physician engagement and more on physician satisfaction. Giving physicians what they wanted—such as access to the operating room and a supportive nursing staff—is what drove good business. Now, however, there is an opportunity through physician engagement—whether with employed or independent physicians—to improve patient access, customer service, quality and costs.
—Stephen Moore, MD, Chief Medical Officer, St. Luke's Health CHI, "Bridging the Divide," 2020

ENGAGING AN ORGANIZATION'S physicians is truly a critical challenge. When I began to discuss the idea for this book, I was struck by how many healthcare leaders indicated that physician engagement was a priority for them and their organizations. They offered several views of both the challenges and the rewards of furthering physician engagement.

"IT'S THE KEY TO OUR FUTURE"

Most of the leaders I spoke with admitted that they were not doing so well with either physician engagement or developing physician leaders. One healthcare leader told me, "Any suggestions you could give me would be worth their weight in gold." One physician leader remarked, "Everyone looks to me to manage this [physician engagement], and I keep telling them it is a job for all of us. We all have to work on it." Several leaders said they were at the point that almost any new idea would be helpful. One CEO simply said, "It's the key to our future. We must get this right."

Conclusion: Physician engagement is key to our future.

"IT'S A HOT TOPIC!"

Physician engagement has become a great concern in healthcare. Some writers and speakers have combined this issue with physician burnout, whereas some healthcare executives see engagement as key to managing the changes in payment mechanisms and enhancing quality of care. Other observers believe that engaged physicians are a critical first step toward true population health. Sadly, some people in the healthcare field see engagement simply as a way to control physicians. And some consulting firms have jumped on the physician-engagement bandwagon, conducting surveys to help organizations measure and improve this feature of physician life.

The topic appears in many published surveys of critical issues facing the healthcare industry. A 2019 American College of Healthcare Executives (ACHE) survey listed physician engagement (which the report called "physician–hospital relations") as one of the top issues faced by healthcare leaders (ACHE 2019). Other issues in the ACHE survey intersect with physician engagement in many ways, especially as it relates to financial challenges, access to care, and patient safety and quality.

Even before the COVID-19 pandemic of 2020, the anticipated changes for healthcare organizations in the few years thereafter were expected to be the most significant ever experienced. The worldwide pandemic has guaranteed that those changes will be massive. As cost and quality pressures continue and as society demands different responses from the healthcare system, many experts predict foundational changes to the healthcare industry. Moreover, much like the introduction of Medicare and Medicaid, these transformations will be profound and will last for decades. To thrive in the next generation, world healthcare organizations will clearly require high levels of physician engagement.

Conclusion: Physician engagement strategies and tactics are needed more than ever.

"IT IS A KEY DRIVER IN HEALTHCARE"

With some hesitation, this book also raises what may be one of the significant leadership challenges in physician engagement. Many leaders in healthcare are seemingly afraid of, resentful of, and unaccepting of physicians. As one CEO told me, "You can't live with them, but you can't live without them." Another leader remarked, "Physicians just don't get it! They are just not team players." And Bradley Knight (2019) wrote, "The differences in perceptions and cultures between doctors and hospital administrators are huge, and represent major obstacles to improving physician engagement."

Others view physicians as merely widget makers—people who only produce revenue or RVUs (relative value units). One CEO said to me, "They are really just factory workers—just high-priced ones!" Controversial as it may seem, some healthcare leaders are just not comfortable with physicians.

However, I hope that readers will sincerely seek approaches for increased collaboration with physicians. They can be a great help to all of us as we try to remake the field and enhance care, improve quality, and control costs.

Conclusion: Physicians are not an alien species; they can be great collaborators.

"PHYSICIAN ENGAGEMENT IS A COMPLEX MATTER"

The challenge of increasing physician engagement and decreasing the conflict between administration and clinical sides of healthcare is far more complex than most assume it to be. If organizations expect to successfully deal with pandemic preparation, accountable care organizations, population health management, bundled payment programs, value-based purchasing, cost containment, improved quality and safety, care management, Medicare management, and other complex challenges, physicians must be engaged and involved. Their deep engagement is no longer a luxury. Now is the time to focus on this issue.

Conclusion: Physician engagement is not tied to an on-off switch; it is a multifaceted, intricate subject.

WHY THIS BOOK?

Physician engagement is hard to define, and the literature on the topic is short on details. Despite a good deal written about it, no universal agreement exists on its definition. With this book, the other contributors and I hope to rectify this ambiguity about physician engagement and address other challenges to healthcare leaders' views of this aspect of healthcare.

The upcoming changes in healthcare will be profound. The COVID-19 pandemic will certainly drive many of these changes, but so too will economic and other escalating challenges.

First, the field needs a better definition of engagement. I hope that a focused definition and broader understanding of physician engagement will enhance the readers' ability to make meaningful and long-lasting changes in their organizations. Currently, there are multiple definitions and complicating aspects of physician engagement. The contributors and I hope that this book can be a clarifying beacon that will benefit the field.

Second, we also want to provide innovative ideas to enhance engagement. Without the involvement of physicians, the changes coming to healthcare will fail to achieve all that is needed to improve the industry. We hope that, much like the 1999 report by the US Institute of Medicine, *To Err Is Human* (Kohn, Corrigan, and Donaldson 2000), this book can be a rallying cry and a focal point for the field as we enlist the support and enthusiasm of our physician cadre to face the changes ahead.

Third, the book aims to help its readers see individual physicians as just that—individual physicians. We also try to attack and dispel the stereotype that all physicians are alike. This pigeonholing can be harmful in many ways, and a deeper understanding of engagement will help address this inaccuracy.

Finally, we would like this book to start a dialogue in the field—a dialogue centered on a healthy respect for what physicians provide to the healthcare industry and one that does not view physician engagement as "herding cats," a phrase that is, frankly, inaccurate at best and offensive at worst. Physician engagement is not one or more actions that force physicians to change their behavior. Nor is it an action that aligns financial incentives or an attempt to create a regimented, marching group of doctors. For too long, too many healthcare leaders have tried to manipulate and control physician behavior in a somewhat autocratic manner. Many leaders simply do not view physicians as engaged individuals, thinking instead that physicians have to be cajoled and otherwise encouraged to behave certain ways to support healthcare organizations. To the contrary, I believe that the vast majority of physicians are highly engaged individuals. While many may not be engaged in the broad strategic aims of healthcare organizations, they are deeply engaged in patient care. We must move away from the forced behavior that we have seen imposed on physicians in all too many healthcare organizations.

Roy Smythe, MD, said it well in "Stop Trying to Change Physician Behavior": "Proving to them [physicians] that new behavior will allow them to deliver better patient care, and accomplish more of their original goals of 'helping people'—as trite as this sounds—can be powerful in this era of 8 minute primary care visits" (Smythe 2017).

MULTIPLE VOICES OF PHYSICIANS

It is the clear intent of this book to present the voices of several kinds of physicians. Although I am not a physician, great effort was made to enlist the support, viewpoints, and counsel of experienced and knowledgeable physicians. I entered into a great deal of back-and-forth with each chapter author. The process was not as simple as "Send me your chapter, and I will include it." Instead, there was much collaboration between and among the various authors and me. Ultimately this teamwork led to a more robust presentation of different ideas and viewpoints. While there are no major conflicts in the book, there are different points of view and different approaches to issues. Physician engagement is a complex topic; as more viewpoints are given, the counsel should be broader, deeper, and more textured.

As you read, think and reflect on the material to build your own sense of the issues. Be open-minded as you reflect on questions such as these:

- Exactly what is physician engagement? Is there a common definition?
- What does successful physician engagement look like? What are the elements of physician engagement?
- How can physician engagement be measured? Are the measurements valid, reliable, and pertinent?
- What does increased physicians' presence in governance, leadership, and management positions do for engagement levels?
- Is there a difference between input and involvement?
- What role does physician engagement play in quality, costs, value creation, and a unified culture?
- To what extent does economics play a role in physician engagement?

Readers may also consider the companion volume of this book, *Enhanced Physician Engagement*, Volume 2, *Tools and Tactics for Success*. The second volume demonstrates various models and strategies to promote and sustain enhanced physician engagement. The foundational concepts in this volume 1 are seamlessly applied in the practical strategies found in volume 2.

Carson F. Dye

REFERENCES

American College of Healthcare Executives (ACHE). 2019. "Top Issues Confronting Hospitals in 2019." Accessed May 20, 2020. www.ache.org/learning-center/research/about-the-field/top-issues-confronting-hospitals/top-issues-confronting-hospitals-in-2019.

Knight, B. P. 2019. "Differences in Perceptions and Cultures Between Doctors and Hospital Administrators Undermine Physician Engagement." *EP Lab Digest*. Published November 2. www.eplabdigest.com/differences-perceptions-and-cultures-between-doctors-and-hospital-administrators-undermine-physician-engagement.

Kohn, L. T., J. M. Corrigan, and M. S. Donaldson (eds.). 2000. *To Err Is Human: Building a Safer Health System*. Washington, DC: National Academies Press.

Moore, S. 2020. "Bridging the Divide: How the Level of Physician Engagement Can Make or Break Your Hospital." *Becker's Hospital Review*. Published May 20. www.beckershospitalreview.com/hospital-physician-relationships/bridging-the-divide-how-the-level-of-physician-engagement-can-make-or-break-your-hospital.html.

Smythe, R. 2017. "Stop Trying to Change Physician Behavior." *Pulse* (LinkedIn blog). Published January 18. www.linkedin.com/pulse/stop-trying-change-physician-behavior-roy-smythe-m-d-.

Acknowledgments

WORKING IN A LARGE academic medical center, one of the best children's hospitals in the world, and two outstanding Catholic hospitals, combined with more than 20 years of consulting and executive search work, has given me a rich and diverse set of experiences. My career has encompassed a myriad of adventures in all types of healthcare organizations, working with many talented leaders—including many physicians and physician leaders. Over the years, I have conducted numerous physician leadership searches and have had the chance to get to know countless physician leaders in great depth. I have facilitated several affinity groups of physician leaders and have met with them twice yearly to listen to their challenges, solutions, and innovative ideas. Acknowledging everyone here would not be possible because of the many pages that would be required. However, several individuals deserve special recognition.

Exposure to highly effective leaders over the years has taught me much—and I am thinking especially of Sister Mary George Boklage, Dr. John Byrnes, Michael Covert, Dr. Kathleen Forbes, Mark Hannahan, Dr. Scott Ransom, and Dr. Lonnie Wright. Others with whom I have worked and gleaned great insights include Dr. Imran Andrabi, Dr. John Baniewicz, Dr. Gary Chmielewski, Dr. Michael Choo, Dr. Bob Coates, Dr. Dave Drinkwater, Dr. David James, Dr. Dave Kapaska, Dr. Walter Kerschl, Dr. Mark Laney, Dr. Steve Markovich, Dr. Terry McWilliams, Gene Miyamoto, Dr. Marci Moore-Connelley, the late Dr. Mark Peters, Dr. Ed Pike, Bill Sanger, Randy Schimmoeller, Dr. Herb Schumm, Dr. Sergio Segarra,

Dr. David Shulkin, Kam Sigafoos, Dr. Doug Spotts, Dr. Rodney Stout, Dr. David Tam, Dr. Davin Turner, Dr. Tom Whalen, and Dr. Raúl Zambrano.

Special thanks goes to my friend and coauthor, Dr. Jacque Sokolov, who always has unique and cogent insights into physician leadership and engagement. Our work together on the book *Developing Physician Leaders for Successful Clinical Integration*, published by Health Administration Press in 2013, was insightful and opened many doors for me in my work.

Why am I so focused on *physician* engagement? There are multiple reasons, but a couple stand out. From my very first day at Clermont Mercy Hospital, Sister Mary George Boklage instilled in me a respect for physicians, a deep understanding of what they do and how they fit into the healthcare world. She also helped me gain leadership credibility among physicians early in my career. Even though I was the hospital's chief human resources officer, she expected me to be actively involved in all types of physician matters, and that was instructive. Most important, physicians were never greedy people or mere RVU producers to Sister Mary George. She definitely never saw them as cats to herd. She saw them as partners, collaborators, allies, and coworkers in patient care.

My following years at Cincinnati Children's Hospital and The Ohio State University Wexner Medical Center took me into the core of medical education. Not only was I fortunate to have a front-row seat, but I also often found myself "inside the ring." My experiences in these two great institutions gave me incredible street cred with physicians. I found myself providing informal counsel in all sorts of physician matters to chairs, division chiefs, and other physician leaders. It was also instructive to see and appreciate how these physician-led organizations excelled.

At the close of my hospital career at St. Vincent Mercy Medical Center, I was exposed to expert physicians and several consummate physician leaders. As I began my consulting career, I found myself getting more and more involved in various physician leadership matters. Circling back to the question posed earlier—why am I so focused on *physician* engagement?—I think the answer is clear: I have worked in organizations where physicians were highly engaged and passionate about their craft. I have seen the positives that occur in quality, cost management, organizational pride, and esprit de corps when organizations have strong physician engagement.

My consulting and executive search career continues to keep me deeply involved in physician leadership and physician engagement. Over the course of many searches for chief medical officers, chief quality officers, chief medical information officers, and other types of physician leader positions, I have learned firsthand how highly effective physician leaders drive robust physician engagement. And helping to establish many physician leadership academies over the years has given me invaluable access to cadres of highly engaged physicians in all types of healthcare organizations.

My appreciation for my coauthors in this endeavor is significant. They responded to my call for input and shared my passion for the need for enhanced physician engagement. They are Dr. Jeremy Blanchard, system chief medical officer at North Mississippi Health Services; Dr. Lisa M. Casey, director of the family medicine residency program at Mercy Health–St. Rita's Medical Center; Dr. Robert Dean, senior vice president of performance management at Vizient; Dr. Kathleen L. Forbes, academic group executive vice president at Methodist Le Bonheur Healthcare; Dr. Andrew N. Garman, professor in the Department of Health Systems Management and director of the Rush Center for Health System Leadership at Rush University; Dr. Katherine A. Meese, assistant professor of health services administration at the University of Alabama at Birmingham (UAB) and director of wellness research at UAB Medicine; Dr. Harjot Singh, speaker/trainer/coach; Dr. Douglas A. Spotts, vice president and chief health officer at Meritus Health; Kalen Stanton, managing director for health transformation at Root Inc.; and Dr. Raúl Zambrano, FACHE, senior consultant for The Greeley Company. You will hear their voices, opinions, suggestions, and counsel in this book. They know our field well, they understand physicians, and they have a keen knowledge of physician engagement.

Several others have helped so much and merit recognition. The staff at Health Administration Press (HAP) are at the top of that list. We are so fortunate to have this publisher in our field. They stay on top of our issues and concerns and are rigorous in their endeavors. They offer wonderful and innovative textbooks for those who are advancing in their educational preparation. Michael Cunningham leads HAP and has some great teammates including Andrew Baumann, Jennette McClain, and Nancy Vitucci, among others. Jennette was a steady presence as I tried to recruit and direct multiple authors. Prior to this book, I always wrote solo or was paired with a single coauthor. Having multiple authors with different viewpoints and different styles was challenging, and Jennette assisted me tremendously. Finally, I have saved mention of Editor Patty Boyd to the end—and she deserves the capital *E*. She did more than just edit; she partnered, she added great thoughts, and she made sure the book has both melody and harmony (multiple authors = multiple singers).

I close with mention and recognition of those nearest to me. Over many years, my wife Joaquina has been a helpful friend and companion, and always a kind critic. Her support has allowed me to excel in many ways. The rest of my family is just as special: daughters Carly, Emily, Liesl, and Blakely; sons-in-law Jeremy, Phil, and Nick; grandsons Carson, Benjamin, and Andrew; and granddaughter Celine have all tolerated my frequent absences as I traveled for work and spent lots of time at the computer. This book would not have been possible without their support.

Carson F. Dye

Introduction

Carson F. Dye

I would ask all readers to briefly ponder their answers to the following questions before digging into this book:

- Has the pace of change ever been any faster in healthcare?
- Are the changes ahead seemingly more complex than ever before?
- Has COVID-19 created a demand for an entire reboot of the healthcare system?
- Is uncertainty at a fever pitch?
- Are concerns over physician issues getting more significant and difficult to manage?
- Is physician engagement easy and feasible, or does it seem to be a unicorn?
- Are physicians a critical component of the changes we have to make in our systems of care?
- Do we need more physician leadership?

Many of the serious issues that healthcare is facing require the involvement of all stakeholders in the system. Physicians, as major players in their organizations, must play a major part. For this reason, I and the other contributors to this book see physician engagement and physician leadership as a critical part of improving healthcare.

The following observations about physicians and their engagement—or lack thereof—in their healthcare organizations exemplify why we wrote this book:

- Many physicians have felt completely deserted during the COVID-19 pandemic. Physician salaries have been turned upside down, many primary care offices have been shuttered, numerous physicians have had to work far outside their specialty, and many caregivers died from COVID-19.

- Fifty-one percent of physicians report that they are burned out (Peckham 2017).

- Increasing numbers of healthcare leaders state that physician engagement is one of their top concerns.

- Many organizations have spent millions of dollars on major electronic health record (EHR) projects, and many report financial losses as a result. Will the investments provide a reasonable return? Are these EHR systems creating major roadblocks to physician engagement?

- The American Medical Association has demanded changes to EHR systems. The editor of *Healthcare IT News* describes the problem: "Primary care physicians spend more than half of their workday typing data on a computer screen and completing other EHR tasks" (Monegain 2017).

- Medical errors are the third leading cause of death in the United States (Sternberg 2016).

- Politicians continue to tamper, alter, or otherwise meddle with healthcare and health insurance programs, and the divisions among the elected officials on issues of healthcare remain extremely wide. And after the coronavirus pandemic, politicians will undoubtedly be involved in major ways with the healthcare system.

- Reported physician shortages are widespread (AAMC 2020; Poché and Dayaratna 2017).

Several principles regarding physician engagement have guided our thoughts, suggestions, and counsel in both volumes of this book. I will summarize them here.

STRONG PHYSICIAN ENGAGEMENT IS NO LONGER A LUXURY

Making physician engagement a top strategic and tactical priority is simply mandatory if organizations expect to have success now and in the future. With such complex challenges as the redesign of much of the healthcare industry because of the pandemic, physician shortages, the needs of a large and rapidly aging population, population health management, new and different kinds of payment programs, value-based purchasing, cost containment, quality and safety concerns, care management, and Medicare penalties, physician engagement must be a top-level focus for all organizations.

AS HEALTHCARE ORGANIZATIONS GROW LARGER, CONSOLIDATION IS INEVITABLE

In the future, healthcare organizations will continue to consolidate. Large systems will get even larger, and smaller entities, even those who remain fiercely independent, will join larger systems. In my experience and from my research, engagement seems more difficult to achieve in larger organizations. People do not feel as connected to the missions and visions of larger organizations. Some of the drivers of high levels of engagement include *line of sight*, or the ability of individuals to see how their personal efforts are tied to the overall mission, vision, and outcomes of the organization. Moreover, a body of significant research in the area of personal control theory suggests that individuals are most highly engaged when they have more control over decision-making and how they do their work. But the days of the small hospital, the local community pharmacy, and the intimate one- and two-person physician practices are disappearing. The larger, consolidated organizations face greater challenges to physician engagement. Simply stated, engagement is easier to develop, extend, and sustain in smaller work settings.

PHYSICIANS ARE ALREADY HIGHLY ENGAGED INDIVIDUALS

Most physicians are indeed already highly engaged. In fact, they are arguably among the most engaged workers in our society. Yet their interests and concerns may not correspond with those of the leaders of healthcare organizations. Physicians may not have the same focus that a larger healthcare organization does as it modifies its mission and vision and adapts to different business models, payment schemes, and societal demands on the system. How does physicians' focus differ? Physicians are *highly engaged in patient care activities*. They are dedicated to patient quality and safety and typically develop caring relationships with their patients. In this respect, physicians are truly engaged. While they may have frustrations about how healthcare has changed, they still feel energized and rewarded by the activities of patient care. Physicians also spend most of their time serving in smaller work settings (physician practices or local clinics), in contrast to the behemoth health systems described earlier.

PHYSICIAN ENGAGEMENT IS COMPLICATED

Physician engagement is far more intricate than most assume it to be. While many consulting firms have provided definitions and measures of physician engagement, they are often different and can at times be contradictory. Perreira and colleagues (2019) suggest that the "concept is still poorly understood and measured and that this conceptual 'fuzziness' likely contributes to the lack of evidence in this area, making comparisons across settings challenging." Frankly, my preparations for the development of this book have taught me that the issue is far from straightforward. But leaders should not abandon efforts to improve physician engagement just because there are no cut-and-dried solutions.

ENGAGEMENT IS NOT SYNONYMOUS WITH ALIGNMENT

Unfortunately, engagement has gotten a bad name with many physicians because numerous healthcare executives have equated engagement with alignment and, in some cases, the willingness to "get in line and follow orders." Many interpret engagement as economically tying behavior to financial rewards (the carrot and the stick). As mentioned earlier, much discussion about physician engagement rests on the perception that physicians are not engaged—but this perception is about their engagement in organizational strategies and not their concern with patient care.

THERE STILL EXISTS A PHYSICIAN MYSTIQUE

The physician mystique, or the viewpoint that physicians should not be challenged and are almost infallible, cannot be overstated. Many leaders in healthcare are seemingly afraid of, envious of, or unaccepting of physicians. Many are not comfortable around physicians. Sadly, some readers are only hoping to find suggestions on how to minimize the physician mystique and learn how to "herd these cats." But this is not what physician engagement is all about. Readers who sincerely seek approaches to increase collaboration are on the right track. While the position that physicians hold in society may not be a critical issue, the lines of reasoning around it can be helpful nonetheless.

PHYSICIAN LEADERSHIP IS A KEY COMPONENT OF ENGAGEMENT

For all physicians to be engaged, organizations must have more of them in leadership roles. The increased presence of physician leaders in all levels of the organization is a critical part of engaging all physicians. An organization can take several steps to ensure that physician leaders are involved in key decisions. For example, it can seat physicians in governance, leadership, and management positions. From the boardroom and C-suite to the middle-management hallways, quality, the optimization of value, cost reduction, and enhanced performance will all be tied to the presence of physicians in many leadership roles. Dye and Sokolov (2013) described this approach as having physicians constantly at the table rather than occasionally asking them for input.

PHYSICIANS ARE NOT ALL CUT OUT OF THE SAME CLOTH

There are great differences among physicians; a single descriptor cannot simply portray all these experts. Physicians come from many generations, and someone's age can affect the person's worldview, professional approach, and many other individual characteristics. Different specialties have differing viewpoints. Obviously, the location of the workplace (e.g., hospital-based versus community office practice) creates variations as well. Because of all these differences, attempts to improve engagement can be all the more complicated.

STRONG PHYSICIAN ENGAGEMENT IS POSSIBLE

Strong physician engagement in a healthcare organization is not a unicorn. By their nature, physicians are highly intelligent. If given the chance and if given some voice, physicians can be more highly engaged than many other individuals can be.

TOLERATING A CONCLUSION IS NOT THE SAME AS EMBRACING IT

Finally, the thought leaders at Root, a strategic consulting firm, clearly articulate one of my foundational beliefs about true engagement: "History shows that people will tolerate the conclusions of their leaders, but they will ultimately act on their own" (McNulty 2018). This concept applies to physician engagement as well. Physicians will tolerate the pronouncements and conclusions of health system executives but then return to their clinical work areas and operate on their own assumptions and conclusions. It is not enough to assume that physicians agree with leadership; healthcare leaders need to see that engagement has a psychological component and that physicians must feel emotionally connected to whatever goals the organization wishes to pursue. Ideally, ultimate engagement means that physicians will freely and enthusiastically come to the same conclusions as those of organizational healthcare leaders.

A Side Note

Although this book is concerned with physician engagement, the value and great benefits that other clinicians bring to the healthcare enterprise are earnestly and sincerely recognized. All of us who contributed to the book highly value the contributions of nurses, nurse practitioners, pharmacists, physician assistants, imaging technicians, medical technologists, physical and occupational therapists, and many other clinical staff who care admirably for our nation's population.

(continued)

(continued from previous page)

There are clearly issues of engagement for these healthcare professionals as well. Moreover, we do not wish to minimize the importance of having all who serve in healthcare highly engaged. But this book focuses on physicians. It is physicians who serve most often as the connecting links in healthcare activities. It is physicians who drive a great deal of the costs, the plans of care, the quality, and the ultimate outcomes in the system. Physicians *must* play significant roles in helping redesign our healthcare system after COVID-19. Having physicians—all physicians—highly engaged will greatly benefit those we healthcare leaders serve. As I will explain later in the book, I also believe that elements of physician engagement are different from engagement with others. But suffice it to say, this book acknowledges, respects, and honors *all* those who care and serve patients. No slight or disrespect is intended.

OVERVIEW OF CHAPTERS

This book is organized in a simple and logical way. The first chapters focus on a critical element: *defining* engagement and physician engagement. In chapter 1, I examine the concept of employee engagement, which has received much more evidence-based research than has physician engagement. An overview of the research in employee engagement in this chapter helps lay the foundation for how it applies to physicians. In chapter 2, I examine some of the academic articles (albeit few) written on physician engagement and the views of the major consulting firms that do substantive work on this issue. In chapter 3, I use models to highlight various perspectives of physician engagement and to help readers more precisely define it.

The models also provide a framework for developing strategies and tactics to improve engagement.

Many of the remaining chapters, most of them written by physicians, contain concrete suggestions on how to enhance physician engagement. One of the more important ways to achieve this goal is to understand physicians themselves. In chapter 4, Douglas A. Spotts, MD, provides a psychological view of physicians, presents some of the stereotypes about them, and shows why these stereotypes may be misleading. A subtitle of this chapter, which is about understanding an organization's physicians, might be "And Really Liking Them." For healthcare leadership to truly engage physicians, all leaders and managers must truly enjoy working with them.

Lisa M. Casey, DO, argues in chapter 5 that to enhance physician engagement, organizational leaders need to move more physicians front and center in their organizations. Physicians should also be given more authority and higher levels of involvement (thus a "bigger paddle"). In some respects, this chapter forms a centrum for the holistic idea of physician engagement.

In chapter 6, I contend that all physicians are leaders, no matter their specialty, age, or position in an organization. This chapter deals with the pure definitions of management and leadership. Some physicians can engage comfortably in these activities; others cannot. The chapter examines this phenomenon and suggests approaches to deal with it.

Chapter 7, by Kalen Stanton, explores visualization techniques that have radically helped get individuals involved in change and in organizational vision and mission. In chapter 8, Harjot Singh, MD, introduces the concept of flow and how it can greatly increase physician engagement. He explains why engagement is so vital to a healthy sense of existence.

In chapter 9, I address one of the most challenging and sometimes divisive questions about physician engagement. For many in the field, the simple answer to physician engagement is an economic one. Give them money, and they will be engaged. This chapter briefly presents some of the academic research viewpoints contrary to that viewpoint and suggests that money is not always a prime motivator for physicians.

In chapter 10, Jeremy Blanchard, MD, provides conceptual and practical insight into conflict. He explains that conflict should not necessarily be avoided, and he discusses its impact on physician engagement. Chapter 11, by Kathleen Forbes, MD, examines the sensitive issue of gender in healthcare. With the majority of the healthcare workforce being female and the greatly increasing numbers of women who are physicians, Dr. Forbes looks at ways to better engage women physicians, to the women's and the organizations' advantage. In chapter 12, Raúl Zambrano, MD, confronts many of the tougher issues facing healthcare regarding diversity, inclusion, and equity. Contemporary concerns about racism and diversity cannot be ignored when considering physician engagement.

In chapter 13, Katherine A. Meese, PhD, and Andrew N. Garman, PsyD, address several contemporary approaches to caring for physicians organizationally. They show how organizations can better engage physicians by helping them flourish.

Finally, in chapter 14, Robert Dean, DO, addresses the age-old issue of the conflicts and sometimes open warfare between hospital (healthcare) administration and physicians. Dr. Dean lays out the various issues and suggests how to minimize the disputes. Physician burnout, an increasing topic of concern, is closely related to physician engagement. It does seem somewhat logical that if physicians were highly engaged, they would likely be less burned out.

We hope that readers will finish this book with a deeper understanding of both the complexities and the subtleties of physician engagement. Perhaps the book is best described as an endeavor to answer this key question: What does successful physician engagement look like? There are many answers to this question, and this book provides a guide map.

Volume 2 of this book, *Enhanced Physician Engagement: Tools and Tactics for Success*, delves into specific techniques that can be used to enhance physician engagement. Readers may want to explore the second volume after reading the first.

REFERENCES

Association of American Medical Colleges (AAMC). 2020. *The Complexities of Physician Supply and Demand: Projections from 2018 to 2033.* Washington, DC: HIS Markit Ltd.

Dye, C. F., and J. J. Sokolov. 2013. *Developing Physician Leaders for Successful Clinical Integration.* Chicago: Health Administration Press.

McNulty, N. 2018. "When Self-Discovery Leads to Lasting Health Behavior Change." Root Inc. Published May 23. www.rootinc.com/blog/when-self-discovery-leads-to-lasting-health-behavior-change.

Monegain, B. 2017. "AMA Demands EHR Overhaul, Calls Them 'Poorly Designed and Implemented.'" *Healthcare IT.* Published September 12. www.healthcareitnews.com/news/ama-demands-ehr-overhaul-calls-them-poorly-designed-and-implemented.

Peckham, C. 2017. "Medscape Lifestyle Report 2017: Race and Ethnicity, Bias and Burnout." *Medscape.* Published January 11. www.medscape.com/features/slideshow/lifestyle/2017/overview#page=2.

Perreira, T. A., L. Perrier, M. Prokopy, L. Neves-Mera, and D. D. Persaud. 2019. "Physician Engagement: A Concept Analysis." *Journal of Healthcare Leadership* 11: 101–13.

Poché, N., and K. Dayaratna. 2017. "How to Address the Looming Crisis of Physician Shortages." *Daily Signal*. Published April 21. www.dailysignal.com/2017/04/21/how-to-address-the-looming-crisis-of-physician-shortages.

Sternberg, S. 2016. "Medical Errors Are Third Leading Cause of Death in the U.S." *U.S. News & World Report*. Published May 3. www.usnews.com/news/articles/2016-05-03/medical-errors-are-third-leading-cause-of-death-in-the-us.

CHAPTER 1

Employee Engagement: Precursor to Physician Engagement

Carson F. Dye

WHERE DOES ONE begin when writing a book on physician engagement? As many writers do, whether they are in school or at work, before tackling a topic, they seek out a definition of the matter being considered. Thus this chapter reviews the various definitions and conceptual approaches to engagement.

The majority of the academic literature about engagement applies to employee engagement. Discussions of this topic began to surface in the early 1990s. The term *employee engagement* was likely coined by William A. Kahn, of Boston University. Kahn (1990) believes that "people can use varying degrees of their selves, physically, cognitively, and emotionally, in work role performances." This concept has been applied in academic studies of organizational behavior, leadership, human resources management, and industrial/organizational psychology. Additionally, the vast majority of healthcare organizations have regularly been conducting employee engagement surveys for the past two decades.

Because much less has been written about physician engagement, we begin this book with a review of employee engagement. However, physician engagement has significant differences from employee engagement. Even if physicians are employed by a corporate entity (hospitals, health systems, other corporations), the nature of their education and training, the work they do, and their professional autonomy makes them exceedingly different from all other employees. Like it or not, the captain-of-the-ship sensibility among physicians seldom applies to other employees. This attitude particularly holds in clinical decision-making and usually carries over to any other aspect of physician interactions. Despite these differences, though, many concepts around employee engagement provide useful insight.

AMBIGUITY ABOUT THE CONCEPT OF EMPLOYEE ENGAGEMENT

The literature on employee engagement offers many definitions of, and much discussion about, the term. Fried and Fottler (2015) suggest that engagement is a "measure of employees' positive or negative emotional attachment to the job, which influences their willingness to learn and perform at work." According to Kruse (2012a), "engagement is the emotional commitment the employee has to the organization and its goals." And Eldor and Vigoda-Gadot (2016) suggest that "employee engagement represents a work-related state of mind characterized by feelings of vigor, fulfillment, enthusiasm, absorption and dedication."

Many of the definitions emanate from consulting firms rather than academic research. Consider these comments about employee engagement:

- Engagement is "those who are involved in, enthusiastic about and committed to their work and workplace" (Gallup 2017).
- "Conducting an employee survey is only the beginning of an effective change process" (DecisionWise 2020).
- "Korn Ferry research shows that companies with high levels of both engagement and enablement have up to

4.5 times more revenue growth than those with low levels" (Korn Ferry 2020).

- "The bottom line is that leadership creates engagement, higher employee engagement equals better organizational performance, and lower employee engagement equals worse organizational performance" (Chamorro-Premuzic 2015).

Despite the many definitions, descriptions, and explanations of employee engagement, there seems to be no consensus. Markos and Sridevi (2010) write, "To date, there is no single and generally accepted definition for the term employee engagement." Truss et al. (2013) concur: "Engagement has emerged as a contested construct, whose meaning is susceptible to 'fixing, shrinking, stretching and bending.'" Another viewpoint comes from Dominika Cechova at PeopleGoal, Inc. She suggests, "Employee engagement definition has been addressed by the business leaders as well as scholars for years. Yet, it remains challenging to find a unified definition for this unique concept" (Cechova 2019).

Where does the vague definition of engagement leave us? It likely means that we must be cautious about any absolute pronouncements about employee engagement. There is clearly much subjectivity to the concept. While the idea of employees being enthused about, inspired by, and animated in their work and their organizations is a great one, wise leaders must recognize the lack of conclusive objectivity about engagement. Definitions vary, and surveys often evaluate engagement concepts that lack hard-core evidence. Engagement is not a science. This same caution applies to physician engagement.

THE LITERATURE ON EMPLOYEE ENGAGEMENT

A brief review of the history of employee engagement in both the academic and the popular literature is useful. As mentioned earlier, Kahn (1990) probably coined the term *employee engagement*, explaining that engagement has three dimensions. The first, *meaningfulness*, pertains to the extent to which employees feel worthwhile and valued. The second, *safety*, concerns employees' belief that their work environment is secure and predictable and that they understand the behavioral implications of their actions. The third, *availability*, relates to employees' feelings of capableness at their jobs. Although it was written around three decades ago, Kahn's article still has great relevance today. Shuck and Wollard (2010) also provide another excellent review of the literature. They examine the growth of the concept in both academic and business publications.

In the 1990s, the concept of employee engagement began to surface in business and industry. Gallup gained much attention in the consulting domain of employee engagement surveys, largely building on Marcus Buckingham and Curt Coffman's *First, Break All the Rules* (Buckingham and Coffman 1999). Before the late 1990s, most organizations conducted employee *satisfaction* surveys, not *engagement* surveys. Engagement was simply not a word used often in human resources circles. Only in the past 20 to 25 years have satisfaction surveys been replaced with engagement surveys. This change reflected the thinking that engagement represents a far more sophisticated and broader construct and measurement. Initially, only consulting firms were promulgating the measurement of employee engagement rather than employee satisfaction (certainly, consultants would benefit from a more progressive form of employee survey). And because engagement was a more expansive concept, there was the opportunity for additional consulting work other than simply conducting surveys.

Kahn (1990) describes engagement as the "expression of a person's 'preferred self' in task behaviors that promote connections to work and to others, personal presence (physical, cognitive, and emotional), and active, full role performances." Much of his viewpoint supports the idea that engagement is driven in great part by a person's freedom of choice—choice in what work to do and how that work is done.

As discussed, Gallup popularized the idea of employee engagement around the turn of the new century. The company's Q12 survey provides "the 12 questions that measure the most important elements of employee engagement" (Gallup 2020b). Many organizations of all types and industries flocked to survey their employee populations along these lines. Gallup has amassed large amounts of data on engagement, using its employee-engagement approach. According to its website (Gallup 2020a), "The Q12 was then—and continues to be—the most powerful tool for measuring and managing employees' enthusiasm and commitment to their jobs."

Despite these examples, there is still scarce academic literature on employee engagement. Moreover, the field still lacks a well-accepted—and research-supported—construct and definition of the concept. As Macey and Schneider (2008) point out, "the meaning of the employee engagement concept is unclear." Luthans and Peterson (2002) write that "many complex questions remain" about employee engagement. And Shuck and Wollard (2009) note that the "historical perspective of employee engagement has uncovered areas of inconsistent definitions and interpretations."

A Google search of "employee engagement" returns 423 million results. A narrower search for the "elements of engagement" provides these insights:

- Engagement comprises eight elements: leadership, communication, culture, rewards and recognition, professional and personal growth, accountability and performance, vision and values, and corporate social responsibility (Turley 2015).

- To enhance employee engagement, several undertakings work well: eliminating negative components of the work environment, meaningful work, using employee strengths, and building relationships (Hogg 2013).

- At its heart, engagement is about people—understanding, motivating, and connecting with them. That makes engagement a complex topic. The deeper you go, the more confusing it can seem. Creating an effective engagement strategy sometimes feels like an impossible task (Kelly 2016).

- Four things are important to employee engagement: commitment, motivation, loyalty, and trust. Their level determines the quality of engagement of an employee (Juneja 2020).

THREE PARTS OF EMPLOYEE ENGAGEMENT

Despite the lack of robust academic literature and much disagreement on the definition of employee engagement, the concepts do provide much to consider from a leadership and organizational management perspective. And healthcare organizations clearly need engagement, among both their employees and their physicians.

Most studies of employee engagement discuss three primary contributors (see exhibit 1.1):

- **The work they do:** This part of engagement should not be surprising, because so many people do seek employment in work that they like to do. In the healthcare field, many individuals seek out the chance to have meaningful work that serves and cares for others.

- **The mission of the organization for which they work:** Again, healthcare is a field with a mission that many can strongly relate to and support. Many healthcare workers describe what they do as a "calling," or a compelling undertaking. A large part of engagement means that employees come to work and give their best every day because they are highly committed to what their organization is doing.

- **The rewards for their efforts:** Employees do what they do in some respect because of what they feel they receive in return for this effort (personal pride, pay, recognition, satisfaction, camaraderie with others).

Exhibit 1.1 Three Factors of Employee Engagement

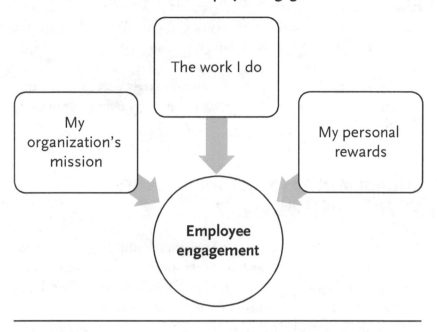

THE EMERGING SCIENCE OF ENGAGEMENT THROUGH VISUALIZATION AND STORYTELLING

Emerging research on employee engagement involves having employees develop a vision of their organization and how their work relates to this vision. Usually called *visualization*, the approach addresses employees' need to see the big picture. Sinar (2016) explains visualization: "Just describing a direction in words is no longer enough; leaders must convert words into visual concepts to make their messages understandable and evocative, and to make them stick." In a similar vein, Chambers (2013) says that storytelling can do the same thing: "The human mind processes information faster and better when in it is in the form of something memorable and cohesive, like a story." Zhang (2018) says that "an image can help people see what other people mean. A visual facilitator can help clarify thoughts and empower holistic thinking. As an illustration morphs and new iterations come to life, people align their points of view to create a common mental model that everyone can own. Art can help people prepare for and adopt a new strategy, initiative, or change. And it's magical."

Visualization is such an important and rarely covered topic that it merits its own chapter. Chapter 7 discusses visualization in more depth.

ENGAGEMENT: MORE THAN HAPPINESS OR SATISFACTION

Employees can be happy but not engaged, and they can sometimes be engaged but not happy. Happiness is also somewhat unidimensional—it pertains more to how an individual feels. Happiness can be affected by many more factors than just those in the workplace. Seligman (2011) says that happiness has three elements: "positive emotion, engagement, and meaning." Engagement drives happiness. Kevin Kruse, author of *Employee Engagement 2.0*, writes that "research is overwhelming that we need to be engaged at work in order to be happy in all areas of our life" (Kruse 2012b).

In similar fashion, this is one reason that employee engagement surveys have replaced employee satisfaction surveys. Satisfaction relates more to individual happiness, while engagement is a more expansive model. And the factors that contribute to engagement may differ from the contributors to satisfaction.

CONCLUSION

This chapter has revealed many points of view but no definitive conclusions. But as Brenner (2013) aptly puts it, engagement is a nebulous concept. Obviously, it's difficult—if not impossible—to improve something when that something is not clearly defined.

While this chapter made no conclusions about engagement, it did show that the concept is extremely multidimensional. Engagement encompasses individual motivation, organizational and departmental cultures, leadership practices, and social camaraderie. In describing motivation, Pink (2009) suggests that it is composed of autonomy, mastery, and purpose. This description of motivation also captures the gist of engagement. Akay (2015) describes Pink's concept as "a new approach to motivation which is based on self-determination. According to it, people have an innate drive to be autonomous, self-determined and connected to one another." Akay's observation too includes some elements of engagement.

Learning various techniques to engage employees is a lifelong journey; no single destination is ever the final goal. Considering the complexity of engagement, we should not distill it into a single definition or a simple model. Rather, we need to aggregate many of the various concepts to gain a broader and deeper understanding of engagement.

With this background behind us, we now consider the issue of physician engagement in earnest. As Obbard (2019) writes, "Physician engagement is a strategy that focuses on building strong relationships and aligning physicians with the values, vision and mission of healthcare administrators. Engaged physicians take greater care of their patients, reduce medical costs and are more efficient than their unengaged counterparts."

REFERENCES

Akay, E. 2015. "Intrinsic Motivation and More." *Learning Is Fun Every Day* (blog). Published January 16. https://esinakay.wordpress.com/tag/daniel-pinks-theory.

Brenner, M. 2013. "What Is Engagement?" *Association for Talent Development* (blog). Published January 7. www.td.org/insights/what-is-engagement.

Buckingham, M., and C. Coffman. 1999. *First, Break All the Rules: What the World's Greatest Managers Do Differently*. New York: Simon & Schuster.

Cechova, D. 2019. "Employee Engagement: The 2020 Definition." PeopleGoal. Published November 13. www.peoplegoal.com/blog/employee-engagement-definition.

Chambers, A. 2013. "Imagery, Cartoons, Visuals and the Story of Your Company." Root Inc. Published January 31. www.rootinc.com/blog/imagery-cartoons-and-visuals-and-the-story-of-your-company.

Chamorro-Premuzic, T. 2015. "The Engagement Epidemic: Why It Begins and Ends with Leadership." *HR Examiner*. Published September 10. www.hrexaminer.com/the-engagement-epidemic-why-it-begins-and-ends-with-leadership.

DecisionWise. 2020. "Employee Engagement Summit." Accessed May 27. https://decision-wise.com/employee-engagement-survey-consulting.

Eldor, L., and E. Vigoda-Gadot. 2016. "The Nature of Employee Engagement: Rethinking the Employee–Organization Relationship." *International Journal of Human Resource Management* 28 (3): 526–52.

Fried, B., and M. Fottler. 2015. *Human Resources in Healthcare: Managing for Success*, 4th ed. Chicago: Health Administration Press, 108–9.

Gallup. 2020a. "Q12 Employee Engagement Center." Accessed December 10. www.gallup.com/products/170969/q12-employee-engagement-center.aspx.

———. 2020b. "Get the No. 1 Employee Engagement Survey and All the Strategic Advice That Goes with It." Accessed November 22. https://q12.gallup.com/public/en-us/Features.

————. 2017. "Gallup Daily: U.S. Employee Engagement." Published July 31. www.gallup.com/poll/180404/gallup-daily-employee-engagement.aspx.

Hogg, B. 2013. "Core Elements of Employee Engagement." Bill Hogg & Associates. Accessed December 4, 2020. www.billhogg.ca/wp-content/uploads/2013/04/Article-CoreElementsofEmployeeEngagement.pdf.

Juneja, P. 2020. "Elements of Employee Engagement." Management Study Guide. Accessed December 4. www.managementstudyguide.com/employee-engagement-elements.htm.

Kahn, W. A. 1990. "Psychological Conditions of Personal Engagement and Disengagement at Work." *Academy of Management Journal* 33 (4): 692–724.

Kelly, S. 2016. "The 9 Pillars of Employee Engagement." Glassdoor for Employers. Accessed December 8, 2020. www.glassdoor.com/employers/blog/9-pillars-employee-engagement.

Korn Ferry. 2020. "Employee Engagement." Accessed December 4. www.kornferry.com/solutions/organizational-strategy/employee-engagement.

Kruse, K. 2012a. "The Difference Between Happiness and Engagement at Work." *Forbes*. Published December 21. www.forbes.com/sites/kevinkruse/2012/12/21/happy-at-work/.

————. 2012b. *Employee Engagement 2.0: How to Motivate Your Team for High Performance*, 2nd ed. Richboro, PA: Kruse Group.

Luthans, F., and S. J. Peterson. 2002. "Employee Engagement and Manager Self-Efficacy." *Journal of Management Development* 21 (5): 376–87.

Macey, W. H., and B. Schneider. 2008. "The Meaning of Employee Engagement." *Industrial and Organizational Psychology* 1 (1): 3–30.

Markos, S., and M. S. Sridevi. 2010. "Employee Engagement: The Key to Improving Performance." *International Journal of Business and Management* 5 (12): 89–96.

Obbard, A. 2019. "Why Is Physician Engagement Important?" *The Exponent* (Marketware blog). Published February 7. www.marketware.com/why-is-physician-engagement-important.

Pink, D. H. 2009. *Drive: The Surprising Truth About What Motivates Us*. New York: Riverhead Books.

Seligman, M. 2011. "The Original Theory: Authentic Happiness." Authentic Happiness, University of Pennsylvania. Published April. www.authentichappiness.sas.upenn.edu/learn/wellbeing.

Shuck, M. B., and K. K. Wollard. 2010. "Employee Engagement and HRD: A Seminal Review of the Foundations." *Human Resource Development Review* 9 (1): 89–110.

———. 2009. "A Historical Perspective of Employee Engagement: An Emerging Definition." In *Proceedings of the Eighth Annual College of Education & GSN Research Conference*, edited by M. S. Plakhotnik, S. M. Nielsen, and D. M. Pane, 133–39. Miami, FL: Florida International University. Accessed December 9, 2020. https://digitalcommons.fiu.edu/cgi/viewcontent.cgi?article=1160&context=sferc.

Sinar, E. 2016. "To Become a More Visionary Leader, Become Stronger at Visualization." *Medium* (blog). Published May 29. https://medium.com/@EvanSinar/to-become-a-more-visionary-leader-become-stronger-at-visualization-4c629e133eb1.

Truss, C., A. Shantz, E. Soane, K. Alfes, and R. Delbridge. 2013. "Employee Engagement, Organisational Performance and Individual Well-Being: Exploring the Evidence, Developing the Theory." *International Journal of Human Resource Management* 24 (14): 2657–69.

Turley, C. 2015. "The 8 Elements of Employee Engagement." *Engage* (Achievers blog). Published September 10. https://blog.achievers.com/2015/09/8-elements-employee-engagement.

Zhang, V. 2018. "The Power of Visualization." Root Inc. Published February 5. www.rootinc.com/blog/the-power-of-visualization.

CHAPTER 2

Literature on Physician Engagement

Carson F. Dye

*Enhancing physician engagement requires a multistep process
that includes making an effort to better understand their world;
encouraging opportunities for input and participation in care
redesign; providing education, training, guidance, and support; and
making the effort to recognize and thank them for what they do.*
—Alan H. Rosenstein, "Strategies to Enhance
Physician Engagement," 2015

READERS EAGER FOR a more definitive discussion of employee engagement than was presented in chapter 1 may find similar frustration with physician engagement. The literature on physician engagement has recently grown, but much like the concept of employee engagement, there is little agreement on the details of the topic. Definitions vary, and vary greatly. In some respects, there is more disagreement on what constitutes physician engagement than on what constitutes employee engagement.

This chapter will examine physician engagement from two perspectives:

- Literature that meets one or more of the following criteria: it is peer-reviewed, it lacks commercial intent, or it is unrelated to selling consulting services or surveys

- Information provided from leading consulting firms and advisory firms

OVERVIEWS IN THE LITERATURE

We first focus on literature that is not commercial. Some articles have been published in refereed professional journals, while some material appears in other noncommercial publications. And as mentioned in chapter 1, there is more literature on employee engagement than on physician engagement.

Probably one of the more complete reviews of physician engagement done without any commercial aim is *A Roadmap for Trust: Enhancing Physician Engagement* (Kaissi 2012). This 38-page report, funded by Practitioner Staff Affairs of the Regina Qu'Appelle Health Region in Saskatchewan, Canada, is comprehensive and as relevant today as it was when written in 2012. Although written much from the perspective of Canada, this comprehensive review of physician engagement has major application in all physician settings.

Another report by the same sponsor is *Anchoring Physician Engagement in Vision and Values: Principles and Framework* (Dickson 2012). Both these reports offer more in-depth discussion on physician engagement. The remainder of this section samples various viewpoints on physician engagement from the literature.

TRADITIONAL VIEWS OF PHYSICIAN ENGAGEMENT

Lee and Cosgrove (2014) probably best characterize the longtime perspective of physician engagement: "Traditionally, hospitals have defined physician engagement as the extent to which doctors saw their future as intertwined with that of the larger organization. Hospitals wanted physicians to be loyal—that is, to refer most or all of their patients to them, thereby increasing revenue." Much healthcare activity focuses on maintaining strong relationships between hospitals and physicians. The word *loyalty* is frequently used by healthcare leaders who are describing their physician ranks.

Many discussions of physician engagement simply apply an economic viewpoint. Walsh, Ettinger, and Klugman (2009) explain that the "lack of physician engagement is due, in part, to competing demands and absence of compensation for participation in quality improvement work." Much of the literature between 2005 and 2010 uses the phrase *physician alignment* and seems to equate alignment and engagement. Unfortunately, *alignment* is still often used as a synonym for *engagement*.

This book strongly proposes that alignment and engagement are different things. Alignment generally relates to some type of economic control done either though an employment relationship with physicians or through a gain-sharing provision for independent physicians. Alignment always involves a carrot-and-stick feature; physicians have to do something to earn something, usually a financial reward. Mertz (2014) describes the relationship between alignment and engagement: "Since the care decisions made by physicians related to hospital-based care influence institutional operating costs, maybe these two concerns are really just one: how to engage physicians in addressing hospital issues." He continues: "My experience is that alignment discussions are initiated by hospitals. They develop the model, perhaps with the help of that consulting company, and present it to physicians, occasionally, as a take-it-or-else option." We must, however, view physician engagement more broadly than just as an economic quid pro quo.

Some people believe that there has always been some type of physician engagement and that the emphasis is exacerbated by cost pressures in healthcare and the increase in organizational complexity. One CEO remarked that physician engagement was not a hot issue until the advent of the electronic health record. This CEO believed that physician engagement simply related to communications with the medical staff and attending to their needs and wants. Although the term *physician engagement* may not have been used in the past, there have been decades of concern about keeping physicians happy.

THE MANY VIEWS OF PHYSICIAN ENGAGEMENT

If you the readers were asked to define physician engagement, your answers would probably vary greatly. When I asked a group of healthcare executives this question, the answers were wide-ranging:

- "It's what we do administratively to keep our physicians focused on our business."
- "It's the quid pro quo of relationships in the practice of medicine."
- "It is the work we do as leaders to get all our physicians on the same page."
- "It can be economic for some and touchy-feely for others, but it involves meeting the needs and wants of our doctors."
- "It is making sure that they bring their patients to us and not to our competitor."
- "It is setting clear expectations (for both sides) from the start and ensuring that roadblocks are removed and bureaucracy is simplified."
- "It is simply one thing—trust."

As these answers suggest, there is simply no clear agreement on what physician engagement is. It is most often in the eye of the beholder. Consider the following observations about physician engagement:

- "This concept is still poorly understood and measured. This conceptual 'fuzziness' likely contributes to the lack of evidence in this area, making comparisons across settings challenging" (Perreira et al. 2019).
- "Engagement as a term is used a lot. But what does it really mean to physicians? Lacking specificity around this— and solid metrics—it's nearly impossible for health care

organizations to achieve an increase in engagement with their physician population" (Whitlock and Stark 2014).

- "Physician engagement is not merely a matter of engaging individuals, but of engaging members of a group, who are likely to be highly identified with their profession, attached to its defining attributes and norms, and motivated to protect its power and status" (Kreindler et al. 2012).

- "There is no single path to physician engagement; planning the way forward requires a careful mapping of the social identity landscape" (Kreindler et al. 2014).

- "Due to the wide use of the term, it remains a quite nebulous concept resulting in little consensus on appropriate measurement and minimal empirical evidence demonstrating the association between the engagement of physicians and improved outcomes" (Perreira et al. 2019).

Physicians' Personal Benefit

Physicians themselves truly want to feel engaged. The passion and other feelings that helped them get through medical school and training do not disappear once a person is in practice. In fact, for many younger physicians, engagement is direct and relevant; the first several years of a person's clinical practice are often stimulating and rewarding. One newer physician expressed this satisfaction: "Finally, I had my own practice!" Whitlock and Stark (2014) write that "feeling engaged is a prime driver of physicians' satisfaction and dissatisfaction with their jobs. When physicians feel a lack of engagement—or are outright disengaged—it manifests itself in various ways, from feelings of hopelessness, anger or cynicism to, ultimately, leaving or wanting to leave their jobs." Physicians—or anyone else, for that matter—gain more satisfaction out of their work and life if they feel engaged.

Organizational Benefit

Rarely does any discussion of healthcare fail to mention physician engagement. Articles abound on the need for strong physician engagement to move to different reimbursement models as the industry tries to move away from pay for performance. The importance of physician engagement in enhancing healthcare quality and addressing cost and organizational performance inefficiencies is obvious. Snell, Briscoe, and Dickson (2011) say that "transforming complex health systems will require the engagement of physicians as leaders in their health care settings, in both formal and informal roles." The Advisory Board (2021) reports that "physician engagement has taken on new urgency. The industry is pushing hospitals to double down on quality and efficiency—and executives can't do it alone."

Physician engagement can be a critical driver of patient safety and the quality of care. Byrnes (2015) makes this observation: "I'm not sure why, but whatever the reason, physician engagement is critical to your success as a quality leader. Your ability to partner with your colleagues in a collaborative, collegial, respectful and honest way spells the difference between creating great quality programs or mediocre ones."

Strong physician engagement takes on increasing importance as the healthcare industry faces significant changes in response to the COVID-19 pandemic. For example, Ninivaggi (2020) writes, "COVID-19 is a disease calling for renewed physician engagement. The engaged physician has a dedicated commitment to studying, enhancing expertise, and applying skills toward safe, high-quality patient care."

Multiple Approaches to Engagement

The complexity of physician engagement means that there are many angles and approaches to engagement. For example, Kaissi (2014) explains that "physician engagement can be conceptualized as an ongoing two-way social process in which both the individual and organizational/cultural components are considered." Rosenstein (2015) also describes the multiple factors involved: "Strategies for engagement may vary in accordance with years in practice, specialty, and current models of practice (e.g., solo, group, foundation, salaried, boutique, locum)." Sears (2011) concurs: "There is no 'one-size-fits-all' approach to physician engagement. Each organization has unique operational and political issues as well as varying levels of communication between the members of its medical staff and its administrators."

Perreira et al. (2019) summarizes the many aspects of physician engagement this way: "'Physician engagement' is regular participation of physicians in (1) deciding how their work is done, (2) making suggestions for improvement, (3) goal setting, (4) planning, and (5) monitoring of their performance in activities targeted at the micro (patient), meso (organization), and/or macro (health system) levels."

Problems Caused by Physician Disengagement

If the need for enhanced physician engagement is not acknowledged, the healthcare system can suffer. Showalter and Williams (2017) describe the financial challenges, the quality and safety concerns, population health issues, physician shortages, and the need for more efficient healthcare systems. They explain that "simply changing the system around physicians will not deliver the results we need to face these challenges. Physicians must be essential participants in changing the system to improve outcomes."

Gunderman (2016) underscores this argument: "Low levels of engagement are associated with higher physician turnover, increased error rates, poorer rates of patient cooperation in treatment, and lower levels of patient satisfaction."

Burnout is an issue that merits its own chapter, but mention of its relationship to physician engagement is appropriate here. Shanafelt and Noseworthy (2017) discuss the manifold problems associated with burnout: "Engagement is the positive antithesis of burnout and is characterized by vigor, dedication, and absorption in work. There is a strong business case for organizations to invest in efforts to reduce physician burnout and promote engagement. Physician burnout has been shown to influence quality of care, patient safety, physician turnover, and patient satisfaction." And Cardarelli et al. (2019) write simply that "staff and provider engagement leads to better quality and experience of care and less turnover and burnout."

Physician Engagement Versus Physician Control

Sadly, an often-held view of physician engagement has caused much administrator–physician conflict. In this view, physician engagement means control. The unfortunate expression *herding cats* is frequently used disparagingly to describe attempts to engage physicians. Breen (2017) summarized his take on these sorts of articles about physician engagement:

> These articles always have the same advice to bring doctors into line: build trust, make physicians partners, convert physician "champions," have an engaging style, and (my favorite) make change not about saving money but their desire to help patients.
>
> That last strategy must really offend doctors. They're asked to change their behavior to "help their patients," but they know the bottom line is money . . . and they know where any money they save will accrue: to the "suits" who'll then crow to their colleagues about bringing their restive doctors into line.

Consulting and Advisory Firms

As mentioned earlier, much of today's information about physician engagement comes from consulting firms. Some may question the utility of information from commercial entities, but consulting and other advisory firms do create useful data. As a consultant myself, I see the value of the broad experiences and insights that can come from these firms.

Many of these firms have extensive databases that serve as substantive evidence in physician engagement. For example, few can challenge the breadth and extensiveness of the survey information that Gallup, Inc., or Press Ganey Associates has on physician engagement. These firms have worked with healthcare organizations of all types and sizes and have huge databases. Much of what they can tell us is not only important insight, but also probably statistically significant.

One note of advice, however: Explore the information, concepts, and definitional models of these firms carefully, and watch for potential bias. Although this chapter briefly reviews several consulting firms' ideas about physician engagement, I recommend caution and a little skepticism when you are viewing physician engagement information from commercial sources. The mention of any firm in this chapter or book is not intended as an endorsement.

Generally speaking, physician engagement consulting is focused mostly on engagement surveys (Gallup, Press Ganey, etc.), helping organizations develop strategies and tactics to enhance engagement, or a combination of both. We now will look at several firms' approaches.

The Advisory Board

The Advisory Board (www.advisory.com) believes that "maximizing engagement is, in large part, about investing in three big opportunities—Giving physicians real authority to lead; keeping communication lines open; and involving physicians in strategic decision-making."

An infographic by Advisory Board (2019) presents the benefits and challenges to focusing on physician engagement: "Strong physician engagement impacts a host of health system priorities, including physician retention, patient experience, care quality, and organizational costs. But many physician executives feel lost when navigating the multitude of potential tactics to improve engagement among both employed and independent physicians. Plus, time and resource constraints make it hard for executives to prioritize where they should invest their efforts."

Not surprisingly, communication plays a significant part in physician engagement. Much of the Advisory Board's approach to physician engagement involves enhancing communications. Sarah Evans of the Advisory Board writes, "Transparent, two-way communication is mission-critical to build physician engagement, as well as to advance large-scale change. Nearly all physician executives dedicate significant time and energy to keeping physicians informed of organizational strategy and change initiatives—yet many physicians still feel out of the loop" (Evans 2020).

Another important aspect of physician engagement is the physician's connection with the organization as a whole, as the Advisory Board (2016) points out: "It's more than satisfaction with one's job: It's the degree to which employees emotionally connect with their organization and are committed to its goals." In addition, the company suggests that "to build support for your organizational goals, it's important to integrate doctors into strategic decision-making. Physicians are more likely to feel engaged with a strategic plan when they know their voices and interests were heard during the decision-making process."

Hurst and Akabas (2018) of the Advisory Board also wrote, "The more engaged physicians are, the less likely they are to be at risk for burnout." Time and again, the connection between physician engagement and burnout continues to surface.

Gallup

Gallup (www.gallup.com) has been a leader in surveying physician engagement and has helped many healthcare organizations assess their levels of engagement. Through their survey research, Burger and Giger (2014) found that they could differentiate "physicians with emotional equity in the health system from those who did not buy in—and discovered a strong relationship between physician engagement and productivity."

Gallup studies also suggest that "fully engaged and engaged physicians gave the hospital an average of 3% more outpatient referrals and 51% more inpatient referrals than physicians who were not engaged or who were actively disengaged. Engaged physicians were 26% more productive than their less engaged counterparts, which amounts to an additional $460,000 on average in patient revenue per physician per year" (Henson 2016).

Gallup reports further insights on physician engagement (Kamins 2015):

Five characteristics distinguish engaged employees from actively disengaged employees . . . :

- loyal to the organization
- willing to put forth discretionary effort
- willing to trust and cooperate with others
- willing to work through challenges
- willing to speak out about problems and offer constructive suggestions for improvements

Kamins (2015) points out that leaders have several shortcomings when it comes to physician engagement. These include:

- Failure to communicate with physicians in a timely way
- Ignoring physicians' input
- Asking about a program or policy that physicians consider unimportant
- Not understanding what physicians want or the stresses they are under

As Gallup's Deborah Paller explains, the idea of engagement is complex: "Since physicians are more emotionally driven than many people realize, healthcare leaders must build strong relationships with their medical staff based on trust, integrity, and personal values" (Paller 2005).

Press Ganey

A well-known firm that has worked with many healthcare organizations in measuring patient satisfaction, Press Ganey (www.pressganey.com) has also done extensive work in physician engagement. Press Ganey (2019) reports several aspects of physician engagement:

- Of the health care workforce overall, physicians are the least engaged . . .
- Employed physicians have lower engagement than contract and private practice physicians.
- Across the health care workforce, physicians demonstrate the lowest resilience, driven largely by their difficulty disconnecting from work.
- The strongest driver of resilience among physicians is the degree to which they feel committed to the organization, while the strongest driver of resilience among employees is the feeling of accomplishment they get from their work . . .

Physicians are the least resilient segment of the health care workforce, driven in large part by an inability to decompress.

Diana Mahoney of Press Ganey says, "The importance of creating and maintaining a culture that allows physicians to stay connected to their purpose, their 'why,' in the face of multiple external stressors such as regulatory changes, administrative burdens, and resource limitations is increasingly understood to be foundational to practice success" (Mahoney 2019).

Deirdre Mylod, also of Press Ganey, discusses the connection between burnout and lack of engagement. She says that addressing burnout means "promoting resilience and wellness to help clinicians cope with the intensity and volume of their work, but it also means making tangible progress in reducing the negatives in the work environment that lead to burnout" (Mylod 2017).

CONCLUSION

Physician engagement is clearly a critical challenge for healthcare leaders. Because engagement lacks a clear-cut definition and is significantly complex, healthcare leaders need a multifaceted and detailed approach to engage physicians. But the return is worthwhile. If physicians are highly engaged, it is likely that their engagement will drive higher levels of patient satisfaction, quality of care, and patient safety. There would be enhanced camaraderie among physicians and better cost management. One CEO said it this way: "As goes my physician engagement goes the entire success of my entire organization—better quality, better expense management, better employee satisfaction, and better service to our community." Some studies suggest that physicians who are more highly engaged are also more productive and more loyal to their organizations. And as the healthcare industry faces unprecedented change after the COVID-19 pandemic, organizations will need high levels of physician engagement as they morph into the next generation of healthcare delivery.

REFERENCES

Advisory Board. 2021. "Rise to the Physician Engagement Challenge: New Tactics for a New Market." Accessed May 5. www.advisory.com/en/topics/physician-engagement-and-burnout/2016/07/rise-to-the-physician-engagement-challenge.

———. 2019. "Navigating the Physician Engagement Challenge: How to Scope an Effective Strategy." Infographic. Published July 2. www.advisory.com/research/physician-executive-council/resources/posters/navigating-the-physician-engagement-challenge?WT.ac=GrayBox_PEC_Info_x_x_x_CMO_2020Jan15_Eloqua-RMKTG+Blog.

————. 2016. "Most Doctors Aren't Engaged in Their Work. Here Are 3 Ways to Change That." Published July 12. www.advisory.com/daily-briefing/2016/07/12/most-physicians-arent-engaged-in-their-work.

Breen, M. 2017. "Why Physician Engagement Is Code for Physician Control." *KevinMD* (blog). Published January 10. www.kevinmd.com/blog/2017/01/physician-engagement-code-physician-control.html.

Burger, J., and A. Giger. 2014. "Want to Increase Hospital Revenues? Engage Your Physicians." *Gallup Business Journal.* Published June 5. https://news.gallup.com/businessjournal/170786/increase-hospital-revenues-engage-physicians.aspx.

Byrnes, J. 2015. "Great Physician Engagement Is Key to Great Quality." *Physician Leadership Journal* 2 (2): 40–42.

Cardarelli, R., M. Slimack, G. Gottschalk, M. Ruszkowski, J. Sass, K. Brown, R. Kikendall, J. J. Allard, K. Burgess, M. Luoma, and W. Gonsalves. 2019. "Translating Provider and Staff Engagement Results to Actionable Planning and Outcomes." *Journal of Patient Experience.* Published July 12. https://journals.sagepub.com/doi/full/10.1177/2374373519862927.

Dickson, G. 2012. *Anchoring Physician Engagement in Vision and Values: Principles and Framework.* Regina Qu'Appelle Health Region. Accessed March 8, 2021. http://www.rqhealth.ca/service-lines/master/files/anchoring.pdf.

Evans, S. 2020. "Rise to the Physician Engagement Challenge: New Tactics for a New Market." Advisory Board. Published July 16. www.advisory.com/topics/physician-engagement-

and-burnout/2020/07/three-ways-to-ensure-all-physicians-hear-your-message.

Gunderman, R. 2016. "Why Are Physician Engagement Scores So Dismal?" *The Health Care Blog.* Published January 25. https://thehealthcareblog.com/blog/2016/01/25/why-are-physician-engagement-scores-so-dismal.

Henson, J. W. 2016. "Reducing Physician Burnout Through Engagement." *Journal of Healthcare Management* 61 (2): 86–89.

Hurst, T., and R. Akabas. 2018. "Want to Reduce Physician Burnout? Start with Engagement." Advisory Board. Published September21.www.advisory.com/research/physician-executive-council/prescription-for-change/2018/09/provider-burnout.

Kaissi, A. 2014. "Enhancing Physician Engagement: An International Perspective." *International Journal of Health Services* 44 (3): 567–92.

———. 2012. *A Roadmap for Trust: Enhancing Physician Engagement.* Ottawa, Ontario: Canadian Policy Network.

Kamins, C. 2015. "What Too Many Hospitals Are Overlooking." *Gallup Business Journal.* Published February 23. https://news.gallup.com/businessjournal/181658/hospitals-overlooking.aspx.

Kreindler, S. A., B. K. Larson, F. M. Wu, J. N. Gbemudu, K. L. Carluzzo, A. Struthers, A. D. Van Citters, S. M. Shortell, E. C. Nelson, and E. S. Fisher. 2014. "The Rules of Engagement: Physician Engagement Strategies in Intergroup Contexts." *Journal of Health Organization and Management* 28 (1): 41–61.

Kreindler, S. A., D. A. Dowd, N. D. Star, and T. Gottschalk. 2012. "Silos and Social Identity: The Social Identity Approach as a

Framework for Understanding and Overcoming Divisions in Healthcare." *Milbank Quarterly* 90 (2): 347–74.

Lee, T. H., and T. Cosgrove. 2014. "Engaging Doctors in the Health Care Revolution." *Harvard Business Review* 92 (6): 104–38.

Mahoney, D. 2019. "New Report Identifies Shared Drivers of Patient Loyalty and Physician Engagement in the Medical Practice Setting." Press Ganey. Published June. www.pressganey. com/docs/default-source/default-document-library/new-report-identifies-shared-drivers-of-patient-loyalty-and-physician-engagement-in-the-medical-practice-setting.pdf.

Mertz, G. 2014. "The True Meaning of Physician Alignment." *Physicians Practice*. Published November 12. www.physicianspractice. com/view/true-meaning-physician-alignment.

Mylod, D. E. 2017. "One Way to Prevent Physician Burnout." *Harvard Business Review*. Published October 12. https://hbr. org/2017/10/one-way-to-prevent-physician-burnout.

Ninivaggi, F. J. 2020. "Physician Engagement: Mindfulness as Part of the Pandemic Solution." *Elsevier Connect* (blog). Published May 21. www.elsevier.com/connect/physician-engagement-mindfulness-as-part-of-the-pandemic-solution.

Paller, D. A. 2005. "What the Doctor Ordered: The Best Hospitals Create Emotional Bonds with Their Physicians." *Gallup Business Journal*. Published September 8. https://news.gallup. com/businessjournal/18361/What-Doctor-Ordered.aspx.

Perreira, T. A., L. Perrier, M. Prokopy, L. Neves-Mera, and D. D. Persaud. 2019. "Physician Engagement: A Concept Analysis." *Journal of Healthcare Leadership* 11: 101–13.

Press Ganey. 2019. "Health Care Workforce Special Report: The State of Engagement." Published October 22. www. pressganey.com/about/news/press-ganey-releases-special-report-on-state-of-health-care-workforce-engagement.

Rosenstein, A. H. 2015. "Strategies to Enhance Physician Engagement." *Journal of Medical Practice Management* 31 (2): 113–16.

Sears, N. 2011. "5 Strategies for Physician Engagement." *Healthcare Financial Management* 65 (1): 78–82.

Shanafelt, T. D., and J. H. Noseworthy. 2017. "Executive Leadership and Physician Well-Being: Nine Organizational Strategies to Promote Engagement and Reduce Burnout." *Mayo Clinic Proceedings* 92 (1): 129–45.

Showalter, J. W., and L. T. Williams. 2017. *Mastering Physician Engagement: A Practical Guide to Achieving Shared Outcomes.* Boca Raton, FL: CRC Press.

Snell, A. J., D. Briscoe, and G. Dickson. 2011. "From the Inside Out: The Engagement of Physicians as Leaders in Health Care Settings." *Qualitative Health Research* 21 (7): 952–67.

Walsh, K. E., W. H. Ettinger, and R. A. Klugman. 2009. "Physician Quality Officer: A New Model for Engaging Physicians in Quality Improvement." *American Journal of Medical Quality* 24 (4): 295–301.

Whitlock, D. J., and R. Stark. 2014. "Understanding Physician Engagement—and How to Increase it." *Physician Leadership Journal* 1 (1): 8–12.

CHAPTER 3

Physician Engagement Models

Carson F. Dye

ONE OF THE better ways to try to understand a complex topic is to develop a model. A model is a representation of a multifaceted concept that is difficult to explain with narrative alone. Often a visualization, a model can graphically or symbolically represent the concept. Because models typically simplify reality, they omit some details.

Chapters 1 and 2 discussed the challenges of understanding engagement and the lack of a precise definition of the term. These challenges are particularly true of physician engagement. As discussed earlier, there is no agreement on what constitutes physician engagement, a multifaceted concept. This chapter examines two models I have developed. While not intended to be comprehensive, they do provide visuals for thought and reflection.

A TWO-FACTOR MODEL

In a two-factor model of physician engagement, the two focal points of engagement are quite different. One centers on patient care; the other centers on the organization. The following observations by different physicians clearly illustrate these divergent goals:

"Most physicians want to be engaged. They want to do what's best for the patient. If you show them something, they're going to want to get better and they'll work with you." (Jeffrey DiLisi, MD, Virginia Hospital Center)

"Physician engagement is proactive physician involvement and meaningful physician influence that move a healthcare organization toward a shared vision and a successful future." (A. Clinton MacKinney, MD, MS, University of Iowa)

Note the dichotomy in the preceding comments. DiLisi (quoted in Pozen 2014) views physician engagement from the perspective of the *patient*. MacKinney (2016) views it from the perspective of the *organization*. Clearly, these are two entirely different viewpoints (see exhibit 3.1). We need to understand this dichotomy to gain greater insight about physician engagement and physicians themselves and to begin to map out strategies and tactics to enhance physician engagement.

While most administrative leaders view physician engagement from the perspective of the mission of the organizations, most physicians view it from the perspective of involvement with patient care. And therein lies an inherent conflict. Keller and colleagues (2019) vividly describe the difference in the two groups' views of healthcare:

Exhibit 3.1 The Two-Factor Model: Physician Engagement Viewed Two Ways

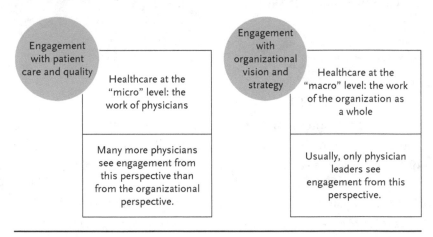

Engagement with patient care and quality	Engagement with organizational vision and strategy
Healthcare at the "micro" level: the work of physicians	Healthcare at the "macro" level: the work of the organization as a whole
Many more physicians see engagement from this perspective than from the organizational perspective.	Usually, only physician leaders see engagement from this perspective.

Patient care occurred in high-acuity, short-time-horizon environments, and so clinical decision making tended to occur in a short V-shape, where a lot of information was distilled quickly into a single best course of action. Organizational care instead occurred in a tall W-shaped approach, distilling information into multiple possible solutions over a relatively longer amount of time. These differences were reflected in a palpable urgency in interactions with physicians, more chaotic work spaces, and less formal clothing. To administrators, the short V-shaped approach seemed impulsive and less resilient to change: "Physicians don't like surprises." To physicians, the W-shaped approach seemed indecisive and excessively bureaucratic.

As a result, when healthcare organizational leaders are talking with physicians about engagement, the two parties may be on entirely different pages. Without a common viewpoint—and definition—of engagement, the groups will likely disagree and reach no conclusions. Matheson and Kissoon (2006) say it well, explaining that physicians "may think they are responsible for ensuring good patient outcomes only, while the administrator may think they are responsible for system efficiency and costs only." Knight (2019) describes another difference between administrators' and physicians' perspectives: "Administrators tend to distill information into multiple options over a time period of months to years in contrast to physicians, who are accustomed to quickly distilling information into a single best course of action within minutes to days." For all these differences, efforts to seek common ground are essential.

Any leader who has spent even a short time in healthcare knows the importance of engaging physicians in all aspects of the operations of the organizations. As Goldsmith, Hunter, and Strauss (2018) explain, "Physicians are complex, highly trained professionals. They cannot be mere employees; they must be owners of the organization's goals and strategies." Shanafelt and Noseworthy (2017) concur: "Having an engaged physician workforce is critical for health care organizations to meet institutional objectives and achieve their mission."

As discussed in previous chapters, employee engagement is significantly different from physician engagement. Contrary opinions aside, physicians are far more central to the business of healthcare than are other employees. Oshiro (2015) writes, "Physicians play a critical role in every aspect of healthcare. Physicians guide processes and decisions that are made inside and outside the hospital walls. Every strategy to fix problems in healthcare today revolves around the buy-in of one critical group—the physicians. Physicians determine 75 to 85 percent of the decisions that drive quality and cost."

Even if they are employees, physicians have a higher sense of independence than do other employees. They identify far more with their profession than they do with the organization for which—or *in* which—they work. While some healthcare employees are licensed, the physician license is more sacrosanct and carries a greater personal risk if lost. Furthermore, physicians spend far more time than any other type of employee spends in educational preparation.

As suggested earlier, most physicians are likely to already be highly engaged—in patient care and quality. As Dickson (2012) writes, "Physician engagement already exists. It exists because a physician invests his or her psychological energy into improved patient care." Physicians may be entirely disassociated with the goals and strategies of the larger healthcare organization in which they work and yet still highly engaged in the clinical work they do. Here might be one of the great dichotomies. Physicians typically feel engaged; administrators believe this group is disengaged. And physician engagement surveys typically focus most of their questions on the issues involving the organization, not patient care. This disconnect between administrators' and physicians' perceptions presents a great learning opportunity.

To explore this dichotomy further during a recent meeting with several physician leaders, I conducted a survey on physician engagement. Before completing the survey, the participants were shown the images in exhibit 3.2 and were asked to think about the question "What is physician engagement?"

Exhibit 3.2 Physician Engagement at the Point of Care

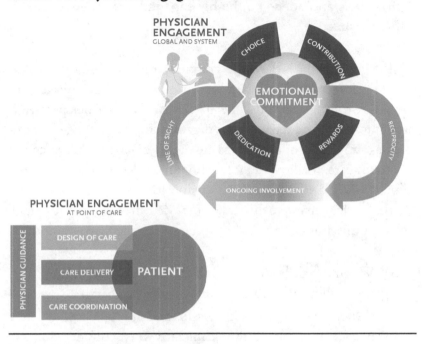

Source: Model drawn by Victor Zhang.

The participants were presented with these two images as a backdrop to the discussion. The top image shows physician engagement from the perspective of the organizations, and the bottom one shows it from the perspective of the point of patient care. (Each element in the exhibit will be explained in detail later in the chapter.) Thus the idea that physician engagement has two sides was planted before their discussions. The following directions were also provided:

> Our discussion today on physician engagement and the survey we will soon give you presents two somewhat contrasting views of physician engagement. One surmises that most physicians are **already actually highly engaged**, especially when considering engagement from the perspective of the point of care. The other views physician engagement from the perspective

of the health system and was based on the theory that many physicians are indeed **not highly engaged** when viewed from this perspective.

The goal of the survey, the graphics, and the discussions that ensued was to make one central point: that physician engagement should be viewed from two perspectives. The first perspective is patient focused, and the second is organization focused. My hypothesis was simple: Most physicians are highly engaged when it comes to patient care, quality, and safety but are far less so when it comes to the goals and strategies of the organization.

The participants were then asked to review the following five statements or questions and rate them on a basic Likert five-point scale:

- When most physicians think about engagement, they think about it from the point-of-care perspective.
- Generally speaking, what is the level of physician engagement for full-time clinicians when considered from the point-of-care perspective?
- When most leaders think about physician engagement, they think about it from the health system perspective.
- Generally speaking, what is the level of physician engagement for full-time clinicians when considered from the health system perspective?
- Engaging physicians under the health system perspective is a critical step toward effective clinical integration.

The results (whose details are provided in the chapter appendix) of the survey are not unexpected. In the words of one of the survey participants who was given the results, "I am not really surprised at all by these results. They simply reflect logic. Of course physicians are highly engaged with patient care—that is not news to me!"

The two conclusions from this group of physician leaders support the idea of a two-factor model of physician engagement:

- Full-time clinicians think about physician engagement from the perspective of where care is delivered. They view the engagement of physicians as being clinical—not corporate.
- Full-time clinicians are viewed as being highly engaged, at least from the point-of-care perspective, *but not very engaged from the health system perspective.*

The observation of one participant was pertinent:

When I first got into management and thought about engagement with physicians, it was totally focused on care delivery. How do we deliver great care? How do we ensure we have no sentinel events? How do we reduce harm? This was my total focus. And when I thought about getting my medical staff engaged, I thought about getting them on board with quality and safety and reducing variation. Honestly, I didn't see this as engaging with the organization. I guess in a way it is, but is it a conscious connection? For me, it (engagement) was on a microsystem level, where we engage in how we design or deliver care in our little realm of influence—the ICU, operating room, or our office, with our patients at the center of the model, not the organization.

Thus we have now defined physician engagement from two perspectives (see exhibit 3.3).

AN EIGHT-FACTOR MODEL

While the two-factor model makes great sense, it is clearly lacking in detail. It ignores the organizational perspective of physician engagement and offers little insight on ways to develop and enhance this type of engagement. To overcome these shortcomings, a model needs greater complexity.

Exhibit 3.3 Physician Engagement: Two Perspectives

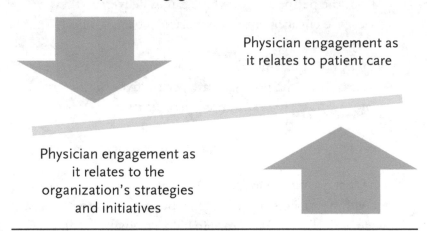

Physician engagement as it relates to patient care

Physician engagement as it relates to the organization's strategies and initiatives

The same physician leaders who helped drive the development of the two-factor model were then asked to further discuss the components of physician engagement as they related to organizational strategy and direction. This discussion resulted in a list of eight primary components of physician engagement and gave examples of physicians' likely comments (see exhibit 3.4):

- **Emotional commitment:** "I care about what I am doing." "I care about this organization." "I feel connected to what we are doing here."
- **Dedication:** "I love what I am doing." "I feel I am making a difference." "I would almost do this for no pay."
- **Choice:** "This is what I have always wanted to do." "If I had to start over, I would do the same thing I am doing now." "I selected this—I want to do it."
- **Contribution:** "I am an important part of this enterprise." "I feel I am making a difference."
- **Reciprocity:** "I get something out of what I do."
- **Rewards:** "I feel I am really getting something out of my work."

Exhibit 3.4 Eight-Factor Model of Physician Engagement

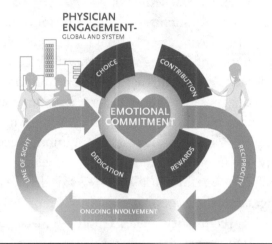

Source: Model drawn by Victor Zhang.

- **Ongoing involvement:** "I am involved with change." "Others give serious consideration to my suggestions." "I feel a part of the decision-making process here."
- **Line of sight:** "Our mission is clear." "I can see what is going on."

Essentially, this eight-factor model shows that these eight components drive physician engagement. We will look at these components in more depth.

But before considering each component, note how the first components or factors relate to the *individual.* Emotional commitment is heartfelt and comes from individuals' value systems and the developmental forces that shaped people as they grew up and made early life choices. Exhibit 3.4 suggests that emotional commitment sits at the core of the person. Another individual component, dedication, is closely related but represents someone who is devoted to something and who is single-minded in focus and energy. Note that physicians can be detached from their systems by fulfilling their needs for emotional commitment and dedication anywhere (in their individual clinical settings).

The next four components—choice, contribution, reciprocity, and rewards—still emanate partly from the perspective of the individual but begin to embrace the *organization*. Choice is the personal freedom to decide between alternatives. A contribution is something that the individual has given to make some situation better or more effective. Healthcare is filled with many individuals who are strongly motivated by this desire to make a contribution. Reciprocity and rewards may be viewed by some as the same, yet for the purposes of our model, they are different. While rewards denote the financial returns (wages, benefits, opportunities for promotion) for what an individual does, reciprocity suggests more of a basic law of social psychology—that we pay back what we receive from others. Or, as some say, we pay a good deed forward.

The last two components—ongoing involvement and line of sight—move the focus more toward the *organization*. Ongoing involvement represents the active participation, enthusiasm for, and contribution to the larger matters that go beyond the individual. It is the ability to have a say in how things occur. And line of sight is a twofold concept. First, it means that individuals can see a connection between their own goals (personal and work-related) and those of the organization. Second, a line of sight denotes congruence between both personal and organizational sets of goals. When personal and organizational goals agree, it's a win–win situation.

We will now look at these eight elements in detail and examine how they apply to physicians.

Emotional Commitment

Johnson and Bangs (2016) speak to the importance of physicians' emotional commitment in a healthcare organization: "Engaged physicians are emotionally committed to your organization, its vision, and the initiatives you are pursuing collectively. While this may sound 'fluffy,' it is emotional commitment that motivates, propels innovation, and drives their investment in the processes that truly create value." There is a distinction between rational commitment and emotional commitment. The latter represents a love or devotion to what one does; the former connotes having to do something, often unwillingly. Clearly, physicians who have an infectious passion for what they do are more likely to be engaged.

Dedication

Robert Pearl (2014) believes that the majority of physicians are dedicated. "Most physicians," he says, "go into medicine with a mission-driven spirit, committed to helping people. They are grateful for the opportunity to care for others, proud of their ability to diagnose and treat, and inspired by the trust their patients put in them." Of course, this level of dedication applies to patient care as well, but the question is clear: How can that dedication to patient care be aggregated into the mission of the organization as a whole? Several years ago, one physician said simply, "If my hospital is fully focused on patient care, I am totally and completely behind all of its decisions and actions. If not, then count me out." Dedication can be hard to define. The *Cambridge Dictionary* suggests it is "the willingness to give a lot of time and energy to something because it is important." But for our purposes here, we think of dedication as the devotion to the care and healing mission of our field.

Choice

An alarming survey done by the Doctors Company (2018) showed that 7 out of 10 physicians are "unwilling to recommend their chosen profession to their children or other family members." Another survey reported in the *Physicians Practice* blog, by Doulgeris (2020), showed less disturbing numbers: "Over one third of physicians would not choose medicine if they had their careers to do over." As demonstrated by these survey results, the belief that you have a choice in what you do is a critical aspect of engagement.

Contribution

Highly engaged individuals, and definitely most of us who work in healthcare, understand this driver of engagement. In many respects, this motivational factor of engagement can be labeled as purpose. A sense of contributing something helps healthcare workers see their work as meaningful. And a meaningful contribution is what many who work in direct patient care look for to sustain their energy during tough days. Feeling as though you have contributed something can be monumental ("I helped saved her life") or something much less consequential ("I kept him company while he waited for his X-ray"). Many primary physicians have told me that it is clearly not about money but is about the many little things they can do to help their patients in life. Copeland (2011) writes that "on the most fundamental level, physicians can give back by listening. It is easy to get caught up in patient throughput, schedules, and goals. But something so basic as taking a few extra minutes to really listen can mean so much to our patients and our practices. Empathy is a gift, and we must not forget that."

Reciprocity

Generally speaking, reciprocity means that we pay back what we receive from others. In essence, "I receive, and I give back in return." Healthcare is filled with many individuals, among them physicians, who view reciprocity as the gift of giving back. Reciprocity involves relationships; the acts between individuals form the satisfaction that continues to drive behavior. Russel Libby (2019), a practicing physician, described it as such: "The privilege of being able to develop meaningful relationships with patients and help them live healthy, productive lives is a unique and wonderful quality of practicing medicine."

Rewards

While a few of the physician leaders in the engagement meeting believed that rewards were the same as, or similar to, reciprocity, most participants saw rewards as the simple factor of what physicians gained out of their activities, clinical or otherwise. Many approaches to physician engagement have historically focused on providing financial rewards to physicians, but the concept of a reward is much broader. Those who cling to the idea that money is everything would do well to immerse themselves in Daniel Pink's book *Drive*. Pink (2009) writes that "we have three innate psychological needs—competence, autonomy, and relatedness. When those needs are satisfied, we're motivated, productive, and happy." In the same book, he explains, "When the reward is the activity itself—deepening learning, delighting customers, doing one's best—there are no shortcuts."

Ongoing Involvement

Lack of involvement is often mentioned by physicians as one of their biggest complaints about administration. Consider the negativity felt by a physician who says, "I did not know that was going to happen; they did not ask me." Physicians feel much more engaged when they are invited to participate in discussions and decisions.

Line of Sight

One of the more critical components of engagement, including physician engagement, is line of sight. If they have a line of sight, individuals can see the purpose of their organization, the way their role and efforts fit in this purpose, and the consistency of what is done across the organization. Perhaps most important, physicians have to see a connectedness between what they are doing (their personal mission, vision, actions) and what the organization is doing. Some call this a feeling of ownership, that what they do is directly tied to their organization's success. For example, organizations whose physicians truly understand the purpose of electronic health records have much less dissatisfaction about these records.

CONCLUSION

While these models may help explain physician engagement, there is no evidence that either model is complete. In fact, the scientific method requires that a hypothesis first be developed and then tested before a model can be developed. Clearly the testing done for these models represents the viewpoints of several healthcare leaders. But in no way are these models absolute, complete, and conclusive. Readers should feel free to add their own insights and conclusions as they review the chapter—and this entire book.

REFERENCES

Copeland, L. R. 2011. "What Giving Back Means to Me." *Physicians Practice*. Published November 11. www.physicianspractice.com/what-giving-back-means-me.

Dickson, G. 2012. *Anchoring Physician Engagement in Vision and Values: Principles and Framework*. Regina Qu'Appelle Health Region. Accessed March 8, 2021. http://www.rqhealth.ca/service-lines/master/files/anchoring.pdf.

Doctors Company. 2018. "The Future of Healthcare: A National Survey of Physicians." Published October 1. www.thedoctors.

com/about-the-doctors-company/newsroom/press-releases/
2018/physicians-unwilling-to-recommend-their-profession-
survey-shows/www.thedoctors.com/about-the-doctors-
company/newsroom/the-future-of-healthcare-survey.

Doulgeris, J. 2020. "New Survey Validates That US Physicians Are
Ailing." *Physicians Practice* (blog). Published December 4. www.
physicianspractice.com/new-survey-validates-us-physicians-
are-ailing.

Goldsmith, J., A. Hunter, and A. Strauss. 2018. "Do Most Hospitals
Benefit from Directly Employing Physicians?" *Harvard Business Review*. Published May 29. https://hbr.org/2018/05/
do-most-hospitals-benefit-from-directly-employing-
physicians.

Johnson, M., and D. Bangs. 2016. "Physician Engagement for the
Established CIN." Veralon. Published May 4. www.veralon.
com/physician-engagement-established-cin.

Keller, E. J., B. Giafaglione, H. B. Chrisman, J. D. Collins, and
R. L. Vogelzang. 2019. "The Growing Pains of Physician–
Administration Relationships in an Academic Medical Center
and the Effects on Physician Engagement." *PLOS One* 14 (2):
e0212014. https://doi.org/10.1371/journal.pone.0212014.

Knight, B. P. 2019. "Differences in Perceptions and Cultures
Between Doctors and Hospital Administrators Undermine
Physician Engagement." *EP Lab Digest*. Published November 2.
www.eplabdigest.com/differences-perceptions-and-cultures-
between-doctors-and-hospital-administrators-undermine-
physician-engagement.

Libby, R. 2019. "Physician Perspective: Russell Libby." *Physicians
Practice*. Published March 22. www.physicianspractice.com/
view/physician-perspective-russell-libby.

MacKinney, A. C. 2016. "Physician Engagement: A Primer for Healthcare Leaders." Center for Rural Health Policy Analysis and Stratis Health. Published February 12. https://cph.uiowa.edu/ruralhealthvalue/files/RHV%20Physician%20Engagement%20Primer.pdf.

Matheson, D. S., and N. Kissoon. 2006. "A Comparison of Decision-Making by Physicians and Administrators in Healthcare Settings." *Critical Care* (London) 10 (5): 163.

Oshiro, B. 2015. "The Best Way Hospitals Can Engage Physicians, Nurses, and Staff." *Health Catalyst Insights* (blog). Published April 21. www.healthcatalyst.com/the-best-way-hospitals-engage-physicians-nurses-and-staff.

Pearl, R. 2014. "Malcolm Gladwell: Tell People What It's Really Like to Be a Doctor." *Forbes*. Published March 13. www.forbes.com/sites/robertpearl/2014/03/13/malcolm-gladwell-tell-people-what-its-really-like-to-be-a-doctor/.

Pink, D. H. 2009. *Drive: The Surprising Truth About What Motivates Us*. New York: Riverhead Books.

Pozen, S. A. 2014. "How to Achieve Physician Engagement in Your Hospital." Published November 11. www.hhnmag.com/articles/3874-how-to-achieve-physician-engagement-in-your-hospital.

Shanafelt, T. D., and J. H. Noseworthy. 2017. "Executive Leadership and Physician Well-Being: Nine Organizational Strategies to Promote Engagement and Reduce Burnout." *Mayo Clinic Proceedings* 92 (1): 129–46.

PHYSICIAN ENGAGEMENT SURVEY

1. When most physicians think about engagement, they think about it from the point-of-care perspective.

Not at all	To a small extent	Somewhat	To a great extent	Totally and completely
0	3	5	7	10

2. On a scale of 1 (lowest) to 10 (highest), generally speaking, what is the level of physician engagement for full-time clinicians when considered from the point-of-care perspective?

1	2	3	4	5	6	7	8	9	10

3. When most leaders think about physician engagement, they think about it from the health system perspective.

Not at all	To a small extent	Somewhat	To a great extent	Totally and completely
0	3	5	7	10

4. On a scale of 1 (lowest) to 10 (highest), generally speaking, what is the level of physician engagement for full-time clinicians when considered from the health system perspective?

1	2	3	4	5	6	7	8	9	10

5. Engaging physicians under the health system perspective is a critical step toward effective clinical integration.

Strongly disagree	Disagree	Neither disagree nor agree	Agree	Strongly agree
1	2	3	4	5

PHYSICIAN ENGAGEMENT SURVEY RESULTS

1. When most physicians think about engagement, they think about it from the point-of-care perspective.
   Survey answer mean: 8.2 (on a scale of 1–10)
2. Generally speaking, what is the level of physician engagement for full-time clinicians when considered from the point-of-care perspective?
   Survey answer mean: 8.9 (on a scale of 1–10)
3. When most leaders think about physician engagement, they think about it from the health system perspective.
   Survey answer mean: 9.1 (on a scale of 1–10)
4. Generally speaking, what is the level of physician engagement for full-time clinicians when considered from the health system perspective?
   Survey answer mean: 4.1 (on a scale of 1–10)

5. Engaging physicians under the health system perspective is a critical step toward effective clinical integration.

   Survey answer mean: 4.9 (on a scale of 1–5, with 5 being the highest possible score; note changed scale for this question)

CHAPTER 4

Aiming to Better Understand Physicians

Douglas A. Spotts

*This is the moment—this is the most important moment right now.
Which is: We are about contribution. That's what our job is. It's
not about impressing people. It's not about getting the next job.
It's about contributing something.*
—Rosamund Zander and Benjamin Zander,
The Art of Possibility, 2002

PERHAPS THE MOST important aspect of physician engagement is
the simple aspect of knowing and understanding physicians. While
this recommendation may seem insulting to many healthcare leaders ("I already know and understand physicians!"), unfortunately,
my experiences suggest that we leaders need a deeper grasp of the
physician mind, spirit, heart, and soul. Read on to explore some
of the nuances of, and insights into, this understanding. With this
knowledge, you can better reflect on various ways to fully engage
physicians.

A UNIQUE LEARNING STYLE

Physicians love to be heard and to share a vast amount of evidence-
based practice experience and knowledge. They look to consensus

statements from specialty societies and the latest journal club findings. Physicians demonstrate their commitment to lifelong learning but seldom share what they have learned in the public arena outside of peer discussions or patient interactions in the clinic unless asked to do so.

Understanding physicians requires insight into the unique way in which physicians are trained. Their training is different from other professional disciplines in medicine, like nursing. Other medical disciplines successfully employ protocol methodology and team-based approaches in their pedagogy. Formal physician training in the United States, while thankfully showing some signs of increased team- and case-based learning, is still largely siloed. It is based on an individual's assessment of medical knowledge and skills. Individual skill development is followed by proof of competency through testing.

The classic example of physician training is participating in medical rounds with attending physicians, higher-level medical students, and resident physicians. Individuals are put on the spot to show that they know their patients' histories, diseases, current labs and studies, and the plan for the day. There is little recognition of other perspectives of care for the patient, especially at critical moments of care transition such as discharge. Physicians are instructed to always be prepared for the unknown, to question everything and everyone, and to beware of reaching rapid conclusions. The average physician, however, reaches a presumed diagnosis or an assessment of the current condition within the first thirty seconds of interaction. Physicians interrupt their patients within 11 seconds of the start of the visit (Phillips, Ospina, and Montori 2019) and seldom assesses the patients' health literacy and understanding of medical instructions (Sim, Yuan, and Yun 2016). These medical professionals train and learn under pressure and rapidly respond to, integrate, and formulate data and clinical judgment using evidence and consensus. This tug-of-war between perfection and rapid diagnosis is a norm in physician training.

A NEVER-FAIL ATTITUDE

A deeply engrained maxim among physicians is "Never fail" and, especially, never fail the patient. To invite them into deeper problem solving, leaders need to understand that physicians will not ask for feedback or invite team perspectives. Healthcare leaders can "enroll" or get physicians involved by simply asking for their perspective or opinion on an issue. Even better, leaders can ask them to help explain the science or evidence behind an intervention. Ask physicians to help solve a problem, and they will rise to the occasion and share a vast amount of that siloed, pent-up knowledge. But can they be counted on to volunteer their knowledge in an open forum? Most readers would say no. Experienced healthcare leaders know that they need to invite physicians in and that a breakthrough moment is often right around the bend. Leaders should understand these aspects of communication when working with physicians on problems and other issues in the boardroom and the C-suite.

COOPERATIVENESS AND CREATIVITY

One analogy for physician education and training is that of childhood play at the playground or especially in the community sandbox. Physicians were the kids who shared their toys with others, cooperated, and creatively entertained themselves and others for hours. Herein lies a problem. The systematic disregard for this spirit of creativity, flexible problem solving, and collaboration in formal medical education is a major failure of the present system. The emphasis on individual decisions and responsibility for outcomes instead of collaboration in matters of quality and safety in patient care is something not encountered in other professional training. Although medical education is undergoing major change, the focus on individualism still exists. Rios (2016) points out the resultant problems: "The medical school environment enables doctors and medical students' feelings of intellectual superiority, selfish and excessive competitiveness; inability to see the patient as a whole; overvaluation and excessive use of technology; role modelling of non-empathic behaviours; and behaviours showing disrespect, discrimination, and violence." Physicians must be asked to be a part of a team and directed toward a clear purpose involving patient care, so that they can rediscover and unleash dormant "sandbox" skills to produce meaningful results (engagement and alignment).

While there are differences among various specialties, ages, and backgrounds, most successful physicians do share several characteristics. These, perhaps, were first learned in the childhood sandbox, but good physicians find a way to incorporate the following qualities throughout their formal education and careers: good listening skills, being organized and conscientious, the ability to work with others to support and advocate for patients, a great bedside manner that makes patients feel cared for, and intellectual curiosity. Physicians can also be forthright, a quality that can, unfortunately, be viewed negatively. Most physicians are also thorough. Any healthcare leader who has been caught using faulty data with physicians will attest to this quality. Physicians with the emotional intelligence to allow their best traits (empathy, compassion, listening, advocacy) to rise above their weaker ones (overt skepticism, reluctance to change) are usually ready to be engaged in leadership opportunity. Exhibit 4.1 categorizes successful physician traits. Intentional rediscovery of the

Exhibit 4.1 Successful Physician Traits

Emotional intelligence	Patient first		
Ability to cooperate	Forthrightness	Thorough	
	Intellectual curiosity	Organized and conscientious approach	Good listening skills

better side of physicians is, thankfully, being built into humanistic and ethical studies and new models of learning in medical school curricula.

A TENDENCY TO QUESTION EVERYTHING

In addition to the highly individualized training of physicians, this group shares another important characteristic: Physicians question everything. And they also question every motive. This skepticism comes from many moments of self-doubt, often thought of as "the times you missed the diagnosis." According to conversations with trusted physician colleagues, their skepticism has a profound impact on their behavior. Physicians do not accept face-value conclusions without first having raised their eyebrows about the issue. They simply have been burned too many times by jumping to the quickest and most apparent conclusion without examining the nuance of human nature, life circumstances of the patient, or something not inherent to the patient story captured by history. This skepticism is even more transparent in an era of dot phrases (auto text) in the electronic health record (EHR) and copy-and-paste functionality in the daily progress note.

Medicine is an art and a science. The art comes from the wide variability of patient personalities and circumstances and the human condition; the science is related to the unique analysis of the data, tests, and studies on the management of patient disease. Preventive medicine, a blend of both art and science, is geared toward maintaining a balance in patient wellness that produces the best quality of life possible.

Social determinants of health play a role in all aspects of patient care and wellness. All that technology has to offer in this electronic era may help the science of medicine, but the art is not as easily addressed by artificial intelligence paradigms and dot phrases geared to capturing ICD-10 billing codes and narrow definitions of disease and treatment modalities. There is a time to act swiftly, decisively, and according to protocol—for example, a patient in cardiac arrest, trauma triage, and cardiac risk calculation. But there is also a time for deeper questioning. For example, a physician might ask why the patient's HgbA1C, once maintained in perfect control, suddenly rises. The obvious answers are that the patient is not taking the medicine correctly or that the medicine is no longer effective. But further questioning might prove these hypotheses incorrect. The physician might listen to a teary-eyed patient who admits having to choose between eating a balanced diet or paying for medication they can no longer afford after the loss of a job and health insurance.

Nothing will further discourage a doctor from engagement than obvious answers to complex and critical problems—solutions handed down from the C-suite without physician input. On the other hand, nothing engages doctors more than does active listening to their questions, perspectives, and concerns by those who invite their input. Readers should consider these physician traits when considering ways to further engage these professionals.

CHANGE MANAGEMENT

Physicians do not readily embrace change. Medicine is full of examples of physicians' slowness to embrace new thinking. Remember the once-accepted and widespread use of leeches for bloodletting as a form of medical treatment? One does not need to travel to the eighteenth century to observe physicians' reluctance either to change or to question established standards of practice. Consider the vast amount of change in practice standards since the mid-1990s. Physicians no longer do routine urine testing in primary care. Cancer screening is changing faster than ever before and now includes factoring in age, comorbidities, symptoms, blood test results, imaging studies, genetic studies, and family history in the final decision-making. And studies have shown that doing more testing is sometimes more detrimental to health and quality of life than is less testing. Computers, electronic solutions, and artificial intelligence constructs are supposed to be guiding physicians in their decision-making, and yet, there is more duplication of testing than ever. In the United States, costs spiral upward, and quality falls to among the lowest scores of healthcare systems in the developed countries of the world.

What are change-averse physicians to do? The overwhelming challenges facing US healthcare will require systemic changes and are precisely where other members of the healthcare team and administrators need to understand the unique capabilities of physicians and invite them to use their special skills and board the train of change. One simple way to do this is to provide physicians with leadership development. When an organization helps physicians improve their leadership skills, physicians not only will board the train but will also become the engineers and conductors of the change process. The following sections discuss some ways to encourage leadership among physicians.

Invite Physicians Early to the Conversation

Physicians will embrace change when the other steps to engagement are followed. Administrative leaders can invite them to the conversation, listen to their perspectives and questions, and finally assist them with competencies to lead change. Like the rest of us, physicians by nature do not want to fail. When you think about the natural progression of life and death, obviously all of us ultimately fail, but no physician wants to be identified as *that* physician who, through incompetence and incomplete thinking, makes a mistake and fails the patient. No physicians want to be responsible for producing an untoward outcome, even death. This fear holds most physicians back from being the innovative investigators, thinkers, problem solvers, advocates, and cooperative team members that administrators seek in solving complex health system and health challenges. Physicians simply do not want to change, because embracing change too quickly has ensnared them too often in perceived failure. If there has ever been a unifying theme in the psyche of the physician, it is this: Never fail. Kotter (2012) writes: "Whenever smart and well-intentioned people avoid confronting obstacles, they disempower employees and undermine change."

How can you gain an understanding of physicians' nature and disposition so that you can address the challenges of their unique training and see these challenges as opportunities for transformation? How does the healthcare leader first seek to understand and then help transform the physician mindset from individualistic thinking, critical skepticism, reluctance to change, and, most of all, fear of failure, into possibilities for continuous change and improvement? These are the questions we'll address in the remainder of this book and in volume 2, *The Complete Guide to Enhanced Physician Engagement: Tools and Tactics for Success*.

Help Physicians Move to Deeper Levels of Engagement

In Jim Collins's well-known book *Good to Great*, he compares a fox with a hedgehog: "While the wily fox knows many things, the simple hedgehog only knows one thing, but that one knowledge bite is highly impactful in protecting itself against danger" (Collins 2001). He conceptualizes the hedgehog as the "sweet spot" where (1) a person's deep passion, (2) what that person can be the best in the world at, and (3) the driver of one's economic engine all converge. For physician leaders, the sweet spot, or hedgehog concept, is in delivering excellent patient care. Exhibit 4.2 presents the physician take on this concept.

Physician engagement is not about making physicians more competent. They have already developed competency many times over and beyond their peers in medicine and other disciplines in their educational journey. Nor is physician engagement about making physicians happier. Happiness and satisfaction is not the same as engagement. Some of the most unhappy physicians are highly engaged—engaged in changing their situations!

Exhibit 4.2 Physician Hedgehog Concept

Developing physicians into hedgehogs by having them focus on such a hedgehog concept as excellent patient care, which entails leading organizational efforts to zero harm or high reliability, better safety goals, or improved quality scores, creates the kind of transformational momentum that truly makes a healthcare entity change from good to great. And the resulting outcome will most certainly be increased physician engagement.

Factors such as meaningful data aggregation and assimilation, patient safety, evidence-based quality of care, competition, and control of processes and care pathways are motivators that enhance the hedgehog concept of excellent patient care. When healthcare systems add these motivators to recognition and appreciation of physician effort, they create the Collins "flywheel," or momentum, of continuous and meaningful change. This flywheel effect is a multiplier of further excellence on the good-to-great journey and places the hedgehog right in the center of unstoppable momentum. And a healthy dose of praise for a job well done will make any physician a friend for life!

FROM ENGAGEMENT TO LEADERSHIP: HOW PHYSICIANS CAN DEVELOP INTO ENGAGED LEADERS

Let us expand on the concept of understanding physicians and developing them into engaged leaders. Note that in our discussion of physician leaders, the focus will be on *all physicians as leaders*, not just those who are paid as leaders. Dye (2017) wrote, "Physicians can serve as leaders on the front lines of care. Health systems would be wise to enlist and develop many of their clinicians as leaders." Essentially, all full-time clinicians can serve in various leadership capacities even as they are practicing medicine each day.

There are challenges to the development of physician leaders, and some aspects of physicians and their training may stand in the way of their development as leaders. Physicians experience long and hierarchical training with extended subordination. They are extensively evaluated on individual performance rather than group- or team-based performance. They may assume that the leadership conferred to them by their clinical authority with patients can be transferred to settings where, unfortunately, that authority is irrelevant. They are deficit-based thinkers because differential diagnostic thinking encourages physicians to identify problems (deficits). This mindset impedes the value of problem solving by focusing on deficits (what is not there) rather than imagining the possibility of what could be, in an ideal state. The latter type of thinking is more indicative of appreciative inquiry, the typical way that organizations solve problems. They look toward creating solutions for "the best of what could be" rather than look at the shortcomings of the present.

The answer to developing physician engagement and alignment in leadership comes down to assessment and development of physician leadership skills in addition to clinical competencies. This approach works in any healthcare environment, whether it is an employed or independent model of physician clinical practice, a closed or an open medical staff model, or a not-for-profit or for-profit health system. It also applies to any other community leadership opportunity.

Organizations and governing bodies that fail to recognize this need for physician leadership development will ultimately struggle in this time of rapid change and challenge in healthcare.

In analyzing physician leadership, Taylor, Taylor, and Stoller (2008) uncovered four attributes: "knowledge, people skills or emotional intelligence, vision, and organizational altruism (dedication to organizational success even at personal sacrifice)." They further suggested that these four attributes characterize effective, successful leaders. These qualities also align with Collins's hedgehog concept discussed earlier.

Another important competency in addition to the preceding four is receptivity to mentoring (exhibit 4.3). According to an informal survey I conducted with physician and nonphysician leaders alike, this attribute alone—receptivity to mentoring—strongly predicts the success of efforts to develop an emerging physician leader. Moreover, receptivity is tightly linked to the physician's chances of greater success, growth, and engagement on the leadership journey.

Returning to the sandbox play of childhood and reflecting on the five competencies discussed, we can conclude that the physicians

Exhibit 4.3 Physician Leadership Competencies

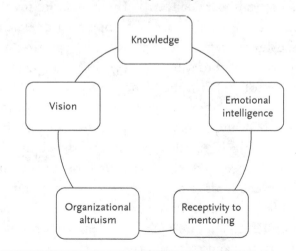

who accepted feedback and guidance at play as children are now those most open to feedback throughout the long years of their professional training. Are physicians who more readily shared their toys and cooperated in the sandbox as children more inclined to be collaborative and engaged leaders? The physicians who have a team of mentors and other advisers from different aspects of their professional education and formation seem to succeed in developing emotional intelligence in addition to their intellectual capacity and competency in clinical skill development.

My informal survey of physician and nonphysician leaders included a question on what special knowledge competencies are required for successful physician leadership development. The respondents widely agreed on the following key knowledge skill sets: (1) basic finance, including balance sheets and reimbursement information; (2) legal and compliance or regulatory aspects of healthcare; (3) fundamentals of strategic and project planning; and (4) information technology systems. The list does not mean that physicians lack capability in these disciplines. But the typical education of a physician centers on evidence-based science and clinical skill building, not on these important aspects of healthcare administration.

Besides these four knowledge skills, four other qualities can transform the excellent clinician into an effective partner-leader for health and healthcare concerns. These qualities involve more personal insight: (1) the ability to develop and articulate a vision, (2) skill at seeking strategic pathways for the best possible outcomes, (3) receptivity to collaboration, and (4) the willingness and ability to receive feedback with the highest level of self-reflection and awareness. Exhibit 4.4 shows how these eight factors fit together.

Note that this competency set could easily encircle the drivers around the hedgehog of excellent patient care shown in exhibit 4.2. The hedgehog defined by the intersection of passion, outcome, and being one's best self leads to overall excellence in any endeavor. The circle of competencies around the motivational drivers that define the hedgehog of excellent care could even represent a round sandbox ready for innovative and creative play!

Exhibit 4.4 Required Skill Sets and Knowledge

| Functional and technical knowledge | • Finance and reimbursement
• Legal, compliance, and regulatory
• Strategic and project planning
• Information technology |

| Personal insight and leadership | • Ability to develop and articulate a vision
• Skill at seeking strategic pathways for best possible outcomes
• Receptivity to collaboration
• Willingness and ability to receive feedback with highest level of self-reflection and awareness |

ADVANTAGES OF HAVING PHYSICIANS AT THE TABLE

For physicians to be effective participants and leaders in transformational change (zero harm, improved quality and safety, and innovation in evidence-based care), they need these critical skills that have been historically overlooked in their medical education. In their clinical roles, physicians act as sole decision makers, using information provided by others to inform their decisions. Clinical work is an individual process; it rarely requires a team of others. But the redesign of healthcare and physician engagement in this transformation is by necessity a collaborative pursuit. Health system leaders need to make a similar transformation, recognizing physicians as partners in care redesign initiatives rather than taking independent action asking physicians to adapt to their decisions. To the contrary, health system leaders should ask physicians to serve as co-architects in the decision-making process (true engagement). Physicians are comfortable dealing with the unknown and are trained to press through uncertainty. Most physicians want to analyze decisions before recommending some action. When clinical ambiguity occurs, they desire consensus from their peers.

Most administrators train to be doers and to take action quickly. This approach can be effective when the variables are known and the expected outcomes are clear: Follow the rules (the protocol), and the expected outcome should happen exactly in the expected way. Physicians do not see solutions to problems in the same way and can often be seen as obstinate and resistant to change because of this myopic viewpoint. But when administrators invite physicians to the table and engage them in the design of the process to achieve a shared goal, the physicians will react with all their best skills brought to the table. They will bring intelligence (intellectual and emotional), dedication, and diligence in completing tasks. They will ask enough of the right questions, using analytic and evidence-based thought, and will take a patient-first approach. Forgetting to both enroll and engage physicians leads to the project's sure demise before it is even launched.

BEYOND ENGAGEMENT TO ALIGNMENT: CASE STUDY

Consider the case of a patient, MS, who fell and fractured her hip and had it surgically repaired at an academic medical center. The patient was mildly confused in the postoperative period and needed long-term rehabilitation. After three days in the acute setting, she was transferred to a local skilled nursing facility for rehabilitation. She had no immediate family members nearby, and her own primary care physician did not attend residents at the skilled facility. On the second evening after arrival at the skilled facility, MS developed chest pain and was transferred to a local community hospital just five minutes away. The patient underwent testing to rule out a cardiac event, and she returned to the skilled facility. On her return, the nursing staff noted three conflicting medication lists and discharge instructions captured on three different EHR systems. She was more confused and had no family member to help sort out her care.

One would like to believe that in the practice of twenty-first-century medicine, patient scenarios like this would not exist. With the advent of specialized interventions; the efficiency of 24-7 hospitalist team care; and improved tests, surgical interventions, and pharmaceutical treatments, careful and coordinated care should be accessible to every citizen. Additionally, artificial intelligence algorithms, best-practice alerts, and "hard stops" in the EHRs should have resolved these transition-of-care issues. Unfortunately, these problems still exist; patient scenarios like the one involving MS are commonplace in the healthcare system. Never was the case more urgent for physician involvement in the quality and safety of patient care than in this example of multiple transitions of care. Inviting physicians to help solve the friction points around transitions of care in this case to improve the patient's health and experience with the healthcare system is a powerful way to better align goals and achieve a shared vision for success.

It ultimately took engaged and aligned physician leadership to ascertain that the patient was confused because of the postoperative effects of anesthesia, the administration of pain medication, and mild underlying dementia. And her chest pain had been caused by constipation; she had not moved her bowels for at least five days. Capturing the patient story revealed that she was lonely and had a poor diet, little access to healthy food, and essentially no means of transportation.

This example illustrates the importance of engaged physician leadership in solving and managing complex health and healthcare dilemmas. Protocols were established for "warm hand-offs" in transitions of care between the three healthcare facilities involved in the care of this patient, for improved "hard-stop" alerts of bowel function and pain assessment in the EHR, and for better communication with a distant relative who was willing to assist with the patient's recovery, transportation, and overall care. Every team member participated in the successful return of this patient to her home (with assistance), but it was physician leadership that helped pull all of the pieces together into systematic improvement.

This example illustrates the need for physician leadership in transitions of care and in life transitions overall. Atul Gawande makes this point in *Being Mortal* (2014): "We've been wrong about what our job is in medicine. We think our job is to ensure health and survival. But really it is larger than that. It is to enable well-being." Physician leaders are positioned to understand the nuance of patient scenarios like this. They must be engaged in these kinds of cases to guarantee systematic outcomes for better safety, quality, and, ultimately, patient well-being.

PHYSICIAN LEADERS IN STRESSFUL TIMES

In times of natural disaster or public health crises, physician leaders also demonstrate the innate ability to solve complex problems and create nimble, flexible approaches to manage chaotic and unclear situations. This ability perhaps comes from another key element of physicians' unique training. Essentially every other professional training course builds leadership through standard pathways following a standardized trajectory. Physicians, on the other hand, possess unique and multibranched learning pathways. The typical medical student experience involves intense focus month by month in constantly shifting environments—from the cardiac catheterization lab, to a student-run free clinic, to a surgical operating theater, to an emergency department sick bay. During the 20,000-plus hours of medical training, the learners are forced to adapt quickly to myriad teams, stressors, conversations, teaching styles, and environments, just to name a few. Long hours, little sleep, multitasking, and strategic prioritization of the daily work before them makes the physician in training fertile soil for further leadership development during chaotic situations. Countless examples of selfless heroism on the front lines of new and unknown infectious diseases like SARS, MERS, and COVID stand alongside treatment of such better-known yet still disruptive infections and diseases as influenza, measles, polio, various bacterial infections, and cancer. The day-to-day work of the physician embraces the ambiguity and humility of what is unknown about a disease and what is unknown about patient care. Unleashing this potential by inviting physician leaders to complex healthcare problem solving yields great results when their engagement is aligned with the strategic priorities of the organization.

POTENTIAL FOR BURNOUT

Another unique aspect of physicians' professional lives is the high potential for burnout. Healthcare executives and organizations must recognize the prevalence of, and predisposition to, burnout, and they need to offer tools to assess physicians' risk of burnout. Physicians rarely ask for help, and if they do, the request is often much too late or in the middle of a spiraling crisis. They seldom reach out to employee assistance programs or state medical society programs addressing burnout and impairment. Why they don't avail themselves of these services is unclear. Some suggest that screening physicians in the same way that patients are screened for loneliness and depression would be beneficial. For example, individuals who answer yes to the question "Are you lonely?" and "No more than five" to "How many individuals can you call on for support outside of immediate family?" are at high risk for major depression and other untoward health outcomes, including suicide, even before they are given further screening questionnaires. In the same manner, answering yes to burnout survey questions or inventories reveals which physicians are at risk for significant effects of burnout. Healthcare system leaders must make screening for burnout a normative exercise for all leaders—physician and nonphysician—to guarantee a healthy and whole workforce. They must understand that physicians are at higher risk for burnout than are other professionals.

What unique aspect of the physician psyche finds physicians reporting close to 50 percent dissatisfaction with the demands of their profession? Whether the physician is employed or in private practice, primary care, or specialty care does not seem to matter.

Why don't lawyers, business leaders, and other professionals report numbers of burnout this high? Is it perfectionism and fear of failure that drives them to the point of 50 percent professional dissatisfaction? Is it tasks in the EHR, administrative burden, or loss of autonomy? Is it reluctance to change and resistance to learning the competencies that will set physicians up for joy and the "best possibility to come" attitude rather than the reality of "what is missing today?" All these possibilities have been proposed as causes of physician burnout, and nothing will undermine engagement and alignment like burnout. If burnout is assessed early, intentionally, and often over a physician's career, and the importance of mentors and mentoring is emphasized as a tool to build resilience, trusted guidance, and feedback, then the physician will succeed in ways that hearken back to the days of collaboration in the sandbox or on the playground. Even if a physician rejects deliberate leadership development, the individual will find professional fulfillment and meaning in deeper ways that enable better relationships with friends, family, patients, and staff alike. Healthcare system leaders must screen for burnout and provide ways for physicians to address this problem to ensure every physician's growth and well-being.

Healthcare systems become a unifying force when a clear, common goal is outlined, when physician input is sought, and when metrics are tied to meaningful strategy and outcomes. When these unified systems face a crisis, even the people most averse to change are willing to work together toward a new approach. Under these circumstances, the value of the physicians' scientific approach and problem-solving deficit thinking combines with the "best is yet to come" mindset. It does not matter who is in or out with management when the system is unified; siloed walls will come tumbling down. Rules and regulations are not ignored, but flexibility is encouraged and barriers are permanently removed. In many ways, moments of crisis expose the worst problems of medicine—glaring health disparities and inequities, for example—and the great potential for its brightest days to come. Effectively, unification helps protect all aspects of patient care from unnecessary interventions, errors, and actual patient harm. Such unified health systems build a firm foundation of better quality, improved safety, and high reliability and focus on those who truly need healthcare. In these unified systems, social determinants are addressed so as to build better infrastructure and community support for those most in need—people who are lonely, poor, or marginalized. In this way, patients like MS live out their lives to the fullest potential in the healthiest way possible.

PHYSICIANS DEVELOP "RANGE"

Epstein (2019) writes that "generalists triumph in a specialized world." He gives great examples of situations where human thinking defeated artificial intelligence constructs. He also describes world-class athletes and musicians excelling at multiple pursuits, not just their individual sport or instrument. He writes about the paradox of knowledge: "Knowledge is a double-edged sword. It allows you to do something, but also makes you blind to other things you could do." In tough circumstances, in times of crisis as well as stability, when generalists need to solve tough problems, the motto "Adapt, improvise, and overcome" defines their point of view. Regardless of their individual specialties, physicians have great potential to be generalist thinkers and lead their clinics, teams, community organizations, and health systems by following "adapt, improvise, and overcome." Generalists are uniquely positioned to apply lateral thinking and a broad range of skills to the most confounding clinical or health system dilemmas they encounter. It is in these dilemmas that the ultimate in physician engagement is needed.

CONCLUSION

Health system leaders can understand the uniqueness of physicians and their training and present them with a fair and honest invitation to leadership by assessing and developing core competencies and motivating factors. When leaders systematically and methodically take these steps to engage physicians, including offerings of mentoring and assessment for burnout, the leaders better enable and motivate the physicians to face every situation that this world throws at them. The hedgehog—a metaphor for a person who knows and does one thing successfully and with deep satisfaction—emerges at the intersection of clinical passion, financial stewardship, and engagement in a greater good and shared vision of success. Hedgehogs perhaps do not lend an image of the speediest of all creatures of nature, but they are resilient and committed. Although they are prickly at times, their exterior blankets purposeful intent underneath. Readers may even find a physician hedgehog digging and playing in the sandboxes of their boardrooms, a downtown free clinic, or the executive suite. When they find such a hedgehog, it means they have found a physician truly engaged in the work, good at it, and deeply involved with the organization. It means engagement to the highest degree, and the journey to greatness—personal and professional—truly begins. Now is the moment for healthcare executives to invest in and expand physician leadership development and opportunity in their organizations. Doing so will certainly drive higher levels of engagement.

REFERENCES

Collins, J. C. 2001. *Good to Great: Why Some Companies Make the Leap and Others Don't.* New York: HarperBusiness.

Dye, C. F. 2017. *Leadership in Healthcare: Essential Values and Skills*, 3rd ed. Chicago: Health Administration Press.

Epstein, D. J. 2019. *Range: Why Generalists Triumph in a Specialized World.* New York: Riverhead Books.

Gawande, A. 2014. *Being Mortal: Medicine and What Matters in the End.* New York: Metropolitan Books/Henry Holt & Company.

Kotter, J. P. 2012. *Leading Change*. Boston: Harvard Business Review Press.

Phillips, K. A., N. S. Ospina, and V. M. Montori. 2019. "Physicians Interrupting Patients." *Journal of General Internal Medicine* 34 (10): 1965.

Rios, I. C. 2016. "The Contemporary Culture in Medical School and Its Influence on Training Doctors in Ethics and Humanistic Attitude to the Clinical Practice." *International Journal of Ethics Education* 1 (2): 173–82.

Sim, D., S. E. Yuan, and J. H. Yun. 2016. "Health Literacy and Physician–Patient Communication: A Review of the Literature." *International Journal of Communication and Health*. Accessed March 8, 2021. http://communicationandhealth.ro/upload/number10/DON-SIM.pdf.

Taylor C. A., J. C. Taylor, and J. K. Stoller. 2008. "Exploring Leadership Competencies in Established and Aspiring Physician Leaders: An Interview-Based Study." *Journal of General Internal Medicine* 23 (6): 748–54.

Zander, R. S., and B. Zander. 2002. *The Art of Possibility: Transforming Professional and Personal Life*. New York: Penguin.

CHAPTER 5

Larger Paddles and Bigger Boats

Lisa M. Casey

No member of a crew is praised for the rugged individuality of his rowing.
—Alfred North Whitehead, "Harvard: The Future," 1936

Physician leadership is critical for better patient outcomes, clinical performance and professional satisfaction. That's true not only during emergencies, but also for managing chronic diseases or improving hospital efficiency.
—Dhruv Khullar, "Good Leaders Make Good Doctors," 2019

What really matters is whether there is leadership at these organizations willing to have the difficult one to one conversations on a consistent basis. I believe that physician leaders, who both have clinical expertise and credibility, are best suited for this role.
—David Liu, "To Change Health Care, We Need More Physician Leaders," 2013

Physicians have many skills and personality traits that can make them among the best, most well-rounded healthcare leaders. They have a true understanding of the intricacies of patient care, which combined with operations and business acumen allows for a potent leadership mix.
—Steve Quach, "How to Prepare Physicians to Be Leaders," 2020

Beyond physician satisfaction, alignment, or cooperation with hospital systems, engaged physician champions serve as a motivating force for quality improvement initiatives and inspiring colleagues.
—Ted A. James, "Engaging Physicians to Lead Change in Health Care," 2020

Increasingly, savvy healthcare leaders understand that physician engagement and physician leadership are closely intertwined; enhanced physician leadership yields enhanced physician engagement.
—Carson F. Dye, *Leadership in Healthcare*, 2017

IT CANNOT BE said enough: We need more physician leaders. We need to give them larger paddles, and we need larger boats or canoes so that we can bring more physicians along with us.

Physicians are the hub of the healthcare team. They make decisions that heavily influence other healthcare team members. Physicians interact directly with patients and their families. They drive much of the quality in the healthcare arena, and they have a significant impact on the patient experience. Much is at stake when physicians are not engaged. Mosley and Miller (2015) write that "after four years of college, four years of medical school, and three to seven or more years of training, many physicians go through their day feeling powerless, despite their unique, specialized knowledge." James (2020) writes that "engaging physicians in leading change is a proven strategy for improving health care. At its foundation, it is a healthy relationship built on trust and mutual support. Addressing issues surrounding burnout, ease of practice, and opportunities for quality improvement are important drivers of physician engagement. However, it is also about physicians embracing ownership."

Larger paddles and larger boats? Organizations have too long relied on the chief medical officers as being the all-inclusive

Source: Drawing by Victor Zhang.

representative of the physician workforce. Although more organizations have, fortunately, been enlarging their physician leadership cadres, the efforts are falling short. Today's healthcare environment demands more physicians. And it requires that physicians be given more substantive roles in influencing policy and tactics.

THE EVOLVING QUALITIES OF EXCELLENT PHYSICIANS

The medical field is always evolving but has done so more quickly since the 1990s. The new environment is a culture of healthcare regulations combined with an abundance of fast-moving changes. The shifting climate of healthcare has added many new qualifications a physician must have to be considered excellent. The practice of medicine has now entered the age of information; an abundance of evidence-based decision-making and organizational efforts takes precedence over the mastery of science and innovation.

Individual initiative is usually what motivates physicians to begin their medical training. The skills that got them admitted to medical school were their competitive instincts and their ability to rise above their peers. They needed a keen understanding of the scientific process and why the body does what it does to understand the abundance of research behind the practice of medicine. The skills that physicians needed to make it through their residency include diligent study and the ability to distinguish between what they know and what they still need to learn as individual practitioners. Each rotation required them to assess their lack of knowledge to round out their intellectual acumen. They obtained habits of combing the literature and other information sources to round out their problem-solving skills. Once they gain these abilities and graduate, new levels of proficiencies are needed as they become practicing physicians in this new stage of their careers.

Physicians need to juggle many perspectives as they continue to evolve in the practice of medicine. Their communication skills in patient care evolve from individual teaching and orator skills to mentoring and other collaborative activities. Research has shown that patient compliance improves with patient-centered or motivational discussions with the patient. Burke, Arkowitz, and Menchola (2003) explain the concept of motivational interviewing, which puts the patient in the driver's seat and in charge of their healthcare decisions. The research shows that motivational interviewing has a significant impact on patient behavior and that physicians should have this set of skills to navigate patient care. No longer are physicians simply providing information during an office visit; they must now understand how to motivate patients and share information in a more interactive style. Another new set of skills, involving virtual healthcare management, has become necessary since the COVID-19 pandemic. Patient care is more than simply knowing how to treat a condition or disease and attempting to pass on that knowledge. Physicians need to communicate in a smarter, more efficient, and motivational way while also learning the technical skills and the art of communicating virtually and in person.

Most agree with Baker and Denis (2011) that the practice of medicine has "traditionally been considered a model of individual professionalism where each practitioner works with his or her own patients in discrete areas of practice and where the defining influence on medical decision making is based on assessing the needs of the patient." But this view has changed considerably. Population health is emerging as an economic force. The medical system itself is adapting to a different mindset as physicians are asked to consider healthcare issues of an entire population, not just the patient in front of them. As society is figuring out how population health affects us all, more and more rules and protocols are being created to handle the new information. Making a living as an independent practitioner, with the shifting billing, coding, and other healthcare rules and regulations, is far more challenging now and has spurred many physicians to decide to be employed instead. As a result, many more physicians find themselves part of bulky healthcare systems that often function as spiraling bureaucracies.

The number of skills physicians need to navigate the world of medicine has quadrupled. Complex systems now challenge physicians who once thrived in small independent practices. Physicians now have to understand clinical science and the rapid changes in medicine, keep up with the latest advances in healthcare, and be able to communicate all this in motivational ways to patients. They then have to understand population health and its effects on the economics of medicine and use their leadership skills to motivate healthcare teams to deliver that care.

Perreira and colleagues (2019) stated it well: "Physicians have long emphasized their critical role as patient advocates and held themselves accountable for effective care." Physicians are taught and trained to be decision makers and to bridge the gap for their patients so the patients have a better understanding of their issues. As physicians navigate these healthcare systems as team members, leaders should remember that physicians' training aimed to help them become critical, innovative thinkers who always put the patient's interest first. As a society, we still need these skills in our practitioners, but as the healthcare landscape shifts, this change can be a setup for conflict if management and physicians are not on the same page.

CONSEQUENCES OF DISENFRANCHISED PHYSICIANS

Naturally, many aspects of healthcare can suffer when physicians are disengaged.

- **Patient satisfaction scores:** Alienated and withdrawn physicians can have adverse effects on patient satisfaction scores. When patients who believe they received high-quality care tell other prospective patients, the organization's market share can increase as word of mouth spreads. The internet is filled with ratings and reviews. These patient satisfaction scores are also being used as quality metrics and incentive bonuses for entire organizations. Press Ganey (2019) reports that high workforce engagement is associated with improved or maintained patient experience scores from one year to the next, whereas no such improvement or maintenance is seen in the presence of low workforce engagement. Disengaged, or worse, disenfranchised, physicians can wreak havoc on these metrics.

- **Momentum for initiatives in the healthcare system:** Employees working with physicians can be affected in positive or negative ways by physician engagement. Frustrated staff may leave to find other employment, leading to higher turnover. High turnover can be a tough problem for everyone, including managers and patients. The constant change of team members makes new healthcare initiatives more challenging, and the shifting roles as staff members turn over adds considerable time to implementing the needed changes.

- **Quality metrics:** Patient care quality is now as much focused on preventive care metrics as on the knowledge of contemporary medical practice. Physicians explain disease processes and treatments to patients, and these conversations set up certain expectations for those patients. For example, good metrics for preventive care like breast and colon cancer screenings can be hard to achieve if patients do not fully understand the importance of these screenings. Engaged physicians can better motivate patients to get these tests; disengaged physicians do a poorer job, and ultimately, costs go up.

In summary, if physician engagement is critical to healthcare success, how can organizations help physicians improve amid the pressures and learn new skills to stay engaged? As trite as it may sound, we will use a boat metaphor: Give physicians larger paddles, and get larger boats so that more physicians can get on board the engagement journey. Moreover, organizations must ensure that all physicians are paddling in the same direction.

THE BOAT AS A METAPHOR

Simplifying the team concept to an activity can help us form a mental image. One such group activity is paddling a boat. A group of people in a canoe or some other boat need to be paddling in the same direction, or the boat will either stop, go in the wrong direction, or even possibly go in circles. The people in the boat need to understand which direction to aim for and be given the paddles to get through the water. More to the point, the paddles must be big enough to move the water. The larger the paddle, the more the boat will move, with less effort.

Anyone on a healthcare team who is daily reading through contemporary data to select the most relevant or important aspects can attest to the frustration and exhaustion that handling data can

Exhibit 5.1 Three Parts of the Paddle

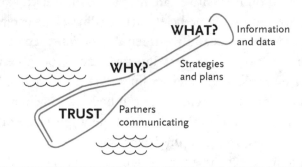

cause. Without a doubt, we are immersed in the information age. Different metrics appear each day, new research on medical care continues to surface, and there is an increasing demand for even greater customer service. It is difficult for any one person to keep up with the latest in medical advances, the always-expanding healthcare rules and regulations, and the ever-changing demands on their time and expertise. We need a team effort to navigate the waters together. Each member of the team has their own part to play and their own paddle—that is, the information they need to put their skills into action to do their part to start paddling in the right direction.

Consider the metaphor further by picturing the three main parts of the paddle: the grip, the shaft, and the blade (exhibit 5.1). All three parts are important to help the team members glide through the waters more efficiently.

- **Grip:** This part of the paddle helps the physician grasp, or grip, *what* is going on with the organization, the physician's practice, and healthcare trends in general.
- **Shaft:** The shaft represents the purpose, or the *why*, of the strategies and plans in place. It considers why certain trends are happening. The shaft symbolizes the administration's best guess and plan of attack to solve problems.

- **Blade:** The blade of the paddle does the actual work of moving the water. It represents *trust*, the two-way street required for physicians and healthcare leaders to work together through the changes they face. This level of cooperative communication is needed if the organization is to survive in the fluctuating world of healthcare. Trust allows a true partnership.

The What

Knowledge (background, pertinent, clear, and concise) is the grip of the handle. It represents what physicians and all other members of an organization must know to function effectively. The types of information needed are described in the following paragraphs.

Background information: Physicians are taught to review clinical literature by looking for the flaws in the articles or guidelines. The questions clinicians need to ask about medical data to treat their patients starts with the validity of the facts. Is this a real phenomenon? Or did this happen by chance? Physicians must weigh information to determine if a treatment can be safely used on a patient, or the patient may suffer. They must be confident that the data is reliable. Society itself wants medical evidence that is real, measurable, and accurate. Physicians are under a great deal of pressure with those decisions. Healthcare leaders need to understand that because physicians apply a critical, scientific viewpoint to information, the leaders must be vigilant in presenting data to physicians.

Cherf (2019) echoes this recommendation on how to include physicians in data discussions: "Ensure that physicians have a strong voice in determining what data to share and how to share it. Physicians frequently prefer a value-based approach that incorporates clinical and patient-centered outcomes. Consistent, relevant benchmarks will keep physicians focused on organizational goals." Paranjpe (2016) talks about timing: "When data is presented untouched and unabridged, it doesn't lie. However, just having the data is not enough. Clinicians need it in real time; only then will they be able to take action, and only then will trust be established in the data." How many times have physicians sat in meetings and questioned the validity or the applicability of data that was presented? How many times have physicians challenged the accuracy of data? Falk, Cherf, and Schuylz (2018) suggest that "health systems should ensure that data is organized and presented in a way that is clinically meaningful and emphasizes high-quality patient care. Beginning a dialogue with physicians by asking them to reduce costs does not always inspire collaboration. To get physicians more involved, analyze cost drivers within the clinical context."

Increasing numbers of healthcare organizations provide some type of financial incentives to employed physicians for meeting specific quality goals. When they are given incentives or quality data that seem arbitrary, it will take time for physicians to be comfortable with the legitimacy of that data. Giving physicians the why and the data behind decisions enhances administrative credibility and shows that their time is respected and valued.

What is relevant and high-quality data? The information must be pertinent, clear, and concise.

Pertinent information: Good data is relevant to medical practice. Physicians must have good data to make decisions. And good data empowers physicians to make changes that matter to clinical care. So often, physicians are given data that is hard to understand or difficult to apply to their daily practices. The understanding of how the organization pulled the data also saves the physician thinking time when processing the information scientifically as they are trained to do. Too much information given at once or information not relevant to an initiative will also frustrate physicians as they wade through it.

Clear and concise evidence: Clear, concise information that tells a story needs less explanation and therefore saves time. Physicians have to process new studies and information for patient care and are accustomed to basing plans on that data. Telling physicians what to think about the data will not be as productive as telling them how administration interprets the data and then pausing to hear, consider, and respect their thoughts. Clearly communicating the information in ways that explain the problems or why decisions have been made helps team members better understand the context and perspective. When physicians can easily process information, they will come up with plans to help. Healthcare leaders should remember that micromanaging has been associated with burnout and that autonomy breeds resilience.

Leaders who can explain information so that others can easily understand it make a tremendous contribution toward building a stronger grip for the paddle.

The Why

Transparent vision of the why (not the how) is the shaft of the paddle. This vision relates to the initiatives, strategies, plans, and tactics in place to respond to current trends and issues. And transparency means openly sharing the administration's best guesses and plans of attack to solve problems.

Once physicians can understand the issues at stake or the changes needed, the next step for administrators is to help them understand why the organization has decided to move in a certain direction. Being transparent about both the information gathered and why the administration wants an initiative to happen helps focus the communication. The leaders should ask themselves, what would physicians want in the communication flow?

Physicians have had to learn the why and how behind the science of medicine to practice medicine. As a result, they anticipate outcomes. It does not help healthcare organizations to curb physicians' tendency to ask why when it comes to healthcare policies, strategies, or tactical plans. Involving them early in discussions can be an invaluable tool in creating the policies that the physicians will more easily follow. Showalter and Williams (2016) write that "engaging physicians is about creating a unified vision and working to achieve the vision." Physician buy-in will increase when they understand the why. They will feel more comfortable anticipating possible pitfalls, because they understand the issues at stake.

When studying physician engagement, several hospital systems have published data on physician communication. Atkinson et al. (2011) found that the organizations that communicated widely and effectively with physicians were using a variety of methods and persistence. They found that face-to-face communication, especially from senior leaders, was crucial. Atkinson and his colleagues went on to say that routine open and honest discussions with an emphasis on listening, responding to others, and closing the feedback loop were the best practice.

Background: If physicians know the background behind a decision and understand why it was made, they will usually support the decision, even when they disagree with it. Moreover, understanding how leadership reached those conclusions enhances transparency, which improves trust.

Goals: The why behind goals can make a vast difference in how teams work toward achieving those goals and reduces misunderstandings about which goals are priorities. As teams work together to attain the targets, they may come up with different ideas on how to achieve them. Making the purpose (the why) clear also helps team members avoid wasting energy. Unclear goals can frustrate the members and derail their efforts.

If a healthcare organization moves in one direction and physicians perceive it is moving in a different direction, reconciling the two paths can be quite a challenge, especially when each party is acting on incorrect assumptions. Knowing the why behind a strategy can prevent these misunderstandings before the physicians have to course-correct. These scenarios are among the most frustrating to physicians, and multiple misunderstandings will eventually lead to mistrust.

Feedback: Information exchange must operate as a two-way street. For example, leaders might be using incomplete data to make decisions while the physicians may have the missing information. If physicians are involved early in the decision process, they may be able to provide those facts and better decisions will result. Leaders must be sure to routinely seek out physician input. These efforts alone will be a huge step toward ensuring that trust and transparency work both ways.

Trust

The bulk of the paddle, the blade, represents trust. Physicians must trust the information they receive about their practices, their workplace or organization, overall healthcare trends, and other issues that confront them.

Communicating what an organization is striving for and why it is moving in a certain direction guarantees transparency and opens pathways that head off or clear up confusion. Trust can help to move all on the boat through the waters of change. Building trust can vary according to person, but most people have similar requirements. MacLeod (2019) writes that trust is the "firm belief and confidence in the reliability, integrity and ability of another." Dependability, or knowing what to expect coupled with believing that you can rely on someone, is the essence of trust. A person in a boat with others can trust the team only after getting to know each team member, learning what each is capable of, and knowing how to interpret other team members' signals. MacLeod adds that "trust is the foundational bedrock upon which everything else is built." Let's look at how we can build trust.

Trust administration to lead. Most physicians have traditionally had an ambiguous relationship with the organization, practicing in it but never actually feeling part of it. Kaissi (2012) reports that these feelings of separateness, "coupled with increasing external and internal pressures for efficiency, cost control, and improved quality and service have resulted in a strained relationship between physicians and managers." Part of the trust with administration comes from regular communication and a personal knowledge of the administrators who are making the decisions that affect the physician's practice.

Chokshi and Swensen (2019) write that "the more layers between frontline clinicians and those making momentous decisions about how care should be organized, the more cynicism and disengagement you are likely to experience." In a survey they conducted, Chokshi and Swensen (2019) found that "the number one initiative that is most effective at engaging clinicians at their organization was involving clinicians in organizational decision making." Getting to know the decision makers in administration helps physicians understand the reasons and values that drive these leaders. Being acquainted with the decision makers helps physicians better understand the logic and thinking behind the conclusions.

Knowing what the administration is doing and why, and being involved in the decision-making helps physicians build trust with the administration.

Trust your team members and gain their trust, so that they can follow and participate in organizational planning and action. A considerable part of this trust is understanding each person's duties in the office and on the team. A clear delineation of duties and an understanding of each person's role makes for a smoother day at the office, as skills are not wasted and responsibilities are not duplicated. Getting to know the values and communication styles of team members can also make a big difference and help avoid miscommunication. Providing time for some socialization (e.g., lunch breaks and group outings) will also improve communication, increase understanding, and, ultimately, build trust.

Much research has been done on teamwork and the values of honesty and accountability in groups. Open and frank discussion in which each team member is respected and valued is the basis for great relationships, which will then build a great team. Trust in a team makes the workday and the experience of providing patient care better for everyone involved. This means increased engagement for the whole team as well as physicians.

Help physicians trust themselves to lead. Leadership training and opportunities for skills acquisition for new and potential physician leaders are essential to helping them have faith in themselves. Just as medical knowledge increased physicians' self-assurance as they obtained their medical licenses, leadership training will make them feel more comfortable taking on extra leadership roles. Once physicians feel competent at their trade of medicine, many look for that next step in their careers. Most physicians hunger for all types of knowledge, and this desire certainly applies to leadership.

Knowledge about healthcare finance, marketing, and strategy even at a basic level will give physicians better insight into what healthcare organizations are doing. It will also increase their confidence in the decisions that leaders make for their organizations. The language of administration and the world of the MBA can be intimidating unless there is at least a rudimentary knowledge of the vocabulary.

Interestingly, many physicians do not believe they are leaders. As Quach (2020) observes, "The few doctors who do end up in leadership roles often struggle because they do not know how their own strengths and weaknesses line up with leadership. There is often a fundamental mismatch between the skills and mindset that served them well as clinicians and those demanded by their new role." He adds, "That's a shame, because physicians have many skills and personality traits that can make them among the best, most well-rounded healthcare leaders. They have a true understanding of the intricacies of patient care, which combined with operations and business acumen allows for a potent leadership mix. Indeed, there's evidence that hospitals run by physicians perform better than those that aren't. Doctors also tend to possess several personality traits—conscientiousness, emotional stability, and extroversion—that correlate to good leadership." Helping physicians see the part they play and the influence they have with teams will increase their own expectations and trust of themselves as leaders.

CONCRETE IDEAS TO EMPHASIZE THE WHAT, THE WHY, AND TRUST

Helping with the What

- Help physicians gain knowledge by offering leadership training, providing funds for education, and encouraging them to attend conferences to get energized.
- Promote active quality-improvement projects, helping to obtain the data for these projects and analyzing physician concerns.
- Conduct brief hospital meetings that include educational elements, and have an active continuing medical education department.
- Compacts, discussed in the following paragraphs, can highlight the organization's expectations and call attention to the issues at hand.

Compacts are different from a physician code of conduct. A physician compact, an agreement between a physician and one or more parties, spells out the expectations that each side has for the other. While some expectations may be written and others are unwritten, a compact should develop a shared sense of what physicians expect to give to the organization and what physicians expect to get from it in return. As a healthcare administrator, you cannot make a compact by simply adding to the professional code of conduct a few extra sentences that address the agreement you would like to have with the physician. The information will be overlooked and get lost in the midst of the yearly paperwork we all sign.

A good compact will instead spell out the rules of engagement and communication, the two most important parts of the compact. A compact can be a great way to let physicians know how valuable they are and that you, they, and everyone else are all on the same team.

The compact can serve as the outline of a great conversation on expectations with the physician's leader. The language used can be as simple as the following:

- "We promise to do this for you."
- "We would like you to promise to do this for us."
- "This is the reason why, and here is what we are trying to accomplish through these behaviors."

An excellent resource on physician compacts is Mary Jane Kornacki's *A New Compact: Aligning Physician–Organization Expectations to Transform Patient Care* (Kornacki 2015).

Helping with the Why

- Make sure you have clear communication tools. Work diligently to reach physicians in the way that is the most effective (e.g., e-mails, face-to-face conversations), and use clear language. Seriously consider creating a physician intranet with newsworthy information.
- Compose brief e-mails, and consider the receiver's point of view when you write them.
- Add some websites explaining new government regulations and the rationale behind them.
- Use an intranet to explain changes that affect physicians—and explain the reasoning behind the changes as much as you can.

Building Trust

- Help the team get to know each other. Introduce new clinical staff formally via e-mails and the physician intranet.

- Plan some social events (e.g., hospital-wide picnics, office retreats, and other social events), and provide workshop support from the administration.
- Assign mentors for new physicians. Develop more formalized onboarding and mentoring programs.
- Make sure that new-personnel orientation sessions to the health system include members of the administration team.

CONCLUSION

Physicians need many new qualities and skills in this changing era of healthcare. Healthcare leaders who understand and acknowledge the challenges physicians face to stay current will have the ear, the respect, and the engagement of their physicians. Disenfranchisement or disengagement can come from many directions, but many tools can help physicians work more efficiently and lead more effectively. The paddle metaphor can help. Paddles can have many shapes and sizes, but the basics are the same. Enthusiasm, engagement, and partnership are the outcomes when physicians know the what and the why and have trust in their organization's leaders.

REFERENCES

Atkinson, S., P. Spurgeon, J. Clark, and K. Armit. 2011. *Engaging Doctors: What Can We Learn from Trusts with High Levels of Medical Engagement?* Published March 1. Academy of Royal Medical Colleges. www.aomrc.org.uk/wp-content/uploads/2016/05/Engaging_Doctors_trusts_with_high_level_engagement_2011.pdf.

Baker, G. R., and J.-L. Denis. 2011. "Medical Leadership in Health Care Systems: From Professional Authority to Organizational Leadership." *Public Money & Management* 31 (5): 355–62.

Burke, B. L., H. Arkowitz, and M. Menchola. 2003. "The Efficacy of Motivational Interviewing: A Meta-Analysis of Controlled Clinical Trials." *Journal of Consulting and Clinical Psychology* 71 (5): 843–61.

Cherf, J. 2019. "Doctors Need Data to Drive Cost and Quality Decisions." *Medical Economics*. Published May 23. www.medicaleconomics.com/view/doctors-need-data-drive-cost-and-quality-decisions.

Chokshi, D. A., and S. Swensen. 2019. "Leadership Survey: Why Clinicians Are Not Engaged, and What Leaders Must Do About It." *NEJM Catalyst* (blog). Published August 8. https://cdn2.hubspot.net/hubfs/558940/Insights%20Council%20Monthly%20-%20Files/Why%20Clinicians%20Are%20Not%20Engaged%20and%20What%20Leaders%20Must%20Do%20About%20It.pdf.

Dye, C. F. 2017. *Leadership in Healthcare: Essential Values and Skills*, 3rd ed. Chicago: Health Administration Press.

Falk, S., J. Cherf, and J. Schuylz. 2018. "Better Ways to Communicate Hospital Data to Physicians." *Harvard Business Review*. Published October 31. https://hbr.org/2018/10/better-ways-to-communicate-hospital-data-to-physicians.

James, T. 2020. "Engaging Physicians to Lead Change in Health Care." *Lean Forward* (Harvard Medical School blog). Published January 9. https://leanforward.hms.harvard.edu/2020/01/09/engaging-physicians-to-lead-change-in-health-care.

Kaissi, A. 2012. *A Roadmap for Trust: Enhancing Physician Engagement*. Ottawa, ON: Canadian Policy Network.

Khullar, D. 2019. "Good Leaders Make Good Doctors." *New York Times*, November 21.

Kornacki, M. J. 2015. *A New Compact: Aligning Physician–Organization Expectations to Transform Patient Care*. Chicago: Health Administration Press.

Liu, D. 2013. "To Change Health Care, We Need More Physician Leaders." *KevinMD* (blog). Published August 9. www.kevinmd.com/blog/2013/08/change-health-care-physician-leaders.html.

MacLeod, L. 2019. "Trust: The Key to Building Stronger Physician Relationships." American Association of Physician Leaders. Published February 28. www.physicianleaders.org/news/trust-key-building-stronger-physician-relationships.

Mosley, K., and P. Miller. 2015. "Our Fragile, Fragmented Physician Workforce: How to Keep Today's Physicians Engaged and Productive." *Journal of Medical Practice Management* 31 (2): 92–95.

Paranjpe, P. 2016. "How to Use Data Analytics to Engage Physicians." *Healthcare Innovation*. Published February 23. www.hcinnovationgroup.com/analytics-ai/article/13007598/how-to-use-data-analytics-to-engage-physicians.

Perreira, T. A., L. Perrier, M. Prokopy, L. Neves-Mera, and D. D. Persaud. 2019. "Physician Engagement: A Concept Analysis." *Journal of Healthcare Leadership*. Published July 26. www.dovepress.com/physician-engagement-a-concept-analysis-peer-reviewed-fulltext-article-JHL.

Press Ganey. 2019. *Health Care Workforce Special Report: The State of Engagement*. South Bend, IN: Press Ganey Associates.

Quach, S. 2020. "How to Prepare Physicians to Be Leaders." *Medical Economics*. Published February 13. www.medicaleconomics.com/view/how-prepare-physicians-be-leaders.

Showalter, J. W., and L. T. Williams. 2016. *Mastering Physician Engagement: A Practical Guide to Achieving Shared Outcomes*. Boca Raton, FL: CRC Press.

Whitehead, A. N. 1936. "Harvard: The Future." *Atlantic Monthly*, September.

CHAPTER 6

Physicians as Leaders

Carson F. Dye

"I GIVE ORDERS, and the staff follow them."

The preceding quote suggests the very essence of clinical leadership. So from a clinical standpoint, physicians are leaders. We also know that leaders have a significant influence on engagement. These two contentions form the backbone of this chapter.

CAN WE SAY ALL PHYSICIANS ARE LEADERS?

Isn't one function of leadership to provide direction and guidance? Isn't another function of leadership to anticipate the future? Isn't an important task of leadership to correct errors and lead teams toward high-quality work? Aren't physicians exercising leadership because they "command" most of the aspects of care delivery? Don't physicians anticipate the future? Aren't physicians the ones who "give the orders" to implement care to patients? So, if physicians do the following in clinical settings, are they not leaders?

- Have a vision and share it
- Help people work toward common goals
- Praise good work
- Correct bad habits
- Set standards

Some would contend that all physicians act as leaders as soon as they begin to care for patients and make decisions about clinical care. This form of leadership is often referred to as *frontline leadership*. It represents one place in a three-tier continuum of leadership: *frontline*, at the point of care as the head of the care delivery team; *middle management*, for example, the lead physician of a practice or a department or a committee chair; and *senior leadership*, for example, the chief medical officer (CMO).

In this view, new residents or new physicians right out of medical school or residencies and fellowships are acting as leaders. Quach (2020) says that "doctors get results by being authoritative and decisive. The whole clinical system revolves around physicians' usually unquestioned decision-making." The brief quote at the beginning of the chapter has many meanings, and while its primary function was to elicit an emotional response to the information in this chapter, it also means that physicians are, in fact, leaders. No matter their title or role or age, physicians function as leaders in a clinical sense.

DOES CLINICAL PRACTICE HAVE SIMILARITIES TO LEADERSHIP?

Traditionally, clinical practice tends to be more autonomous than administrative work. The nature of clinical work is changing with the upsurge of team-based care. In his well-known commencement address to the Harvard Medical School in 2011, Gawande (2011) described the critical skill required of all physicians: "the ability to get colleagues along the entire chain of care functioning like pit crews for patients." Moreover, physicians are increasingly finding themselves the head of teams and needing to lead those teams. Van Dyke (2019) indicates that "some medical schools and residency programs are beginning to address this issue by bringing different professions together for team-training exercises, including simulations of patient care scenarios. But the majority of practicing physicians have to learn teamwork on the job."

Consider the key aspects of clinical care. Haines, Kliethermes, and Sorensen (2017) describe patient care as follows: "The patient care process includes five essential steps: collecting subjective and objective information about the patient; assessing the collected data to identify problems and set priorities; creating an individualized care plan that is evidence-based and cost-effective; implementing the care plan; and monitoring the patient over time during follow-up encounters to evaluate the effectiveness of the plan and modify it as needed." Compare this description with the process of leadership (summarized in exhibit 6.1).

Consider also the linkage between engagement and leadership. While this connection may seem simply intuitive and logical, research also clearly suggests that effective leadership contributes to high levels of engagement. Xu and Cooper-Thomas (2011) provide a review of the research and supporting literature. They write, "Leadership that

Exhibit 6.1 The Responsibilities of Clinical Leadership Versus Organizational Leadership

Clinical Leadership	Organizational Leadership
Collecting subjective and objective information about the patient	Collecting subjective and objective information about management issues and strategic challenges
Assessing the collected data to identify problems and set priorities	Assessing the collected data to identify problems and set priorities
Creating an individualized care plan that is evidence-based and cost-effective	Creating a plan of action that is evidence-based and cost-effective
Implementing the care plan and monitoring the patient over time during follow-up encounters to evaluate the effectiveness of the plan and to modify it as needed	Monitoring the strategic and/or tactical plan over time to evaluate the effectiveness of the plan and to modify it as needed

provides a supportive, trusting environment allows employees to fully invest their energies into their work roles." Furthermore, they conclude that "research confirms that leadership behaviors (*supports team, performs effectively,* and *displays integrity*) are positively associated with followers' engagement." Drew and Pandit (2020) agree: "Senior leaders must be role models. Their behaviour is amplified throughout the organisations they lead, whether they recognise it or not. Staff will judge what is important by where and how leaders spend their time rather than by what they say."

If being a leader generally means a higher level of engagement with staff, shouldn't physicians—even those who are functioning as full-time clinicians—become more engaged by seeing themselves as leaders and learning leadership skills? Most would agree that leaders are usually more engaged than anyone else in organizations. So if physicians—even full-time clinicians—see themselves as leaders and seek leadership education and development, it is likely they too will become more engaged.

HOW DO PHYSICIANS BECOME LEADERS?

Wolter and colleagues (2015) write that "traditionally, physicians were put into leadership positions by virtue of their clinical skills, seniority or ownership of the practice. These characteristics were considered sufficient to place physicians in positions of authority." Most physician leadership traditionally has involved the more senior physicians acting on behalf of an organization that is interfacing with members of the medical staff. And until the last couple of decades, the vast majority of physicians in any medical staff were independent practitioners working in professional corporations that were separate from the larger, sponsoring healthcare organization. For years, healthcare administration spoke to the "three-legged stool" that ran healthcare organizations: the board, the administration, and the medical staff. Hino (2013) noted that the "three-legged stool of hospital operations—board of trustees, medical staff and executive management—works seamlessly together for the good of the hospital organization and the community as a whole." And often, because of this tripartite structure, physician leaders saw their role as being advocates of the medical staff. Kornacki (2017) explains that "physicians have long been used to an implicit social contract that includes the promise of autonomy, protection from change, and status and privileges in exchange for healing, helping, and comforting patients. This compact shapes doctors' expectations of organizational life, be they employed, contracted, or voluntary members of a medical staff."

This form of healthcare organization is rapidly disappearing as more and more physicians move to an employment relationship with healthcare systems. Progressive physician leaders now find themselves serving as advocates of the organization, not of the medical staff, and they now are more intertwined with the strategy and business aspects of healthcare. Fromson (2011) describes this change: "Physicians who have the drive to lead, the willingness to test their skills, and an interest in an initial part-time management role and who augment their real life experiences with formal management education are the perfect candidates to lead the business side of medicine." American Medical News (2011) reported that "physicians leaders are viewed as more important than ever to closing the divide between clinicians and the administration as they try to create accountable care organizations, reduce readmissions, improve care and implement electronic medical records."

First, the Desire

The first real sign of a leader is the desire to be a leader. In essence this desire is a mindset and an outlook that signifies that an individual wants to assume some control over the direction of a situation or an organization. It can also indicate that a person wants to improve something. As already mentioned, physicians need to see themselves as leaders. While this observation may seem intuitive, it is a critical aspect of becoming a physician leader. Physicians must want to lead.

Innate Attributes

Next, some individuals have traits that propel them toward leadership roles. Lawrence G. Smith, MD, executive vice president and physician in chief, and dean of the School of Medicine at North Shore University Hospital & Long Island Jewish Medical Center, shared ten characteristics that his health system uses to select leaders for its physician leadership development program—and to judge leadership potential (Becker's Hospital Review 2013).

1. Collaborative and cooperative
2. Strong listening skills
3. Communication skills
4. Self-confidence and mental resilience
5. Humility
6. Lack of arrogance
7. Appreciative of others
8. Mentoring
9. Values life balance— "Real doctor, real person"
10. Vision

These characteristics seem to support the belief that leaders are most often born as leaders and not made. Essentially this viewpoint suggests that certain inherent traits and personality tendencies predispose people to be and become leaders. But many believe that leadership is a combination of inborn qualities and learning and practicing skill-building leader competencies. Hogan and Kaiser (2005) write, "Who you are (personality) determines how you lead." "Internal" propensities combine with learning leadership skills. Organizations such as the American College of Healthcare Executives (ACHE) and the American Association of Physician Leaders (AAPL) would likely support this viewpoint since they provide many leadership development programs. In fact, Sabol (2018) reports that the AAPL uses several characteristics to guide its curriculum: "adaptable, ethical, visionary, introspective, vigilant, tactical and knowledgeable. Every successful leader the team could think of—in any industry—exhibited these traits." It follows that these traits serve well to define what physicians who want to advance into positions of leadership should have.

Skilled Behaviors

While certain innate characteristics and tendencies make some people more effective as leaders, there are also specific behaviors and actions that leaders must execute. This concept derives from the belief that leaders are both born and made. Although some people have a predisposition toward leadership, they must also learn effective skills and competencies. Ultimately, leadership is an aggregation of many behaviors. What do effective leaders *do*? How do effective leaders *behave*? What can we observe about effective leaders? Leadership is more about behavior than about tendencies. Using the preceding list of attributes provided by Dr. Smith, the following list of questions shows the conundrum involved in leadership behavior.

Collaborative and cooperative: What behaviors or actions demonstrate these characteristics? Exactly what do individuals do to demonstrate that they are collaborative and cooperative?

Strong listening skills: What do individuals with strong listening skills do? What are their behaviors when demonstrating this?

Communication skills: What actions do individuals exhibit when showing they possess communication skills?

Self-confidence and mental resilience: How do leaders demonstrate behaviorally that they have self-confidence and resilience?

Humility: How do leaders demonstrate humility?

Lack of arrogance: What actions or conduct shows that someone is not arrogant?

Appreciative of others: What deeds and actions suggest an appreciation of others?

Mentoring: How do leaders mentor others? Which prescribed activities support the growth of others?

Values life balance: What do leaders do to demonstrate that they have a work–life balance?

Vision: How do leaders show that they have vision? How is it evident in their behaviors?

A leadership blog from Western Governors University (2020) summarizes the importance of skilled behaviors: "Leader behavior is the traits and characteristics that make some effective as a leader. Leaders utilize their behavior to help them guide, direct, and influence the work of their team. There are many innate characteristics that enhance leadership behavior, however there are strategies and actions that leaders can work to develop in order to improve their behavior and be more effective. Organizations thrive on leaders who use their behavior to share a vision, encourage teams, and ensure everyone is as effective as possible."

Competencies

Dye and Garman (2014) write that leadership competencies are "one of the only theories of leadership that actually offers the chance to 'see' leadership. For example, the trait theory of leadership states that a leader is an effective communicator; the competency theory provides specific behavioral examples of what effective communication is." The leadership competency model widely used in the healthcare field (see exhibit 6.2) fits well with physician leadership attributes.

Exhibit 6.2 Exceptional Leadership Competency Model

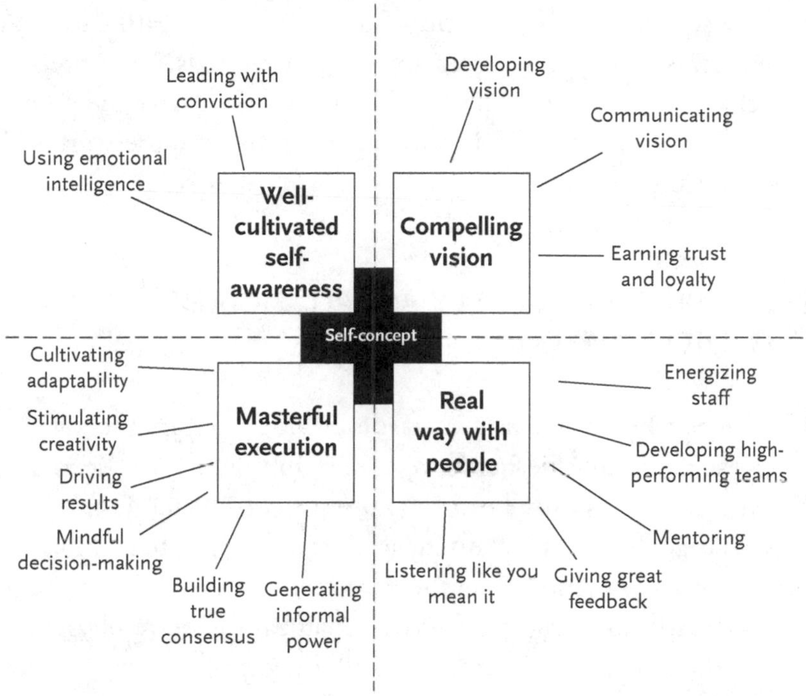

Source: Dye and Garman (2014).

PHYSICIAN LEADERS HAVE A SIGNIFICANT INFLUENCE ON ENGAGEMENT

Physicians functioning as leaders have a significant impact on engagement. By virtue of their stature and respect in society, say Angood and Birk (2014), they are viewed in guidance roles: "It is well-recognized that, at some level, all physicians are regarded by our society as leaders." Carsen and Xia (2006) write, "Leadership roles in medicine, as well as healthcare in general, have both multiplied and grown in complexity, and physicians are being looked at to bridge the gap between practitioner/clinician and manager.

This suggests both a great challenge as well as an unprecedented opportunity. As the next generation of health professionals we can already see the complex world of medicine and healthcare that awaits us. Although it poses many challenges to us, if we prepare ourselves adequately and get involved early on we have the potential to make great strides, both within and outside the worlds of medicine and healthcare."

DO MORE THAN SIMPLY ASK PHYSICIANS FOR THEIR INPUT

Historically, healthcare leaders have asked for input from clinicians when they were considering strategic or significant tactical decisions. But this input has only been sought out occasionally. One of the reasons that clinicians feel disengaged from healthcare administration is the very infrequency of these interactions, especially on major issues. In contrast, highly effective organizations have physicians involved on an ongoing basis with all aspects of strategy, tactics, and operations.

The key differentiator is the matter of "occasional," or "sporadic," versus "ongoing." Obviously, physicians are regularly involved with quality or patient safety matters. They are always seated at decision tables on clinical matters. But many healthcare leaders do not include physicians routinely on issues of operations, finance, or strategy. Dye and Sokolov (2013) write, "Asking physician leaders for input on strategy and decision making is not the same as involving them in these processes and keeping them at the table throughout the execution and implementation stages. Some healthcare leaders may not want to fully involve physicians in this manner. While they may be willing to provide physicians with some level of input, they prefer that the ultimate decision-making authority rest with them." Exhibit 6.3 illustrates how merely seeking physician input differs from making sure that physicians are truly involved.

Exhibit 6.3 Differences Between Involvement and Input

Involvement	Input
Physicians are always at decision-making meetings.	Physicians are sometimes invited.
Physicians are viewed as partners.	Physicians are viewed as tokens.
Executive leadership sees physicians as aligned.	Executive leadership seeks alignment from physicians.
Physician involvement is ongoing.	Physician input is sporadic.
Physicians remain in the process.	Physicians are occasional players.
Seeing physicians at the table is common.	Seeing physicians at the table is rare.

Source: Dye and Sokolov (2013).

In the appendix of their book, Dye and Sokolov (2013) provide an excellent survey tool that can be used to determine the level of physician involvement in the organization. They ask questions such as these:

- Do multiple physicians regularly interact with members of senior management?
- Has a physician (other than the CMO) given a presentation to a routine senior management meeting?
- Do physicians attend any regular meetings of the middle management team?
- Has a physician (other than the CMO) given a presentation to a routine middle management meeting?
- Are physicians part of the budget process?
- Are physicians regularly involved in the entire formal process of strategic planning?
- Do any topic headings of the organization's strategic plan relate to physician involvement?

- Do physicians play a regular part in the ongoing adjustments and modifications to the organization's strategic plan?
- Is the development of the vision for the future of the organization done concurrently with the involvement of the physician leaders of the organization?
- Would informal physician leaders (unpaid but influential) describe decisions made by the organization with the words "We decided"?
- Is additional attention focused on building and maintaining relationships with the physicians who are not closely tied to the organization (e.g., physicians in remote office locations)?
- Would physicians describe the organization as "our organization"?

In brief, to keep many physicians engaged, the organization needs to make sure they are regularly involved in decision-making. Their involvement helps create a true shared partnership and provides transparency for the physician population. Highly effective organizations know that getting large numbers of their physicians to help create the organizational vision and shape policies and practices that support that vision will drive higher levels of engagement.

PROVIDE FOR CAMARADERIE AND COMMUNITY IN THE WORK

In the twentieth century, a large part of the social nature and camaraderie among physicians was exemplified in the physicians' lounge. Practically all physicians visited the hospital daily, and when they did, they came to the physicians' lounge for coffee and perhaps later again for lunch or a break. It was here that professional collegiality flourished. The other quality that developed in the lounge was leadership. The physicians' lounge was often where older physicians would mentor younger ones. Here, wiser, more experienced physicians guided other physicians in informal peer review. Additionally, this was where many aspects of medical staff governance took place. The lounge was therefore the place where much effective communication occurred. Shanafelt and Noseworthy (2017) describe how physicians benefit from these peer-to-peer interactions:

> Physicians deal with unique challenges (e.g., medical errors, malpractice suits) and have a professional identity and role that is distinct from other disciplines. Peer support has always been critical to helping physicians navigate these professional challenges. This support can be formal or informal and encompasses a wide range of activities, including celebrating achievements (e.g., personal and professional milestones), supporting one another through challenging experiences (e.g., loss of a patient, medical errors, a malpractice suit), and sharing ideas on how to navigate the ups and downs of a career in medicine. Historically, such interactions happened somewhat organically during the course of discussing interesting/challenging cases or spending time together in the physicians' lounge. In our experience, these interactions have been an unintended casualty of increasing productivity expectations, documentation requirements, and clerical burden.

However, as inpatient hospitalists replaced the days of primary care physicians' coming to the hospital to see their patients, and as more care moved to ambulatory and office settings, gone was the occasional chance to gather the entirety of the medical staff in the lounge. Moreover, as health systems and physician groups grew larger and as medicine became more complex, the physician lounge lost its allure.

One success story was provided by Janelle Lee, vice president of human resources at Mosaic Life Care in St. Joseph, Missouri. She described the hospital's approach (Lee 2020):

Our physicians indicated they wanted a relaxing space to get away and also to see the executive leadership more, to have conversations. As a response to this, we remodeled a beautiful area with lounge chairs, a television, places to congregate or relax, etc. We also provide a chef-cooked meal once a week for them to enjoy in their own area. To enhance their connection to the executive leadership team, there is a monthly wine-and-cheese evening session. During these events, there is a small array of heavy hors d'oeuvres, wine, and an informal come-and-go setting where the physician and executive leadership group have informal conversations and get any questions answered.

LEADERSHIP CAN HELP WITH BURNOUT

Obviously, increased physician leadership will lead to enhanced physician engagement, which will have a positive impact on burnout. Much has been written about how burnout is reduced if a person derives professional satisfaction from work. Physicians are more engaged in settings that have little organizational complexity or bureaucracy, that seek to receive and respond to their input, and that involve them in both strategic and tactical decision-making. Shanafelt and Noseworthy (2017) write that "although the importance of leadership for organizational success is obvious, its direct effect on the professional satisfaction of individual physicians is underappreciated. Recent evidence suggests that the leadership behaviors of the physician supervisor play a critical role in the well-being of the physicians they lead."

ARE PHYSICIANS DIFFERENT?

To best understand physician engagement and its connection with physician leadership, we should begin with an understanding of physicians and their culture. Understanding someone else's culture is often easier said than done. Some administrators, for example, have simplistic viewpoints about physicians. Unfortunately, many administrative leaders in healthcare view physicians in a rather one-dimensional manner. Many believe that physicians are all alike. Some view the group simply as narrow-minded clinicians; others stereotype them as the "science nerds" they knew in college. Regrettably, some see physicians as greedy and materialistic people seeking fortune. And finally, other administrators are in awe of physicians and are often intimidated by them.

Covey (2004) once gave this well-known piece of advice: "Seek first to understand and then to be understood." While this is wise counsel in all leadership situations, it is particularly true when you are working with physicians. Jain (2016) repeats this advice, from the perspective of a physician: "The very best administrators with whom I have worked have a deep, intuitive understanding of clinical medicine that enables them to speak the same language as their physician counterparts—and, in the process, build meaningful bridges that otherwise would not exist."

Dye and Sokolov (2013) suggest, though, that "physicians do share many traits: their education is long and arduous and focused on getting something done with a minimum of interference or outside input; they expect to control their professional destiny; and they recognize that they play a part in an increasingly complex healthcare system. It's those key similarities that healthcare administrators must be familiar with to maximize the value that physicians bring to the clinical integration table." The authors also provide an excellent short summary of the differences between physicians and administrators (exhibit 6.4).

One thing is certain: To understand the elements of physician engagement, nonclinical leaders must (a) shed their stereotypes about physicians, (b) enhance and deepen their understanding of the clinical practice of healthcare and what physicians do and what motivates them, and (c) be open-minded about the many kinds of people who become physicians.

Exhibit 6.4 Characteristics of Physicians Versus Administrators

Physicians	Administrators
Science-oriented	Business-oriented
One-on-one interactions	Group interactions
Value autonomy	Value collaboration
Focus on patients	Focus on organization
Identify with profession	Identify with organization
Independent	Collaborative
Solo thinkers	Group thinkers

Source: Dye and Sokolov (2013).

A useful starting point for all healthcare leaders in enhancing physician leadership and engagement is to go to the *gemba*, a Japanese term used in Lean management and meaning the place where value is created (or literally "the real place"). While leadership needs to involve many physicians in many ways, there is also a risk in having too many meetings with physicians in boardrooms and executive offices. Meetings like these seldom provide a deep understanding of physicians' clinical work and their concerns.

CHIEF MEDICAL OFFICERS CANNOT DO IT ALL

A final note of caution is appropriate. Practically all organizations have full-time or almost full-time CMOs. Yet many of these organizations believe that their CMOs speak for and fully represent the views of the entire physician organization. This simply cannot be the case. While many CMOs are well connected to the thoughts, opinions, and beliefs of the other physicians in a system, organizations should be careful not to rely solely on these executives as the exclusive voice of all the physicians. Historically, the role of the

CMO was poorly defined and varied greatly from organization to organization. Some officers merely ran the medical staff office and oversaw credentialing and monitoring medical staff bylaws. Others focused heavily on quality, whereas still others simply played the role of "chief mother hen of happiness" and served more as ambassadors to the medical staff lounge.

As the CMO role has progressed, most CMOs today are heavily involved in strategy, operations, and clinical informatics, and in some cases, they serve as line operations executives. With the increased complexity of the role, it is even more difficult for CMOs to be fully tuned in to all the issues of the entire medical staff. Couple CMOs' varied role with the increasing number of physicians who rarely visit the health system offices or set foot in the acute care facility, and we can see that physicians' experiences and viewpoints have become more diverse. Highly effective organizations will certainly use their CMOs to guide and enhance physician engagement, but to place this responsibility solely on the CMO is shortsighted and likely destined to fail.

CONCLUSION

Physicians are called on more than ever to step into leadership roles. Their work as leaders will definitely enhance levels of physician engagement, which will, in turn, create more physician leadership. In this way, inclusion in leadership creates a virtuous cycle with engagement. Lee and Cosgrove (2014) explain how physician leadership in the organization ultimately helps patients: "Engaging doctors, even the old guard, is a management challenge that can be tackled, measured, and improved. The organizations that can help physicians to live up to their aspirations as caregivers—to understand that giving up their autonomy is not actually surrender but a noble act of humility in the interest of their patients—will be the ones that improve efficiency, deliver the best outcomes, increase their market share, and retain and recruit the best people." Angood and Birk (2014) concur: "Physician leadership is critical to shepherd health care into the future, creating a delivery system grounded in better health and better health care at lower costs." It is a simple formula: To enhance physician engagement, increase physician leadership.

REFERENCES

American Medical News. 2011. "Hospitals' New Physician Leaders: Doctors Wear Multiple Medical Hats." Published April 4. https://amednews.com/article/20110404/business/304049965/4.

Angood, P., and S. Birk. 2014. "The Value of Physician Leadership." *Physician Executive* 40 (3): 6–20.

Becker's Hospital Review. 2013. "10 Characteristics of Physician Leaders." Published November 20. www.beckershospitalreview.com/hospital-physician-relationships/10-characteristics-of-physician-leaders.html.

Carsen, S., and C. Xia. 2006. "The Physician as Leader." *McGill Journal of Medicine* 9 (1): 1–2.

Covey, S. 2004. *The 7 Habits of Highly Effective People*. New York: Free Press.

Drew, J. R., and M. Pandit. 2020. "Why Healthcare Leadership Should Embrace Quality Improvement." *British Medical Journal*. Published March 31. www.bmj.com/content/368/bmj.m872.

Dye, C. F., and A. N. Garman. 2014. *Exceptional Leadership: 16 Critical Competencies for Healthcare Executives*. Chicago: Health Administration Press.

Dye, C. F., and J. J. Sokolov. 2013. *Developing Physician Leaders for Successful Clinical Integration*. Chicago: Health Administration Press.

Fromson, J. A. 2011. "Physician Executive Career Options Abound." *New England Journal of Medicine* Career Center. Published November 2. www.nejmcareercenter.org/article/physician-executive-career-options-abound.

Gawande, A. 2011. "Cowboys and Pit Crews." *New Yorker*. Published May 26. www.newyorker.com/news/news-desk/cowboys-and-pit-crews 2011.

Haines S. T., M. Kliethermes, and T. D. Sorensen. 2017. "The Patient Care Process." In *Pharmacotherapy: A Pathophysiologic Approach*, 10th ed., edited by J. T. DiPiro, R. L. Talbert, G. C. Yee, G. R. Matzke, B. G. Wells, and L. M. Posey. Accessed March 8, 2021. https://accesspharmacy.mhmedical.com/content.aspx?bookid=1861&sectionid=174720532#:~:text=The%20patient%20care%20process%20includes,care%20plan%3B%20and%20monitoring%20the.

Hino, R. 2013. "Finding Common Ground Between Hospital Leadership and Staff." Fierce Healthcare. Published March 6. www.fiercehealthcare.com/hospitals/finding-common-ground-between-hospital-leadership-and-staff.

Hogan, R., and R. B. Kaiser. 2005. "What We Know About Leadership." *Review of General Psychology* 9 (2): 169–80.

Jain, S. H. 2016. "Physicians and Healthcare Administrators: Friends or Foes?" *Forbes*. Published June 29. www.forbes.com/sites/sachinjain/2016/06/29/physicians-and-healthcare-administrators-friend-or-foe/.

Kornacki, M. J. 2017. "Three Starting Points for Physician Leadership." *NEJM Catalyst* (blog). Published August 7. https://catalyst.nejm.org/doi/full/10.1056/CAT.17.0440.

Lee, J. 2020. Interview with author. September 17.

Lee, T. H., and T. Cosgrove. 2014. "Engaging Doctors in the Health Care Revolution." *Harvard Business Review* 92 (6): 104–38.

Quach, S. 2020. "How to Prepare Physicians to Be Leaders." *Medical Economics*. Published February 13. www.medicaleconomics.com/view/how-prepare-physicians-be-leaders.

Sabol, E. 2018. "Seven Characteristics That Define a Physician Leader." American Association of Physician Leaders. Published April 26. www.physicianleaders.org/news/seven-characteristics-that-define-a-physician-leader.

Shanafelt, T. D., and J. H. Noseworthy. 2017. "Executive Leadership and Physician Well-Being: Nine Organizational Strategies to Promote Engagement and Reduce Burnout." *Mayo Clinic Proceedings* 92 (1): 129–46.

Van Dyke, M. 2019. "Redefining the Physician's Role as Care Team Leader." *Trustee Insights* (American Hospital Association blog). Published November. https://trustees.aha.org/redefining-physicians-role-care-team-leader.

Western Governors University. 2020. "Successful Leadership Attitudes and Behaviors." *WGU* (blog). Published June 17. www.wgu.edu/blog/successful-leadership-attitudes-behaviors2006.html.

Wolter, N., S. L. Tarnoff, and L. Leckman. 2015. "Recruiting and Retaining Physician Leaders." *Healthcare*. Accessed September 23, 2020. www.researchgate.net/publication/283453560_Recruiting_and_retaining_physician_leaders.

Xu, J., and H. D. Cooper-Thomas. 2011. "How Can Leaders Achieve High Employee Engagement?" *Leadership and Organization Development Journal* 32 (4): 399–416.

CHAPTER 7

Visual and Participative Concepts That Apply to Physician Engagement

Kalen Stanton

THE ART AND SCIENCE of engaging human beings—physicians in particular—in a meaningful dialogue about a strategic journey aims ultimately to arrive at a twofold outcome: a collective mental model of a situation with shared meaning among the participants, and self-discovered conviction about the individual's role in, and accountability for, reaching a desired future state.

Healthcare leadership can best accomplish these two outcomes by engaging physicians or clinicians as human beings through their most human faculties: visualization, interaction, dialogue, and discovery. Through these human-centric experiences, true engagement, alignment, and transformation can begin. This process also serves as a sustainable reference point for recalling connections between the why, what, and how of a strategic change as they progress together into the future. Finally, there is a contemporary resurgence of using visual narrative and dialogue through smartphones and social media that nearly all generations have embraced, and it has proved instrumental in navigating unprecedented events like the COVID-19 pandemic. In these times, not only do visuals speak thousands of words—they also spark movements.

VISUALIZATION

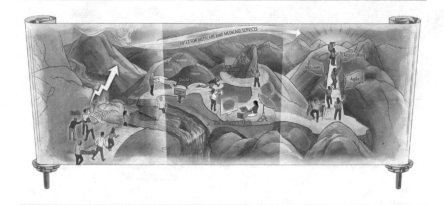

Source: © 2020 Root Inc. Used with permission.

It's Human

Throughout humankind's known history, pictures and stories have been the fabric of change. Any event, custom, behavior, or record of note was documented as a visual narrative and told over the proverbial campfire. Those who have ever had the opportunity to see or hear a story told without written words may remember the deep, intrinsic connection you felt to the story. The immediate recognition, the emotion, the sustained recall—story is in our history, forged by generations, nearly written into human DNA.

Besides any evolutionary advantages it may have had, this method of *visual language* has been so effective over time because it helped illustrate facts. For example, there was an elephant. It was big. There were many hunters, and they overcame the elephant. The village had food. They ate.

But an even more important facet of visualization was that it illustrated emotion. In that same example, the elephant wasn't just big. It was strong and ferocious. It provoked fear.

Nevertheless, the hunters worked together as one. They were triumphant and joyful after their victory. The village was happy because it was saved. A visual tells many details—both intellectual and emotional—that create a story and an understanding for the viewer or participant while also driving conclusions or actions from the story. For example, the villagers could be motivated to overcome fear or learn from the experience and remember how to respond in the future. They didn't have to be afraid when working together!

It's Collective

Perhaps more important than what visualization brings to one human being is what it brings to many: a shared image and understanding. Because today's organizations require other humans to work together in building bigger, more complicated systems or efforts, this important concept of a shared understanding is often left out in clinics or workplaces. To continue with an elephant example, most readers have probably heard the story about the blind people feeling and describing a part of an elephant. Each person explores a different example or attribute of the elephant and concludes that the totality of the object explored is something different, such as a snake or a brick wall. Haudan (2008) applies the fable to systems: "The same problem exists when people can't think in terms of systems. Because they touch only a piece of the system, they conclude that it is the whole system."

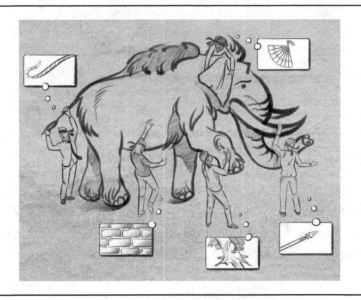

Thus, when people are shown or imagine a holistic visual of the system—or elephant—the system becomes apparent. But even more important, they share a common understanding of what the system looks like without bias or fragmentation. The whole itself is imprinted in their minds.

One way to obtain a collective, realistic understanding of the "elephant," or the current state of a healthcare system, is by paying attention to chat around the proverbial watercooler. Watercooler talk is usually thought to be informal and laid-back conversations unrelated to workplace matters. The watercooler, or coffee room, lunch room, or lounge area, is usually perceived to be an area where people congregate to relax and get away from the pressures of work. But reality teaches us that some of the most useful conversations—and ones that focus directly on work—often take place informally in these areas. The running joke is that people tell the truth in three places: the hallway, the bathroom, and the watercooler—or in healthcare, the physicians' lounge or nurses' station! So embracing this reality and taking it head-on, for example, using a visual to create a safe way to bring it together, has proven most successful. This method can also add humor, which creates an environment of psychological safety that we know is imperative for meaningful dialogue on any healthcare issue.

For example, imagine if someone sat quietly in the CEO's office throughout the day, taking notes and drawing pictures of the statements that were made—by anyone, but particularly by leaders—about clinical matters and physician challenges. At the same time, what if other quiet observers sat in the chief medical officer's room, the physicians' lounge, and the hallway after medical staff meetings and similarly captured statements and mental images conveyed throughout the day? What if these observers then gathered to create one truthful, candid picture about a system challenge?

Contrast this with the opposite picture: that all meaningful conversations take place in the formal settings of an office, a conference room, or a boardroom. While important discussions certainly do take place in these settings, the use of more informal settings combined with the use of visuals can create significant openness not found in the formality and stiffness of typical business meeting settings. Healthcare leaders who have begun to use daily safety huddles will attest to the value of conversations that can surface through this technique. Leaders handling more complicated strategic matters can use the same approach.

Here's an example of the current state of a national health system that was trying to accelerate its path to high reliability. The system had an agreed-upon goal: "Invigorate every human being's commitment and ability to reduce variation or adverse events, and set clear, shared expectations for our high-reliability journey." It was a noble and reasonable goal. Yet when the observers listened to, and watched, the team members who were allowed to speak and act with complete transparency, they observed some of the challenges to achieving this desired goal. Exhibit 7.1 depicts the challenges as the observers saw them.

Exhibit 7.1 Current-State Behaviors on the Path to High Reliability

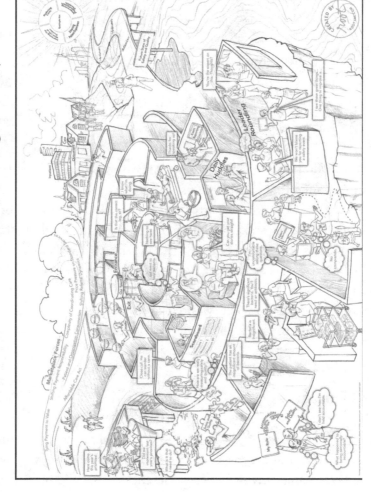

Source: © 2017 Root Inc. Used with permission.

The cultural maze of getting from intention to execution and finally to the goal of high reliability was surprisingly complex—operationally and culturally. Not only was it difficult for stakeholders to envision what the organization must do to achieve consistent success, but they were also unclear on how all the pieces fit together when the stakeholders were honest with themselves. They shared statements such as these:

- "I'm uncomfortable asking questions about certain demographics."
- "We're hearing conflicting stories."
- "I don't really feel safe reporting a safety event."

Remarkably, all these statements of confusion and distrust were coming from a highly ranked institution.

Root Inc.'s watercooler process, anchored in the visual of the maze in exhibit 7.1, shone a light on the complexities and the shared challenges of the organization's current state. Physicians, nurses, and administrators could see their respective vantage points of "the elephant" assembled as one collective image. The process also enabled them to say what they had wanted to say for years but didn't feel able to. A picture safely said a thousand words.

It's Clinical

Interestingly, most physicians will describe their years of clinical study and training as full of drawings, diagrams, and physical specimens. What anatomy or biology reference doesn't contain a visual depiction of the subject? Physicians operate through mental models, diagrams, and pictures that have been imprinted in their minds from endless repetition of investigative learning.

Moreover, physicians are trained to think in terms of systems. Every part connects to others, and every effect has a cause—or multiple causes. Often the surest way they can figure out the solution, or at least the best one, is by examining and understanding the whole system.

And yet, most organizational town halls, e-mails, clinical staff meetings, and strategic planning efforts contain no collective picture of the system and what success looks like—at least no more detailed than a flow chart on a slide. Once physicians are enticed or promoted from clinical responsibilities into the realm of *administration*, the visuals magically vanish. In fact, in many of the largest businesses and organizations today, there is little visualization of what people do or how systems work. Coincidentally, there is also no end to the amount of confusion, silos, misalignment, and non-value-added activities going on in healthcare systems that hire consultants to help translate and reassemble these complexities. Whether we see it with our eyes or in our minds, we humans picture our reality. And this reality is what guides our decisions and our performance.

GETTING PHYSICIANS IN THE GAME

So what is an alternative to the overused, uninspiring, unengaging methods of communication we continue to see in healthcare today? How might the age-old concept of visualization, a common practice of some of our most highly capable and trained minds on the planet (physicians), be reapplied to engage clinical experts in the leadership of healthcare? Consider another exercise to further expand stakeholders' understanding of a system so that they can form their own conclusions about how to respond to challenges in the system.

We will again use as an example a visually immersive and participatory activity that Root offers to help organizations with this more detailed understanding. Root calls its method a *learning map*. Other organizations have started to use a similar process that includes visualization but also some steps that help participants either develop a strategy or better understand the complexities of an organization's strategies. Called *learning roadmaps, strategy maps,* or similar terms, these exercises aim to promote thoughtful reasoning, active participation, and open and frank conversations.

To understand why and how this method works, we first need to introduce the rest of the elements that distinguish a learning map from simply showing a picture:

- **Visualization:** A holistic, shared picture of a current or future state is conveyed by an image or a visual metaphor. This crucial element is an iterative output of listening, conversing, and processing the reality of a situation from the perspectives of the real people involved in it.

- **Data:** The participants in this activity need factual, contextual, simplified data to further understand the implications of the situation and to decide how to respond. Like many other scientists, physicians thrive on plentiful, accurate data. Yet it's not all about the data— just bring enough to the table to inform and validate the discussion and interaction.

- **Interaction:** The Root learning-map method includes intentional, designed crossfire between similar or distinct skill sets convening in Socratic dialogue around the same image and data. The interaction may also call for participants to play distinct roles in the dialogue (e.g., a reader, a timekeeper) so that those with different learning styles are equally engaged.

- **Dialogue:** Structured questions and discussion allow the participants to examine the situation through the visualization and data as though the situation were a cadaver and they were conducting a postmortem. Through dialogue, the participants unlock meaning from the visual image by critically thinking about the why, what, and how of the organization's current state, and they begin to bring to life the future state.

- **Discovery:** A formula driven by the participants combines the visual image, the data, and the dialogue to unearth a collective solution to the challenge the group is facing. The participants discover a shared conviction and must-do actions in response to the situation. Instead of being told what to do, they arrive at their own conclusions. Because of this level of self-direction, the entire process is a much more inspiring journey for everyone involved.

BRINGING IT ALL TOGETHER

One preeminent academic health system on the East Coast used the image depicted in exhibit 7.2 to build a system view for a group of more than two thousand clinical and nonclinical leaders. The goal was to share and collectively understand some of the statewide and nationwide market forces that were necessitating systematic changes in the system's strategy, its operating model, and even its culture.

The image provided a compelling visual map that intellectually and emotionally appealed to people, especially physician leaders. Combined with timely and verified data, the map provoked dialogue among these leaders in small groups, and the discussion became highly engaged and system-focused. How can you *not* talk about your work and your expertise in light of the entire state or system when the whole thing is sitting there in front of you?

In only one hour, these leaders became immersed in the reality of such issues as shifts in their state population demographics, evolving patient behaviors, changes to research funding and clinical trials, and the ever-persistent disruption by new competitors. They answered questions like these:

- What might this shift in behaviors mean for our current communication channels and access for our patients?

Exhibit 7.2 A Case for Change

- How will we fund our research with only the traditional approaches we have today?
- What will happen if we don't evolve our current clinical care model?

As they answered these questions together, applying their own expertise and experience to solve various complex issues in an open discussion, they collectively became a system—or a group of aligned human beings—ready to change.

IT'S WORTH IT

In the preceding example of an academic healthcare provider attempting to transform itself into one unified system, you can imagine how frequently leaders and other team members asked, "How much time will this take?" Probably few leaders in healthcare or any other industry have asked this question more often than physicians have. With good reason.

Dr. Walter Ettinger, former chief medical officer and president of notable northeast health systems, said it best (Ettinger 2018):

Administrators tend to think that physicians only care about money or control when they aren't engaging physicians with the right priorities at the forefront. The real priorities for physicians are fairly universal:

1. I want to know that what we're trying to do is in the best interest of my patients.
2. I want to know my time is valued.
3. I want to know that my input and involvement makes a difference.
4. I want the economics or financial value of my work to be respected as well.

Leaders at this health system were essentially saying the same thing, but in different words. "How much time is this going to take?" However, after engaging in a visual experience together, the physicians and other leaders across the organization almost universally agreed on what needed to be done to serve the *best interests of their patients*. They had a shared mental model, instantly recalled through the visual map they had created with the help of an artist and the data and dialogue to navigate the way forward. *Their time was valued.*

In fact, you can even measure if this type of strategic engagement is worth a clinician's time. In another part of the preceding health system's process, dialogue groups and visuals were set up to increase the clinicians' and administrators' leadership potential and skills together. Some 98 percent of the participants thought the effort was worth their time, and 97 percent would recommend it to others. This buy-in was important since it is no mystery how much physicians appreciate the test data! And the process also opened the door to the next part of the strategic conversation necessary for effective change: input and involvement.

JOIN THE VISUAL MOVEMENT

Although visuals and interactive discovery have accelerated change in the past, newer generations routinely use and expect visualizations of data, because of the ease of technology. Generation Z (born 1997–onward) in particular knows the power of a picture or video.

Think about your social channels or even e-mail. If you only share a few words, the ten or so connections will respond. But share an image, and millions may hearken to your cause. There is a marked reason that visuals work, particularly on social media. Because images or visual stories intrinsically reflect reality either as it is or as you would like it to be, they are readily trusted and accepted far more quickly and completely than words in an e-mail would be accepted.

According to Pew Research, millennials, or Generation Y (born 1981–1996), are not far behind; nor are other generations on the adoption curve (Vogels 2019). By 2020, nearly 90 percent of millennials had adopted social media, more than 75 percent of Generation X (born 1965–1980), and nearly 60 percent of baby boomers (born 1946–1964). Combine these percentages with a statistic such as these provided by Cooper (2013): Pictures garner 104 percent more comments, 53 percent more likes, and 84 percent more clicks on links than do text-based posts. Quite simply, people are communicating increasingly visually. Not only do they communicate more often with images, but they also want to do so. They enjoy this mode of communication. They engage because of it.

So again, why would we ask clinicians—who were trained through visual and kinesthetic techniques, who communicate with one another and in life through visual media and interaction, and who are used to being engaged (by advertising or other actors) in visual media—to give up that entire part of their brains to engage in the business of healthcare? This wasteland of corporate communication and collaboration is something that my colleagues and I often observe in nearly every industry of cross-functional teams and businesses. Just as a clinician feels dehumanized when clicking boxes in an electronic health record, millions of employees feel robbed of their purpose when they work together in ways that no longer feel human at all. Human beings need to visualize what they value and see what matters to them.

VALUE IN REAL TIME

Let's apply an example solution to this need for value and what matters to people by way of a brief case study. We will use the word *value* and portray it in an easily demonstrated way. In 2018, a large multistate health system in the southeast United States needed a way to unify its culture across geographic locations in support of a new strategy and brand—or *identity*. The common denominator for connecting the different locations' concepts of *value* was their shared system values and culture. It was the collective *why* that people, whether clinical or administrative, shared, and this common denominator inarguably drove engagement and the success of the entire system's health outcomes and business.

First, the system's leadership implemented a Root learning map experience to engage each clinician and team member across the system in what it meant to provide whole-person care. Through this experience, the participants developed a shared understanding of the why and what of their new system identity and strategy. But the how, it seemed, needed to be even more personal and relevant than what a team of artists could create. The idea needed to be real. How would a visualization do that?

Visual connection: Through a little brainstorming, a little programming, a lot of simplifying, and finally a refocusing of the camera toward the people themselves, the organization unleashed a culture and a connected team that was equipped to engage in the strategic conversation. By creating a visual and storytelling platform on mobile devices and personal computers via an *engagement app*, the organization invited clinicians and team members to capture the living of their values in a similar manner to how they interacted outside work. Using images, videos, and stories, the participants began recognizing and challenging each other on the premise that their values were a story worth showing. With at least 80 percent of this workforce already engaged in social platforms outside of the health system, it was an easy methodology to introduce. No longer did clinicians and other team members need the weekly e-mail or monthly newsletter to hear about how Tammy or Dr. Wilson exemplified the organization's cause and strategy—people could show it as it happened and could discuss how they felt about it.

CONCLUSION

The timeless value of visualization in amplifying collective human effort is increasingly apparent in healthcare, primarily in how this technique engages individuals both intellectually and emotionally, creates a common mental model for leaders and groups, and shows a system with all its connections and parts. Visualization is natural for human beings to use when they are interpreting information. It is an integral part of medical training itself, and it often creates a safer version of reality for people to process truthful challenges or cultural dynamics. Finally, visual language is quickly evolving and taking over the public sphere at a scale that is inevitably flowing into work and broader communication. Images, videos, and virtual connections are all outpacing and outperforming the PowerPoint slides and e-mails of old. So why miss out? Imagine a world where your physicians are working together in the same direction, building a bridge across a canyon. On the other side waits green pastures and a road where the parts of your strategy fit smartly together to lead up a mountain of strategic prominence. You just pictured that.

REFERENCES

Cooper, B. B. 2013. "7 Powerful Facebook Statistics You Should Know About." *Fast Company*. Published December 2. www.fastcompany.com/3022301/7-powerful-facebook-statistics-you-should-know-about.

Ettinger, W. 2018. Interview with author, November.

Haudan, J. 2008. *The Art of Engagement: Bridging the Gap Between People and Possibilities*. New York: McGraw-Hill.

Vogels, E. 2019. "Millennials Stand Out for Their Technology Use, but Older Generations Also Embrace Digital Life." Pew Research Center. Published September 19. www.pewresearch.org/fact-tank/2019/09/09/us-generations-technology-use.

CHAPTER 8

How Physicians Feel Engagement; How Leaders Enhance It

Harjot Singh

It was a young guy, and the two teams had a big fight about it. He had a tibial fracture, and the popliteal artery was transected. The vascular surgeon wanted to repair the artery first, but the orthopedic team wanted to go first and stabilize the fracture first. I told them if they waited any longer, they might have to amputate. There wouldn't be any leg to save. They agreed to let the vascular guys go first, and then the orthopedic surgeon took his turn. And I was with both teams. My work is always controlled chaos, but this time, it felt like a controlled dance. Almost like they were just mechanics fixing parts of a machine, but I was the real doctor who knew what was going on with the patient.

—Anesthesiologist describing monitoring a patient during two procedures that took eight hours

ENGAGEMENT IS ONE of the most positive aspects of human experience and well-being. Workplace engagement has been studied and dissected for years from the leadership and management perspective. These studies generally stress the needs of the organization and the leader's performance. This chapter will investigate the other side of the issue, uncovering how engagement, or lack thereof, affects physicians and what both organizations and individual physician leaders can do to enhance it. Engagement is a two-way street—it cannot exist effectively without both parties' understanding the other's experience.

Lack of physician engagement is not a new problem. Studies going back several decades note the lack of physician engagement as a challenge common to hospitals and other healthcare organizations. From an organizational perspective, Gallup (2021) defines engaged employees as "those who are involved in, enthusiastic about, and committed to their work and workplace." Or to put it more precisely, HRZone (2020) states that "employee engagement is the emotional attachment employees feel toward their workplace, their role and position in the company, their colleagues, and the company culture and the effect this attachment has on an employee's well-being and productivity." Employees who feel emotionally connected to their positions are more likely to go the extra mile, remain loyal, and perform to the best of their ability. This emotional connection is the anchor that keeps employees motivated during difficult economic and personal times. While there may be some differences between employee and physician engagement, these definitions can provide great guidance when a leader is considering how to address physician engagement challenges.

Though engagement can be defined easily, lack of engagement is an elusive condition difficult to identify. Few leaders wake up in the morning feeling the need to engage physicians. And fewer still stay up at night worrying about a lack of engagement. Yet the fallout from poor engagement shows up clearly in three categories: employee turnover and satisfaction, leadership performance, and customer satisfaction. And a sizable amount of money is tied to the success or failure of these measures.

Engagement measures exist on a spectrum. Gallup provides one of the larger sets of databases on engagement and ongoing updates on its engagement measures. Writing for Gallup, Harter (2020) summarizes some engagement numbers: "Combining Gallup's measurements for 2020 so far—a sample of 30,278 U.S. workers—36% of employees are engaged and 14% are actively disengaged or a ratio of 2.6-to-1 engaged to actively disengaged workers. If this level of employee engagement were to continue until the end of 2020, it would represent a slight increase from 2019 and another new high in the percentage of engaged workers from Gallup's historic measurement." However, this same article shows that the measures have gone through a roller coaster of ups and downs. Additionally, Harter (2020) observes that "Gallup research has shown that employee engagement is very changeable inside organizations when leaders focus on the right practices."

Here, studies by Maslach and Leiter (2014) provide a bridge between organizational engagement and individual engagement. The Maslach Burnout Inventory (MBI) and its twin, Areas of Work/Life Survey (AWS), measure engagement on a spectrum from engagement on one end to burnout on the other. In between are the employees who are ineffective, overextended, and disengaged. Just as the components of burnout are exhaustion, cynicism, and inefficacy, the opposite—energy, involvement, and efficacy—are the components of engagement. The burned-out people on one end of the spectrum succumb to their situation, whereas engaged workers on the other end thrive (exhibit 8.1). The leftover 53 percent in the middle are languishing, neither fully burned out nor thriving at work. This view focuses organizational understanding of engagement on the individual.

Exhibit 8.1 Burnout to Engagement

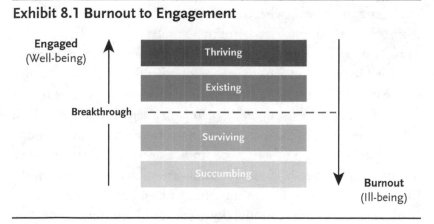

Source: Harjot Singh, MD (www.HarjotSinghMD.com).

ENGAGEMENT AT AN INDIVIDUAL LEVEL

Engagement at an individual level has been studied for nearly five decades. The one field that has contributed the most to this study is positive psychology. Most of the early empirical studies in the mental state of engagement were conducted by Mihaly Csikszentmihalyi, who popularized the concept of flow. In his years of research into creativity and productivity as well as his interviews with people who were successful in a wide range of professions, he discovered that the secret to their optimal performance was their ability to enter a state he called *flow*. Flow is so named because during these interviews, several people described their "flow" experiences using the metaphor of a water current carrying them along (Csikszentmihalyi 1975).

Csikszentmihalyi defines flow as "being completely involved in an activity for its own sake. The ego falls away. Time flies. Every action, movement, and thought follows inevitably from the previous one, like playing jazz. Your whole being is involved, and you're using your skills to the utmost" (Geirland 2017). Flow, characterized by complete absorption in what one is doing, results in a loss of sense of space and time.

Consider this state of flow on an individual level. When immersed in certain activities, people often report completely losing track of time. Perhaps they are participating in a beloved activity like playing music or a sport, where hours pass by without notice. Times like these are not passive, leisurely, or relaxing, but they are not unpleasant; rather, they are active moments when body and mind are stretched in pursuit of achieving something difficult and worthwhile. Those in a state of flow may not describe the experience as fun or happy. In fact, the sense of enjoyment is an aftereffect, during which a person recognizes the time as essential for growth and mastery. The experiences don't have to be unpleasant—but they are active moments when our bodies and minds are stretched to their limits in active pursuit of something challenging and rewarding.

This altered state, colloquially termed as being in the zone, is accurately described by one of the participants interviewed in the earliest stages of flow research: "My mind isn't wandering. I am not thinking of something else. I am totally involved in what I am doing. My body feels good. I don't seem to hear anything. The world seems to be cut off from me. I am less aware of myself and my problems" (Csikszentmihalyi and Csikszentmihalyi 1992).

Returning to individual engagement, data collected by Daniel Goleman shows that most people are either bored or stressed at work, where "15% never enter a state of flow on a typical day and only 20% enter flow at least once per day" (Goleman 2013). Note that flow-producing situations occur more than three times more often when people are at work than during their leisure time. This difference arises because, as previously stated, flow is most easily accessed when engaged in a challenging activity. In this study, Goleman (2013) recorded any time that participants scored above their personal average in both the challenge faced and skills being used at the time of study. Another important element is that flow experiences at work occur at all levels of employment: among managers, clerical staff, and blue-collar workers alike (Csikszentmihalyi 2009).

The phenomena of flow and engagement have a few major elements. Across many studies, people reflecting on experiences of flow mention at least one, often all, of several building blocks. The following sections will examine these essential elements.

Challenges That Require Skill

The match between a person's skills and challenges creates an optimal state where flow can occur. This is also the state of engagement where active and effortless activities happen. Exhibit 8.2 illustrates the balance between the level of challenge and the level of skill necessary to achieve flow (Jain 2018). Enjoyment and engagement are experienced precisely when the opportunity to tackle a challenge is equal to an individual's skill level. If the challenge exceeds an individual's skill level, people will experience anxiety. And if their skills exceed a particular challenge, boredom sets in. Engagement

Exhibit 8.2 Flow

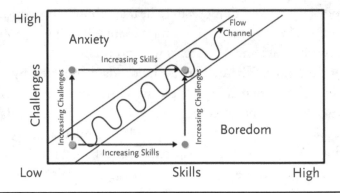

Source: Jain (2018). Used with permission from Saurabh Jain.

occurs just in between boredom and anxiety, where challenge and skill are perfectly balanced.

When a challenge and an individual's skill are mismatched, flow and engagement are disrupted. For example, a medical resident in early training may feel anxious when asked to engage in individual patient care, since the person has little experience and skill in that area. However, this physician may feel boredom with the same work after ten years of doing the same thing. The challenge has diminished, and the physician's skill set has exceeded it. When and where a person reaches a flow state will necessarily shift over the individual's career.

Blend of Action and Awareness

During flow, there is a merging of action and awareness. When individuals have all the relevant skills, their attention is absorbed by the activity. They become so involved in what they're doing that their actions appear automatic. Additionally, they are not aware of themselves as separate from their actions, which take place seamlessly, without self-questioning or other doubts. From the outside, the experience appears to be effortless, when in reality it requires stamina, hard-earned skill, and focused mental energy. The experience is much like how a pathologist is absorbed in interpreting valuable information from what look like blobs of ink to an observer.

Clear Goals and Feedback

People experience flow when they are given clear and immediate feedback. Even if their goals are long-term and take months or years to accomplish, short-term goals and feedback are extremely important. Unfortunately, clear goals and immediate feedback are not always available at work, and physicians must often use their own experience and support to develop this feedback internally.

Short-term feedback that a surgeon receives during surgery is a different experience from that of a psychiatrist who seeks long-term functional improvement. The surgeon may consider the blood, the incision, or the vital signs the most important feedback, whereas the psychiatrist considers small changes in the patient's mental status significant feedback. Without this feedback, over time, the work becomes meaningless and lacks the ability to engage the individual doing the work. As the comparison of the surgeon and the psychiatrist clearly shows, feedback and goals must be individualized to be effective.

Concentration on the Task at Hand

When the mind is engaged, it requires complete focus that leaves no room for irrelevant information. During day-to-day life, the mind is preoccupied with multiple thoughts, worries, and other distracting, unwanted drains on concentration. When experiencing flow, the mind has exquisite focus that improves the quality of experience by diminishing the interference of chaos. At any given moment, a great deal of information is available to every individual.

Yet psychologists have found that the mind can only attend to a certain amount of information at a time, about "110 bits of information per second" (Csikszentmihalyi 2008). That may seem like a lot, but simple daily tasks like decoding speech take about 60 bits of information per second, over half an individual's capacity! For the most part, people decide where they want to focus their attention. When in a flow state, the mind is completely engrossed with the task at hand and, without consciously deciding to do so, loses awareness of all other things: time, people, distractions, and even basic bodily needs. According to Csikszentmihalyi and Csikszentmihalyi (2000), this loss of awareness of other matters occurs because all the attention of the person in the flow state is on the task at hand. There are no more attention resources left to be allocated.

Heightened Sense of Control

As a practitioner's skill set grows, the person develops a sense of mastery of it. Then, the individual takes on a new set of challenges and gradually, with practice and training, gains more control over even tougher challenges. At one level of expertise, resetting a broken bone feels like the height of achievement, and at a greater level, a triple bypass feels like a no-brainer. While people are in the state of flow, they feel in control and are aware of exercising that control.

Loss of Awareness of Self

Typically, people spend a great deal of time thinking about themselves. It is human nature. This preoccupation with the self absorbs much of a person's time and energy, especially when an individual perceives a social or physical threat to the self. As mentioned, flow invokes an intense focus, allowing the rest of the world to disappear from awareness. Simultaneously, there is also an obliviousness to the sense of self. This loss of self is sometimes described as a feeling of oneness with the environment. And even after such an episode is over, "one feels more together than before, not only internally but also with respect to other people and to the world in general" (Csikszentmihalyi 2009). Stress is a common threat that exposes our vulnerable self to constant worries. During flow, especially if the activity has clear goals and if the challenges are well matched to a person's skills, there is no threat to self.

A Changing Sense of Time

Subjectively, people sense the passage of time in different ways. The Greek language explains this phenomenon by using two words for time: *chronos* and *kairos*. *Chronos* refers to measurable, objective time, whereas *kairos* refers to the subjective experience of time (Liddel and Scott 2007). Sometimes this subjective feeling is forced on us. For example, "my whole life flashed before my eyes" is a common statement made after near-death experiences. Individuals often describe a slowing sense of time during this ordeal. This sensation, obviously, is not flow or engagement. An individual feeling flow has entered such a state voluntarily and, if the conditions are suitable, may repeat the experience again and again. During a procedure, a fully engaged physician still knows how much time has passed and how much is remaining. The individual is aware of time and yet simultaneously outside of it.

The key element of the flow experience is that it is an end in itself. The activity is intrinsically rewarding. Csikszentmihalyi (2009) describes it as an *autotelic* experience (*auto*, "self," and *telos*, "goal"). It is done not with expectation of some external benefit but because the doing is the reward. While seeing patients and helping them get better is not necessarily autotelic, doing so because one enjoys seeing them and interacting with them can be. During such an experience, the physician is focused on the activity for its own sake and not on its consequences. Throughout it all, people describe flow as a highly pleasurable event. They enjoy being in control of a task and the ongoing feedback they receive, and they find what they are doing highly self-rewarding. Engaged employees are those with the opportunity to experience flow at an individual level at regular intervals during their work.

THREE PERSONAL BENEFITS OF FLOW

Besides the many organizational benefits from having engaged physicians and physician leaders, the physicians themselves gain personal benefits when they are in a state of flow. We will look at three main advantages in the following sections.

Personal Well-Being

Since the turn of the new century, the concept of flow has been integrated into the five elements of well-being: positive emotions, engagement or flow, positive relationships, meaning, and achievement (PERMA) (Seligman 2018). These five elements constitute the state where human beings flourish. The construct of well-being is conceptualized in two ways—subjective well-being and psychological well-being. Both types are necessary for survival, are strongly related to each other, and affect each other. The subjective type of well-being focuses on the hedonic aspect of well-being: the pursuit of happiness, pleasure, and fun. The psychological type, on the other hand, focuses on eudaemonic well-being: the fulfillment of human potential and search for a meaningful life.

Engagement, the experience of flourishing and thriving, is an essential part of psychological well-being. Engagement helps humans flourish by broadening their experience and building the foundation for future experiences. To help people move from burnout to engagement at work, leaders need to understand the human experience of engagement.

Personal Productivity

Having flow makes life more meaningful, improves positive emotions, gives a sense of achievement, and improves overall well-being. Naturally, in such a positive environment, individuals are more productive, as they enjoy what they do.

Reduced Chance of Burnout

Long-term studies show that burnout has no cutoff but instead exists on a spectrum. Maslach and Leiter (2014) recognize person–job mismatch as the root cause of burnout and lack of engagement and outline six different types of burnout: workload (too much work, not enough resources); control (micromanagement, lack of influence, accountability without power); reward (inadequate pay, acknowledgment, or satisfaction); community (isolation, conflict, disrespect); fairness (discrimination, favoritism); and values (ethical conflicts, meaningless tasks). A pediatric neurologist who later sought coaching for burnout describes many of these elements of burnout:

> I was at this hospital for two years. I saw patients from four states because I was the only pediatric neurologist within 150 miles in any direction. I was busy, and every month, there was one more thing I was told to do. Nobody asked me what I thought of it. I had many ideas on how we could make things better. My staff was always leaving because they would get more money somewhere else. One of them wrote me up when I tried teaching them their work. That was the last straw. I didn't want to be labeled a disruptive physician. I said the heck with it; I can't take it anymore. When I told them I was leaving, there was nothing they could offer me that could've kept me there.

The higher the mismatch between the person and the job, the greater the burnout. In light of these observations, any burnout mitigating strategy cannot simply aim to lower burnout but must also include opportunities to increase engagement as an equal or even a primary goal.

COMMON MISSTEPS IN EFFORTS TO ENHANCE PHYSICIAN ENGAGEMENT

In preparing to engage physicians, leaders face a complex mosaic of people, environments, and goals. With this in mind, they must be careful to avoid the common mistakes outlined in the following sections.

Lumping All the Physicians Together

Engagement is an individualized and personal experience, especially for physicians. Each physician is a separate human being who has spent years accomplishing some of the most demanding physical and intellectual tasks to get to this level of expertise. Each has unique reasons for becoming a physician and has spent years honing critical skills. The individual's physical, emotional, financial, and spiritual needs are distinct from one another. And in the same way, the experience of feeling engaged at work is individual as well. To help their physicians find flow daily, a leader must understand their unique needs and challenges. A fresh graduate with a young family has vastly different engagement needs from those of a physician nearing retirement.

Additionally, each physician on a leader's team contributes anywhere from a few hundred thousand dollars to a few million dollars to an organization's revenue. Owners of champion horses that garner this kind of revenue have special diets, groomers, caretakers, and strategies for each of their horses. The owners understand each animal's individual temperament, and they design care around the horse's needs. They would not expect a win from a poorly fed, overworked, and neglected horse—especially one whose individual needs were ignored. Although people are obviously not horses, the comparison is solid, and physicians must be considered individual assets in a similar way. This observation leads to another mistake often made by healthcare leaders.

Ignoring the Business Case

To ignore the financial aspects of physician engagement, or lack thereof, is a rookie mistake. No margin, no mission. As noted earlier in this chapter, each physician is a clear monetary asset to an organization. In this data-driven world, no emotional appeal holds water against the realities of money in an organization. Engaging physicians undeniably improves an organization's bottom line by boosting productivity, reducing turnover, improving patient outcomes, improving patient satisfaction ratings, reducing violence in the workplace, reducing medical errors and litigation, and lowering burnout. Currently, healthcare organizations spend copious amounts of money to improve *patient* experience, with new clinics and buildings. But these process improvements boost organizational performance by only a little. Buildings and patient experience cannot have a lasting impact with a team of disengaged and burned-out physicians.

Search for the Perfect Survey

A survey is the starting point for many physician engagement initiatives, and rightly so. Whatever gets measured gets the money. In fact, a properly done survey will give a leader the first flavor of the things to come. However, many leaders get sidelined by searching for the perfect survey, wasting months of precious time. Of course, leaders must plan how the survey will be administered. Such questions as how to ask physicians to complete the survey, how to encourage participation, and how to communicate the results should be explored thoughtfully. Additionally, leaders should consider using a survey with an included action plan. For example, both the MBI and the AWS also provide actionable data. Leaders should also be cautious to use surveys that have direct applicability to physicians. Standard employee engagement surveys often have little relevance to physician matters.

Not Having an Engagement Plan

Worse than administering a poor survey is taking no action afterward. Before the survey, leaders should have a preliminary plan in place and then use survey data to adjust the implementation of the plan, as necessary. A physician would not take a patient's temperature or order an MRI without a plan about what to do with the results. A leader risks increasing cynicism and lowering engagement by not having an engagement plan in place and by not communicating or implementing it. Another common mistake is an unending search for a perfect plan. In organizational psychology, a phenomenon called the Hawthorne effect "concerns research participation, the consequent awareness of being studied, and possible impact on behavior" (McCambridge, Witton, and Elbourne 2014). A similar effect is often seen in clinical trials, where attention and observation alone improve clinical outcomes. A physician engagement plan bears some similarity to the well-known placebo effect. Simply put, any plan is better than no plan. A strong leader may begin with a pilot and adjust it along the way, but the fact that any attempt is being made will have its own positive effect.

Short-Term Approach

An effective engagement plan takes time—time for physicians to trust the goodwill of both the leader and the organization and time for physicians to share their pains and observe what leaders do with that information. There are no shortcuts. The most energy, effort, and perseverance are needed up front, when doubt is high and trust is low. During any space shuttle launch, for example, the most fuel energy is spent in the first phase of takeoff. Once the shuttle reaches orbit, the spacecraft needs little fuel to stay there. Implementing a physician engagement program is similar. Think of executing an engagement plan as an S curve. It is a steep climb in a short period to go from the lower curve of the S to the upper one. But eventually, the system previously functioning at a low level begins to function at a higher level, with much less time and energy overall.

Further evidence to keep in mind is that approximately 29 percent of healthcare organizations already have an engagement program (MGMA 2018). Typically, these programs are disjointed and separate from other programs that have direct bearing on physician engagement. A common example is a burnout or well-being program completely separate from an engagement program. The lack of coordination between the two programs ignores the important twin truths that burnout is the opposite of engagement and that engagement is a fundamental element of well-being.

In the current healthcare climate, physicians in most organizations typically speak to their CMO or medical director in one of three situations:

1. **A group meeting.** At these sometimes-optional group gatherings, messages from the top are delivered. Depending on the physicians' style, temperament, or experience, they may choose to attend or not. No matter how much the leader self-identifies as a democratic person, a group meeting is an extremely inefficient use of everyone's time. It contributes little to physician engagement. Physicians come to dread these meetings not just for their futility but also because these occasions are usually when they are told about the next burden they will have to carry.

2. **The physician has messed up.** There is usually an informal or a formal meeting whenever issues must be

addressed and, often, whenever liability is involved. Although this sort of meeting can be an opportunity for engagement, in reality engagement is rare. The atmosphere is charged, and the participants are looking out for their own safety instead of for one another.

3. **The physician is unhappy.** After many requests, a physician is finally able to schedule time alone with "the boss." Because other opportunities to improve engagement were never implemented successfully, this meeting often devolves into desperate ultimatums from the physician. For example, "If you don't pay me X dollars, I am going to leave." This encounter may be the only time when even a haphazard attempt is made to genuinely find out what can be done to make things better, but it is often too little too late.

How many of these three encounters do you think are conducive to engage a physician? Clearly, the answer is none. How many of these meetings give a CMO or another leader a true measure of how engaged the physicians are? Again, none. How many of these meetings allow a leader to understand what creates flow or engagement for a physician? Readers know the answer by now.

This kind of communication infrastructure is a prescription for deteriorating engagement, increasing disengagement, and growing burnout. It moves physicians from well-being and thriving to languishing, and from languishing to ill-being and burnout. It also creates stress for the CMO and medical director because they are unable to improve performance because of high turnover, reduced full-time employees, low productivity, and failed implementation of initiatives.

Systemic and Personal Hurdles to Engagement

Beyond the hurdles already discussed, physician engagement also faces systemic and personal hurdles. During medical training, most physicians and physician leaders have not participated in conversations or programs to improve flow and create engagement. Experientially, they have no memory of any help or guidance in this area. And after their training, most physicians work in places that also lack these conversations. Then, the physicians promoted to leadership positions receive little or no training about how to engage their team. This skill rarely comes naturally. Most physician leaders are too busy already. Unless there is a clear incentive to spend time on conversations that engage, engagement will not happen on its own.

Conceptually and practically, the plan must be executed at both the broader, strategic leadership level and the day-to-day tactical managerial level. This is an important distinction. For physician leaders, the boundary between leaders and managers is often fuzzy. In building physician engagement, both physician leaders and physician managers may be responsible for enhancing physician engagement. Practically, consider a CMO as someone in a leadership role and a medical director in a managerial role. Both must be committed to the same strategy and objectives.

The central element of any engagement program must be communication. Susan Scott (2017) writes, "While no single conversation is guaranteed to change the trajectory of a career, a company, a relationship, or a life, any single conversation can." A committed leader will plan a series of communications that will not only target engagement but also tackle burnout and create a connected community that delivers results. The central goal must be to help physicians experience the flow in their daily work. Each conversation should aim to find out the unique challenges and skills of each physician. This information allows a leader to see where each physician is struggling or thriving.

KEY QUESTIONS TO ENSURE THAT ENGAGEMENT HAPPENS

Can physician engagement be made a strategic priority? Prioritizing engagement requires a commitment of time and money.

If a leader is merely paying lip service to this effort, there is little chance of success. Additionally, the bulk of daily communication to enhance engagement will fall on the person in the manager role. Is leadership willing to train the managers to communicate effectively? Some managers may need ongoing coaching, internal or external, to do so. Will the organization budget time and money for that?

How can organizations create flow for physicians? Developing opportunities for flow is a slow and individual investigative process. It must be done one physician at a time. Engagement cannot be enhanced as a monolithic "them." Leaders must directly provide opportunities for engagement; the process cannot be outsourced or otherwise delegated.

ORGANIZATIONS WITHOUT PHYSICIAN ENGAGEMENT PROGRAMS

Without a formal physician engagement program, individual leaders can still increase engagement. If an organization does not formally assess engagement, a leader can nevertheless use many common data points to understand the team's engagement needs. Physician turnover, physician productivity, recruitment woes, staff complaints, patient satisfaction, patient outcomes, and burnout—all these measurements are directly correlated with physician engagement. And any of them can be used to track success or failure of interventions made or programs implemented. Hence, engagement is not the only element to track. The other measures show progress or lack thereof and are an important part of communication back to the physicians a leader wishes to engage. Therefore, at a managerial level, leaders can begin to engage physicians and combat burnout through meaningful communication, whether an organization has a formal physician engagement plan or not.

CONCLUSION

Finally, implementing meaningful engagement measures is an opportunity for leaders to create flow in their own work while simultaneously creating engagement for others. This pursuit of engagement is necessary on both organizational and individual levels for workplace effectiveness, physician job satisfaction, and patient experience. Investing time and money in more successful communication between leaders and physicians—and in programs that address physician well-being, burnout, and engagement—will strengthen workplace culture, lower turnover rates, and increase job satisfaction for leaders and physicians. It is an investment that healthcare organizations must make for a strong future.

REFERENCES

Csikszentmihalyi, M. 2009. *Flow: The Psychology of Optimal Experience.* New York: Harper & Row.

———. 2008. "Flow, the Secret to Happiness." YouTube TED talk. Published October 24. www.youtube.com/watch?time_continue=15&v=fXIeFJCqsPs& feature=emb_title.

———. 1975. *Beyond Boredom and Anxiety.* San Francisco: Jossey-Bass Publishers.

Csikszentmihalyi, M., and I. S. Csikszentmihalyi. 2000. *Optimal Experience: Psychological Studies of Flow in Consciousness.* Cambridge, UK: Cambridge University Press.

———. 1992. *Optimal Experience: Psychological Studies of Flow in Consciousness.* Cambridge, UK: Cambridge University Press.

Gallup. 2021. "What Is Employee Engagement and How Do You Improve It?" Accessed February 15. www.gallup.com/workplace/285674/improve-employee-engagement-workplace.aspx.

Geirland, J. 2017. "Go with the Flow." *Wired*. Published June 4. www.wired.com/1996/09/czik.

Goleman, D. 2013. *Focus: The Hidden Driver of Excellence*. New York: HarperCollins.

Harter, J. 2020. "U.S. Employee Engagement Reverts Back to Pre-COVID-19 Levels." Gallup. Published October 16. www.gallup.com/workplace/321965/employee-engagement-reverts-back-pre-covid-levels.aspx.

HRZone. 2020. "What Is Employee Engagement?" Accessed September 14. www.hrzone.com/hr-glossary/what-is-employee-engagement.

Jain, S. 2018. "Education Needs Flow." *Medium*. Published January 13. https://medium.com/@skjsaurabh/education-needs-flow-bdc08c659baa.

Liddel, H. G., and R. Scott. 2007. *A Greek-English Lexicon*. London: Simon Wallenberg Press.

Maslach, C., and M. P. Leiter. 2014. *The Truth About Burnout: How Organizations Cause Personal Stress and What to Do About It*. San Francisco: Jossey-Bass.

McCambridge, J., J. Witton, and D. R. Elbourne. 2014. "Systematic Review of the Hawthorne Effect: New Concepts Are Needed to Study Research Participation Effects." *Journal of Clinical Epidemiology* 67 (3): 267–77.

Medical Group Management Association (MGMA). 2018. "Practices Are Slow to Adopt Staff Engagement Programs."

Published February 20. www.mgma.com/data/data-stories/
mgma-stat-poll-practices-are-slow-to-adopt-staff.

Scott, S. 2017. *Fierce Conversations: Achieving Success at Work and in Life, One Conversation at a Time.* London: Piatkus.

Seligman, M. 2018. "PERMA and the Building Blocks of Well-Being." *Journal of Positive Psychology.* Published February 16. DOI: 10.1080/17439760.2018.1437466.

CHAPTER 9

The Economic Model: Does Money Generate Engagement?

Carson F. Dye

The economic model of human behavior is based on incentives applied from outside the person considered: people change their actions because they are induced to do so by an external intervention. Economic theory thus takes extrinsic motivation *to be relevant for behavior.*
—Bruno S. Frey, *Not Just for the Money,* 1997

THIS CHAPTER COULD perhaps be written as follows:

Question: Does money generate engagement for physicians?
Person 1: "Yes, of course it does."
Person 2: "No, it does not."
Person 3: "Sometimes it does and sometimes it doesn't."
Person 4: "None of you seem to know that much about intrinsic or extrinsic motivation."
Summary: It is hard to answer this question, so we should move on to other subjects related to physician engagement.

From an all-encompassing perspective, there are two aspects related to physicians and monetary payments. When the view is the impact of economics on physicians, the focus is on broad-based reimbursement. This viewpoint applies to team-based compensation models or situations involving payments based on government or private gain-sharing or shared-savings programs. The second viewpoint refers to specific compensation paid to physicians under employment relationships. The literature speaks to both (1) the reimbursement aspects of healthcare (e.g., pay for performance, pay for quality, and pay for patient satisfaction such as that measured by HCAHPS [Hospital Consumer Assessment of Healthcare Providers and Systems Survey]) and (2) individual pay. While these two viewpoints are somewhat different, they do intersect. Because of this intersection, the discussion in this chapter will consider both viewpoints. The central question is a simple one: Does money create engagement for physicians? Unfortunately, the answer is not simple.

Because there is no clear-cut answer, the topic of monetary compensation and engagement is challenging. The opinions on this topic vary widely, as evidenced by the opening vignette comments. Consider also the following thoughts by various physicians, health practitioners, and researchers:

> Physicians care first and foremost about their patients' well-being, but that doesn't mean financial incentives are not of great interest to them as well. This motivational tool can be very effective, especially when the incentives are aligned with the organization's shared purpose. . . . Physicians, like everyone else, are motivated by financial incentives and job security. Even if their organization's noble shared purpose resonates deeply with them, they also care intensely about what measures are being used to gauge their performance and how the data are collected and analyzed. This natural self-interest can be channeled to reinforce engagement in a number of ways (Lee and Cosgrove 2014).

> Doctors are unique animals in that the things that motivate them don't necessarily motivate other people and moreover,

they aren't always motivated by the same things that motivate everyone else. So to make your hospital work, you have to know what makes them tick (Allen 2017).

If one implements a financial incentive plan, there are many factors that will increase the probability of success. Relative social ranking (benchmarking to peers and national norms) should accompany or precede a financial incentive, as doing so may yield the results desired without expenditure (for metrics unrelated to additional hours of work). It must be sized sufficiently to attract notice (recommended at least 10 to 15% of salary) and be paid without contingency. Paying too little can yield perverse results by devaluing the work and leading to lower effort overall. It should be paid as close as possible to the work done to avoid significant (hyperbolic) discounting of its dollar value. Withdrawing incentives can result in worse than baseline performance unless changes are hardwired into the workflows (Lubarsky et al. 2019).

Put simply, money isn't everything. Incentives, as important as they are, need to be matched by essential guidance, coaching, and encouragement (Schaff 2019).

Pay-for-performance programs aim to upgrade health care quality by tailoring financial incentives for desirable behaviors. While Medicare and many private insurers are charging ahead with pay-for-performance, researchers have been unable to show that it benefits patients. Findings from the new field of behavioral economics challenge the traditional economic view that monetary reward either is the only motivator or is simply additive to intrinsic motivators such as purpose or altruism. Studies have shown that monetary rewards can undermine motivation and worsen performance on cognitively complex and intrinsically rewarding work, suggesting that pay-for-performance may backfire (Himmelstein, Ariely, and Woolhandler 2014).

Swensen and Chokshi (2019) describe a recent survey of physician engagement. When asked, "What are the top two initiatives that are most effective at engaging clinicians at your organization?" only 15 percent of respondents placed "Financial incentives for organizational priorities" in the top two. This result compares with 57 percent indicating "Involving clinicians in organizational decision-making" among the top two initiatives, and 27 percent placing "Communication about organizational objectives" among the top two. The complete results are summarized as follows:

- Involving clinicians in organizational decision-making: 57 percent
- Communication about organizational objectives: 27 percent
- Providing clinicians with performance data compared with peers: 24 percent
- Designating clinician champions or leaders: 22 percent
- Addressing burnout among clinicians: 21 percent
- Financial incentives for organizational priorities: 15 percent
- Training programs: 12 percent
- Sharing financial results with clinicians: 8 percent
- Financial penalties for ignoring organizational priorities (e.g., quality and good corporate citizenship): 2 percent
- No clinician engagement initiatives are needed: 1 percent

FACTORS AFFECTING MOTIVATION

In discussing physician incentives, Lubarsky and coauthors (2019) describe some forms of motivation that are not necessarily financial: "Intrinsic motivation is powerful when dealing with jobs that require cognitive work, such as creativity and problem-solving. Inherent motivation (free!) can be engaged by healthcare leadership by improving the systems that support the work of physicians." And MacKinney (2016) states, "Although compensation is typically considered in monetary terms, physicians may be rewarded in multiple ways other than through salary."

The first step in considering the impact of economics on engagement is to define motivation. As if the contrast between group reimbursement and individual pay did not confuse the topic enough, another aspect of the impact of economics on physician engagement complicates the issue: motivation. There are many definitions of, and views on, motivation. But suffice it to say that most scholars agree on two aspects of motivation—extrinsic and intrinsic.

The next question, "Is motivation the same as engagement?" presents an additional conundrum. In other words, does it matter if motivation and engagement are the same, slightly related, or not related at all? Ryan and Deci (2000) explain that "to be motivated means to be moved to do something. A person who feels no impetus or inspiration to act is thus characterized as unmotivated, whereas someone who is energized or activated toward an end is considered motivated." They also write, "The most basic distinction is between intrinsic motivation, which refers to doing something because it is inherently interesting or enjoyable, and extrinsic motivation, which refers to doing something because it leads to a separable outcome." While it may be a slight oversimplification, exhibit 9.1 shows the opposite relationships between the two types of motivation.

Since most scholars consider engagement closely related to motivation, people who believe that economics can drive physician engagement would probably see extrinsic motivation as a key factor, and sometimes *the* key factor, in engagement. Conversely, those who view physician engagement as having no direct correlation with economic factors would think that engagement is more intrinsically motivated.

Pink (2009) suggests that "too many organizations still operate from assumptions about human potential and individual

Exhibit 9.1 Extrinsic Versus Intrinsic Motivation

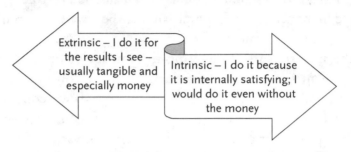

Extrinsic – I do it for the results I see – usually tangible and especially money

Intrinsic – I do it because it is internally satisfying; I would do it even without the money

performance that are outdated, unexamined, and rooted more in folklore than in science. They continue to pursue practices such as short-term incentive plans and pay-for-performance schemes in the face of mounting evidence that such measure usually don't work and often do harm." Certainly healthcare leaders have been thoroughly involved with various pay-for-performance schemes for physicians. These schemes include compensation models based on relative value units (RVUs—or a measure of productivity for clinicians) and compensation bonuses for positive performance in quality, citizenship, or even meeting attendance.

Lubarsky and coauthors (2019) describe the conflict between what truly motivates physicians and what the industry thinks will motivate them: "Physicians enter the field of medicine for its unique opportunities as well as an inherent desire to deliver compassionate and quality patient care, demonstrate high levels of competency, and earn the respect of their peers. The Hippocratic Oath compels physicians to rise above the pressures of cost controls, insufficient value attributed to patient-centric primary care, administrative burdens, long hours, and declining reimbursements to help and heal. While physicians struggle to maintain the meaning of their calling in the rapidly changing world of healthcare, the industry seems focused on how to motivate physicians to adopt desirable behaviors (defined as enhanced productivity and adherence to quality metrics) by focusing on economic gain using financial incentives."

Bruno S. Frey, in his classic *Not Just for the Money*, challenges traditional economic theory and argues that people neither act in expectation of monetary gain alone nor work solely because they are paid (Frey 1997). Furthermore, he claims that higher monetary compensation as well as regulations crowd out motivation in important circumstances. The offer of higher pay may make people less committed to their work and may reduce their performance. They thus behave in exactly the opposite way predicted by the fundamental price-effect theory of economics.

In a similar vein, because motivation and engagement are apparently closely related, we must further ponder the question investigated in this chapter: Are physicians motivated by money (an extrinsic factor)?

Joseph (2020) summarizes the general viewpoint quite well: "Compensation for physicians typically consists of several components, including base salary, bonus, incentives, benefits, and other components. The compensation policy should provide for an optimal and appropriate balance with respect to each of the components." Floyd (2014) writes that "most systems will still keep a significant portion of the physician compensation based on productivity to ensure that physicians have a desire to remain busy and that primary care physicians continue to grow panels (an important need for later capitation)." Kane (2020) summarizes results from the 2020 Medscape Physician Compensation Report: "Incentive bonuses are tied to performance objectives, and are intended to motivate people to work more or be more productive. Among physicians who have an incentive bonus, about a third of both PCPs and specialists say the prospect of an incentive bonus has encouraged them to work longer hours." But note that if this statement were worded differently, it would report that about two-thirds of physicians would say that the prospect of an incentive bonus would *not* encourage them to work longer hours.

INSIGHTS FROM PHYSICIAN LEADERS

To add to the viewpoints presented in this chapter, the editor sought input from several individuals with significant experience in physician engagement and physician compensation. The following pages present their thoughts on the issue.

Lily Henson, MD, MMM, FAAN, FACHE

"I don't think money creates engagement by physicians (or else they shouldn't be in the field). I think engaging physicians by involving them in decision-making is the most important thing you can do."

Margot Savoy, MD, MPH

"This topic comes up every year, and I find I am usually the minority opinion. Money seems like a good incentive, but in under one week, people forget about a monetary bonus. They never really saw it, because it went to direct deposit and got heavily taxed. Early in your career, when you are paid a lot less, typically in more debt, and looking to make large personal investments like a home or a child's education, the extra money is a great incentive.

"At this stage of my career, most incentive plans fail to offer me what would drive me to improve. What drives me, now that my basic needs are met, are time and opportunity. To get more opportunity, I need time. To get more time, I need support and resources. So investing in my practice—giving me appropriate staffing, the tools to see patients efficiently and effectively so I can go home on time and take vacations without being tethered to an EMR—would be worth me putting in extra time. That makes my work now an investment in achieving my future aspirations. The practice investment would create more income from the payers, allowing for even more financial resources to invest in the support staff and tools. Then I can do the other aspects of what I love about medicine—community work, teaching, writing and research. When the incentive addresses all the aspects of the quadruple aim, we all win."

Jeremy Blanchard, MD, CPE

"My perspective is that money is a threshold, similar to concepts delineated in Daniel Pink's descriptions in *Drive* [Pink 2009]; it is not a motivator or sustainer. Money does not create engagement; the physician must feel they are valued, and meeting that threshold allows one to begin the engagement conversation.

"Engagement does seem to have some generational commonalities. It is much less likely for me to see younger physicians define their value to the world as physicians; they more often seem to see medicine as a job. They find the fulfillment in making a difference and being valued.

"Being valued is not monetarily defined. Other attributes to the employment model are valuable once the monetary threshold has been reached (often the 50th percentile of the MGMA compensation survey or other similar survey). For example, they value time—ensuring that they will have time to enjoy their earnings, PTO [paid time off], CME [continuing medical education], leadership development, paid time for quality efforts, paid time for leadership efforts.

"In summary, I believe that the currency of engagement is the physician's feeling valued and that money is just a threshold that, when achieved, allows the individual discussion with the physician to determine what 'being valued would look like.' If the physician feels valued, they will engage with you."

John Byrnes, MD

"At one organization in which I worked, we had a very robust incentive program for physicians. It rewarded them for meeting top decile HEDIS targets (such as HgbA1C <7.0, mammogram rates, colonoscopy rates, etc.). The bonus for the average primary care physician was five figures. In some years, we found that 25–30 percent of physicians left most of their incentive bonus on the table. When asked, many said the money was not a motivator.

"Also, until paying for quality became widespread, I rarely found that I needed financial incentives to engage physicians in moving their performance into the top decile (on clinical outcomes) and beyond. I asked for their help. The medical directors reviewed physician level performance information with the front line monthly, or at least quarterly. We had physician-directed QI [quality improvement] teams standardizing care according to the recent evidence and designing dashboards so they could track their performance. At another healthcare system in which I worked, medical directors' bonuses or incentives for delivering best-in-class quality were rarely required. The one time we did, the contract was executed before I knew about it."

Walter C. Kerschl, MD, CMD, FACP

"If you pay doctors what they are worth (i.e., take money out of the equation by paying fairly), then engagement is all about the vision and the mission.

"Docs don't engage because of money. They engage because of shared values as long as fair pay is provided."

Terry R. McWilliams, MD, FAAFP

"Money alone does not guarantee engagement. In fact, experience has shown that the opposite effect can occur. Besides the well-accepted axiom that employment does not guarantee alignment or engagement, there are many instances of physicians in acquired practices completely abdicating active involvement in either the practice or the health system once employed—and of health systems completely abrogating that involvement ('Just see patients, and we will take care of everything else').

"I fully believe that money will never be a sole engagement vehicle. So many other factors promote or deter engagement.

Involvement in the formal leadership structure, feeling that your perspective is listened to (even though you may not get what you want), transparently sharing information, and feeling valued in and respected by the organization will have a much greater impact than compensation alone. For some physicians, 'you can't pay me enough to . . .' [is their response]. For others, there is no alignment between level of compensation and productivity (a proxy for effort and engagement—though an inadequate one), which tends to support the notion that you can pay physicians a lot of money—even compared to peers—and not engender active engagement in the organization and its success.

"Having said that, I do think that the type of compensation model in place can help better align physician incentives with organizational goals and objectives. Some models do not do this at all (e.g., straight salary and straight individual productivity models traditionally do not align with organizational incentives at all—only with the individual physician's goals and objectives). Depending on the manner in which base plus incentive compensation models are constructed—market competitive rate, individual and group productivity and nonproductivity incentives, downward adjustment risk if clearly defined base expectations are not met, and regular re-evaluation to ensure pertinent incentives exist—compensation *can* be a tool to align physicians and organizations. They will just not do it alone and must exist in systems that have actively and sincerely worked on the other previously mentioned elements."

Harjot Singh, MD, FAPA

"Money is important, and trying to undermine that won't work. And sometimes, it is all about the money—we have had some doctors who were like that. In my experience, these people are in the minority.

"For most physicians, there is a difference between how to get them in, and how to keep them in—and money plays a different role in these two different situations.

"Money is usually what gets doctors in the door and is not usually enough to keep them in by itself.

"If you look at research by [Maslach and Leiter 2014], there are six paths to engaging people—workload, control, fairness, community, reward, and values. Mismatch in any or all of them disengages people and creates burnout.

"Reward is one of six, and monetary reward isn't the only kind of reward out there.

"Sometimes, even though the talk is about money, the root cause is something else—usually fairness, or workload, or control. And if the administrator keeps on ignoring physicians' needs, they do play money as the trump card, giving rise to the thinking 'These doctors are all about the money only.'

"It takes work to figure out which one out of six need to be addressed, and as I discuss in my chapter, it takes work to help figure out what creates the flow for them."

Kevin Casey, DO

"This is a difficult question, not only for the reason that there are some (a small minority, in my opinion) for whom money is the motivating factor.

"Most people, particularly in Western cultures, are competitive. We almost continually gauge our value to something by comparing ourselves with others. Unfortunately, in healthcare, we have set money as the most objective way for us to gauge our value to administration/the institution/group/etc. As long as healthcare leaders use dollars as a tool to try to keep or 'control' physicians, this will continue to be the measuring stick physicians use to determine the level of appreciated value they provide. This has clearly demonstrated over the years more a sense of *compliance* on the part of physicians, but certainly not *commitment*, which is what I believe most leaders would prefer. As far as I can tell, the presence of autonomy, mastery, and purpose, along with well-demonstrated appreciation, is a much more effective way to engage and obtain *commitment* from physicians. This would require some degree of vulnerability on the part of the administrator and more work than just negotiating a dollar amount and therefore is much less likely to be used by healthcare leaders.

"There are a few places (Mayo, CCF [Cleveland Clinic Foundation]) that do not pay their physicians as much as other institutions do, but the prestige and respect (mastery, purpose) that go along with working for those names make payment less of a measuring stick, it appears to me."

Michael Choo, MD, FACEP, FAAEM, CMRO

"When it comes to money, I strongly believe that the majority of physicians simply want to be compensated fairly for their work. It is important that the reimbursement should appropriately account for the high degree of clinical expertise/skillsets needed as well as the increasing administrative burdens now required of our physicians that do not correlate to improvements in care but rather are consequences of mandates from nonclinical stakeholders in healthcare. I personally believe money is not the primary driver of physician engagement; but rather physicians finally started to 'react' and 'adapted' to the primary 'lever' most familiar to the nonclinical stakeholders in healthcare industry. Since money is the key indicator or driver for the nonclinical stakeholders in healthcare, physicians have developed a 'conditioned response' to a system whose attention and focus is more about the money than something else—like true quality of care and outcomes. Physicians are very intelligent, and they figured out that to get the attention of the nonclinician stakeholders in the current healthcare system, they had to focus on the one factor that is critical to the given stakeholders—money. If our healthcare system would start to return the control of healthcare decision-making to physician/clinicians . . . I think physician engagement can be regained and amplified through nonmonetary factors.

"With this said, there will always be a small percentage of physicians who are 'bad actors' motivated by greed and selfishness. But if our physician community would become more accountable to better policing these bad actors, we may actually have a better healthcare system with higher value."

Katherine A. Meese, PhD

"According to Herzberg [Herzberg 2003], money is not a satisfier. Compensation needs to be high enough to make people feel they are fairly paid for their time and expertise, but at best, it will only take a job from bad to just okay. It is not enough to make a job great.

"Compensation is an expression of value, however. As physician compensation has gradually reduced over the last two decades, leaders need to be aware that cuts to overall compensation are likely more demoralizing because of the message of devaluation.

"Engaging physicians in compensation design is key. Financial needs and trade-offs for the physician are likely to vary by career stage and debt burden. It might be that new physicians want the ability to earn as much as possible with a heavy incentive-based structure to pay off their med school debt, mid-careerists may want the flexibility to work less while they have young children, and other stages may prefer options for partial FTEs [full-time employees] or FTE sharing. Compensation models that offer flexibility to the physician based on their desired working arrangements may be ideal."

CONCLUSION

While readers may come away from this chapter still feeling uncertain about the role of financial matters in physician engagement, the chapter does highlight the complexity of this issue. Nevertheless, readers will have at least learned to exercise caution as they initiate compensation programs or other types of payment schemes for physicians in the hopes of enhancing engagement. As Black (2020) advises, "The use of extrinsic incentives in health care may not only be misguided, but it could also be dangerous. Daniel Pink points out many ways that extrinsic incentives can be harmful by diminishing performance, crushing creativity, 'crowding out' ethical behavior in favor of the incentivized action, fostering short-term thinking, and encouraging cheating, and taking shortcuts. None of those are things we want in health care." Judson, Volpp and Detsky (2015) add to this list of concerns: "As health care financing evolves toward reimbursement schemes in which physicians assume risk, there are important questions to consider regarding the balance of extrinsic motivators (e.g., financial reimbursement or other forms of recognition such as awards) and intrinsic motivators (e.g., personal satisfaction derived from doing good work, or internal desire to achieve a particular objective)."

I will conclude by simply suggesting that money is not the only factor that gets physicians engaged. Although a financial reward can significantly contribute to engagement for some physicians, money is simply not a major consideration for others. But for most physicians, many other factors come into play for leaders trying to enhance physician engagement in an organization. Healthcare leaders who place exclusive emphasis on economics alone when trying to enhance physician engagement will miss the mark.

REFERENCES

Allen, J. 2017. "The Nine Things That Motivate Doctors." *Hospital Medical Director.* Published April 20. https://hospitalmedicaldirector.com/the-nine-things-that-motivate-doctors.

Black, C. 2020. "The Pitfalls of Extrinsic Motivation in Health Care." *Op-Med* (Doximity blog). Published May 8. https://opmed.doximity.com/articles/the-pitfalls-of-extrinsic-motivation-in-health-care.

Floyd, P. 2014. "Roadmap for Physician Compensation in a Value-Based World." *Physician Leadership Journal* 1 (1): 14–20.

Frey, B. S. 1997. *Not Just for the Money: An Economic Theory of Personal Motivation.* Brookfield, VT: Edward Elgar Publishing.

Herzberg, F. 2003. "One More Time: How Do You Motivate Employees?" *Harvard Business Review* 81 (1): 87–96.

Himmelstein, D. U., S. Ariely, and S. Woolhandler. 2014. "Pay-for-Performance: Toxic to Quality? Insights from Behavioral Economics." *International Journal of Health Services* 44 (2): 203–14.

Joseph, M. 2020. "Compensation Policies for Physicians Employed by Hospitals and Health Systems." *McAfee and Taft* (JD Supra blog). Published September 14. www.jdsupra.com/legalnews/compensation-policies-for-physicians-13430.

Judson, T. J., K. G. Volpp, and A. S. Detsky. 2015. "Harnessing the Right Combination of Extrinsic and Intrinsic Motivation to Change Physician Behavior." *Journal of the American Medical Association* 314 (21): 2233–34.

Kane, L. 2020. "Medscape Physician Compensation Report 2020." Published May 14. www.medscape.com/slideshow/2020-compensation-overview-6012684.

Lee, T. H., and T. Cosgrove. 2014. "Engaging Doctors in the Health Care Revolution." *Harvard Business Review* 92 (6): 104–38.

Lubarsky, D. A., M. T. French, H. S. Gitlow, L. F. Rosen, and S. G. Ullmann. 2019. "Why Money Alone Can't (Always) 'Nudge' Physicians: The Role of Behavioral Economics in the Design of Physician Incentives." *Anesthesiology* 130 (1): 154–70.

MacKinney, A. C. 2016. "Physician Engagement: A Primer for Healthcare Leaders." Center for Rural Health Policy Analysis.

Published February 12. https://ruralhealthvalue.public-health.
uiowa.edu/files/RHV%20Physician%20Engagement%20
Primer.pdf.

Maslach, C., and M. P. Leiter. 2014. *The Truth About Burnout:
How Organizations Cause Personal Stress and What to Do
About It*. San Francisco: Jossey-Bass.

Pink, D. H. 2009. *Drive: The Surprising Truth About What Motivates Us*. New York: Riverhead Books.

Ryan, R. M., and E. L. Deci. 2000. "Intrinsic and Extrinsic Motiva-
tions: Classic Definitions and New Directions." *Contemporary
Educational Psychology* 25 (1): 54–67.

Schaff, S. J. 2019. "Fostering Physician Motivation: Compensation Is Just the Beginning." *Becker's Hospital Review*. Published
November 13. www.beckershospitalreview.com/hospital-
physician-relationships/fostering-physician-motivation-
compensation-is-just-the-beginning.html.

Swensen, S., and D. A. Chokshi. 2019. "Leadership Survey: Why
Clinicians Are Not Engaged, and What Leaders Must Do
About It." NEJM Catalyst. Published August 8. https://catalyst.
nejm.org/doi/full/10.1056/CAT.19.0630.

CHAPTER 10

Mining for Conflict

Jeremy Blanchard

Dans les champs de l'observation le hasard ne favorise que les esprits préparés (In the field of observation, chance favors only the prepared mind).
—Louis Pasteur, lecture at Université de Lille, 1854

CEOs OFTEN SHARE with their executive teams their expectations and goals. However, many teams never fully embrace the necessary robust debate over these matters. They hesitate to disagree in public, and they walk away from meetings and discussions acting in a way that some would describe as passive-aggressive. Lencioni (2012) suggests ways to avoid this problem: "One of the best ways for leaders to raise the level of healthy conflict on a team is by *mining for conflict* during meetings. . . . By looking for and exposing potential and even subtle disagreements that have not come to the surface, team leaders—and, heck, team members can do it too—avoid the destructive hallway conversations that inevitably result when people are reluctant to engage in direct, productive debate." Consider Lencioni's idea of "mining for conflict." The embrace of conflict is a polarizing idea: It resonates with some and is kryptonite to others. Conflict frequently surfaces during a leader's career. Although conflict doesn't discriminate about whom it affects, the stakes seem to increase as the leader rises to more prominent roles. It clearly has an enormous impact on physician engagement.

In a physician's journey toward executive leadership, there are four common categories of conflict.

CONFLICT OVER DELIVERY OF CARE

All physician executives have been, or still are, participants in the delivery of clinical care. Whether their background is surgery, internal medicine, neurology, pathology, or some other field, clinicians always conduct some type of evaluation and then hand off care to someone else. Although much of medicine has scientific investigation and conclusions to support clinical decisions, on deeper discovery, we find that few decisions are truly well defined. In fact, they are conclusions from available data and exposed to subjective interpretation.

Example: An internist, fresh out of training, began her career in a community hospital. She worked in an employed model with ambulatory, acute care and intensive care unit responsibilities (pre-hospitalists). A senior member of the practice, who was on call, admitted a young patient with pneumonia and acute respiratory distress syndrome. Lung protective management approaches were early in development. The young internist was set to take over the clinical service, including the previously described patient, the next day. At that point, the patient was being managed without any end expiratory pressure, and no guidelines were being followed; the patient was not doing well. In anticipation, the young internist approached her colleague and suggested a guidelines approach to care. When the senior physician refused to do so, the team was left with a *conflict over delivery of care*.

CONFLICT OF PROFESSIONALISM

The broad category of conflict about professionalism relates to individuals' interpretation of professional behavior and their workplace culture. Healthcare cultures continue to evolve at a staccato pace, with an organization's status quo approach periodically interrupted by dynamic bursts of rapid changes in expectations. Conflicts of this type are affected by least three influences: generational perspectives on work expectations (often defined as work ethic), definitions of acceptable behavior, and models of remuneration.

In each physician's practice, there are three to five clinical generations of fellow physicians (Mathews et al. 2012). Generational differences could consequently seed many conflicts. Each generation shares similar core values that led to that generation's choice of becoming physicians. Interestingly, the interpretation of core values can end up creating conflict. Consider accountability. In the older generation, physicians may believe they have accountability for protecting the model of medicine that has brought them fulfillment in their professional lives. Younger physicians, on the other hand, may believe they are accountable for protecting a model of medicine that assures them a joy of practice that they think provides fulfillment. Such a model may include limiting hours in the hospital and thus decreasing the physicians' involvement in the institution, outside of delivering care.

These conflicting perceptions of the ideal practice of medicine may also influence what professionals consider acceptable behavior. Healthcare is no different from other business environments in that racism, a lack of diversity, and chauvinistic behavior were tolerated in the past and are deemed unprofessional now. Finally, there is a strong movement to change the business model of physician remuneration. These changes affect employment, accountable care organizations, unionizing, and other influences on remuneration.

Example: In a medium-sized rural community where general surgeons do not do bariatric surgery, an independent bariatric surgeon created a medical center to offer bariatric surgery. This surgeon came from out of town for a day of clinic and a day of ambulatory bariatric surgery. The following morning, the surgeon would then fly to other communities to do a similar practice. If any patients had complications, they were managed over the phone or asked to go to the emergency department since the bariatric surgeon was not present and did not have admitting privileges. The general surgeon on call would then be asked to see, evaluate, and, if necessary, admit the patient. This arrangement created a major *conflict in professionalism* between the bariatric surgeon, who did not seek privileges at the hospital, and the general surgeon, who was left dealing with a colleague's complications.

CONFLICTS OF LEADING WITH POWER

The third conflict, possibly the most innocuous, is often unrecognized by leaders and develops out of their own personal insecurities. It is often perceived by others as a moment of bullying or intimidation. Leaders often face times when higher-ranking leaders inadvertently or even blatantly act or speak in ways that are meant to degrade or intimidate others.

Example: A CMO in a rural hospital faced the challenge of recruiting surgical subspecialties. The hospital had been looking for a urologist for 15 years unsuccessfully, even investing in a robot as a possible incentive to recruitment. The recruiters had identified an excellent candidate from a highly regarded program. In an attempt to recruit this urologist, the CEO asked his strategy executive, to whom recruitment reported, to offer an incentive that the strategy executive believed was a violation of law. In an e-mail exchange that included the entire executive team, the CEO used an expletive to describe the strategist's desire to seek legal review before offering the incentive. This exchange was detrimental to the health of the executive team and threatened to undermine the sense of trust and cohesiveness. The strategy executive was intimidated and would not confront the CEO. The CMO, recognizing the potential for further damage from this incident, asked the CEO to publicly apologize. The CEO's behavior is an example of a *conflict of leading with power*.

CONFLICT OF THE STORY THAT NEVER HAPPENED

Every situation has multiple interpretations. All of us can think of times we have been part of an incident where our actions were perceived differently than our intentions. Part of the role of leaders is to manage these perceptions. Interestingly, postponing a decision to deliberate on it is often perceived as procrastination. But good leaders determine when and at what level of the organization decisions need to be made. In human interactions or when mistakes happen, the natural impulse is to resolve the issue quickly. This rush to resolution is often a mistake, as the true nature of the situation is seldom as it was initially described. For decision-makers, hearing two sides of the story and, many times, a third or fourth side can be invaluable. An extremely helpful part of a leader's efforts to hear all sides of a conflict is to assume that all conflicting parties have good intentions. Sometimes the good intent is hard to find, but if someone is acting nefariously, it will be discovered as the situation is reviewed.

Example: A physician executive of a moderate-sized community hospital was actively recruiting physicians. In the meantime, the facility had a large number of locum tenentes. One such physician, an intensive-care clinician, had a very extroverted personality and was disliked by some of the nurses. One day, responding to a code in the emergency department, he threw his dirty gloves toward the trash can, but they hit a nurse in the upper body. Following the code, she submitted an incident report. Because of this physician's challenging personality, many who reviewed the report thought he should be reprimanded and potentially fired. The physician executive investigated the matter and was able to resolve the concern with an apology from the physician, who also told the nurse that he had not intended to hit her. Before this apology and conversation, false and inaccurate stories of the incident had been "written" in many people's minds. This example illustrates *conflicts over stories that never really happened.*

HEALTHCARE, THE PERFECT MILIEU FOR BREEDING CONFLICT

Leaders in healthcare live in four very different worlds: the world of societal perceptions and expectations, the scientific and clinical world, the business world associated with healthcare, and the world of their own personal lives. The complexity of reconciling these different worlds in itself creates natural conflict. Add to these challenges the intimacy of delivering healthcare. Only four professions have this level of intimacy—healthcare provider, coach, spiritual adviser/minister, and teacher. And only healthcare has the added challenge of encroaching on people's physical privacy. To be a physician or any other healthcare worker is truly an honor. Interestingly, conflict in healthcare can arise from very different perspectives. When conflict is identified early, it can be defined and managed in more collaborative and generative terms such as shared decision-making, productive conversation, and team empowerment. Conflict is truly an intellectual nutrient that has led to fulfillment in many a servant leader's journey.

Healthcare is ripe with all types of conflict. Struggles abound between physicians and administrations regarding productivity, electronic medical records, attribution of care, and resources. Other conflicts proliferate on issues of personal or professional lives; there is also the litigious side of healthcare, reflecting disagreements that patients or their families have about the care delivered. Also common are scope-of-practice conflicts (where one party is concerned that another party has performed some role outside the other's scope of practice) between physicians and advanced-practice providers and between nurses and physicians. Leaders who mine for conflict have the opportunity to be pioneers. Since conflict has such a negative connotation, stories of how organizations handle conflict productively have been rare. When leaders can welcome productive conflict and help parties truly resolve differences, their value to the organization quickly grows, allowing their own careers and those of the healthcare system's other professionals to accelerate and increasing people's professional fulfillment.

HOW DOES CONFLICT MINING ACCELERATE YOUR LEADERSHIP SUCCESS?

Why should leaders want to mine for conflict? Mining for conflict has several benefits:

- Participating in conflict interaction requires the other party to be, by definition, engaged. Participants must feel strongly involved, have done some research, feel their voice is important, and believe they have something to offer to the discussion.
- Entering into conflict is seldom done without a commitment to accept a negative outcome; it requires courage.
- Conflict means that the other party is at least engaged and involved in the matter or, at the very least, sees value in approaching you with a concern.
- People who initiate a conflict conversation believe they have good intentions; if they are successful at bringing you to their recommendation, something will improve in their mind.
- A conflict represents a relationship that you can somehow nurture; if the other party did not feel you had either influence or value, the person would not have taken the risk of entering into conflict with you.
- Conflict that seems small to you may feel huge to the other party. Being aware of these differences in perspective can help open up your eyes to others' point of view.

Servant leaders mine for conflict because this effort provides one of the greatest opportunities to learn, to show respect, and to build credibility and trust. Leaders can only garner trust after all the parties establish a foundation of mutual respect. Trust is not controllable, because it depends on another party to trust you. But respect and expecting to be treated with respect is totally within the control of a servant leader. This approach allows the leader to be vulnerable, and a willingness to be vulnerable is an essential trait of servant leadership (Greenleaf 2018).

In many crises or other stressful situations (e.g., the COVID-19 pandemic, start-up companies, hospital mergers and affiliations, mass catastrophes), servant leadership is an extremely effective way to guide an organization. This servant model makes it much easier to empower smarter and more competent team members to strive for excellence. And in all crisis situations, communication channels are often down or threatened. Mining for conflict allows leaders to push decisions down to the appropriate levels, leading to nimbler and safer team responses.

HOW TO MINE FOR CONFLICT

Mining for conflict is not a skill that you learn one day and then apply the next. It is a form of pattern recognition. Often, you can recognize a conflict by monitoring specific individuals on your team, topics of controversy, and actions with known high stakes.

Paying attention to the strong "feelers" on teams increases sensitivity to conflict. Two groups can often be the canaries in the coal mine to help leaders identify conflict early: the naysayers and the Pollyannas.

Naysayers

Many leaders devalue naysayers at their own peril. Effective naysayers do their research, have passion, and speak up and out. These elements make naysayers ideal people to provide information never thought of or assumed to be incorrect. Many executives do not know their organization's true culture, and by engaging naysayers, they can often identify early concerns worth discussing. Naysayers can often become great champions and valuable colleagues.

Pollyannas

The Pollyannas are slightly different as "canaries." Because they want everything to be pleasant, their concerns often surface later in discussions than do naysayers' doubts. Frequently serving as a litmus test, Pollyannas change when circumstances become less optimistic.

Distinguishing the Journey from the Destination

A key tactic for mining for the right conflict is actively identifying the journey the organization wishes to traverse and not confusing it with desired destinations. A good metaphor for reflecting on this tactic is the physician's journey. Physicians finish residencies, get jobs, and earn money. Do these equate to fulfillment? Probably not, as most physicians get true satisfaction from caring for others and feeling appreciated in doing so.

For example, a recent subspecialty fellowship graduate finished her rigorous training, but on the day she finished, she asked herself, "Now what?" Her times of greatest fulfillment were such distinctive moments as when she worked on a patient with hantavirus, or when a young nurse whom she had given clot buster to while doing CPR compressions for a pulmonary embolism had survived an otherwise certain death. The physician felt tough times when a 12-year-old boy injured in a motocross died in her arms with the parents at the bedside. One of the common mile markers on these type of journeys is conflict. Often serving as a mile marker or marking a change in direction, these events help individuals become more comfortable with mining for conflict.

CONCRETE TACTICS FOR FACING CONFLICT

Almost all leaders encounter predictable and unpredictable conflict. These circumstances help leaders learn how to mine for conflict and then manage it. Let us now look at how you can prepare to mine for conflict and then actually face a conflict for the benefit of your organization.

Preparation and Just-in-Time Tactics

1. **Breathe:** Begin all potential conflicts by trying to pause and take a breath. You will want to focus on the four steps of a breath—inhale, pause, exhale, and pause. By focusing on the breath, you bring yourself to present. This approach is excellent for preparing for anticipated emotional conversations or times when you want to make sure you are managing your emotions. For many, this is a simple go-to technique to manage their emotions.

2. **Invest:** Look immediately for something you like or respect about the other party; you are investing in them and the conversation. In desperate times, this observation can be as simple as thinking, "That is a nice sports coat." Sometimes, this step is easier, because you like lots of things about the person or people, or you have great rapport. Seeking out something you like helps you mold your nonverbal posture in a way that fosters engagement and trust. There is great controversy over the amount of influence nonverbal cues have in the communication of our message and its intent, but most observers agree that these cues make a difference and reflect what you truly think. A colleague who is seen as a master communicator believes his initial nonverbal cues have more impact than do his words or tone.

3. **Assume good intent:** We all have a tendency to write a story subliminally as we begin all interactions. The story and the ending we choose are totally up to us. To help write the most positive and constructive version, actively

assume the other party has good intentions. Doing so allows you to look at the issue from different perspectives. All stories and decisions are based on assumptions. Pivotal communication like major business decisions are exponentially affected by the underlying assumptions (Lapakko 2007; Levine et al. 2012).

Tactics for the Moment of Truth

Once conversations start, leaders run the risk of being seen as having power. This impression can curb the comfort of others when they approach leaders. For this reason, leaders need to recognize the personal risk and courage of the other person or persons. The following practices can help leaders ease the conversations about conflicts so that everyone feels welcome to share concerns or difficulties.

1. **Choose the right time and the right place:** It is extremely common for someone to approach a senior leader and ask, "Do you have five minutes?" Be mindful that it usually means the other person wants to share something and does not really want a response. Although people who do this may just want to vent, they may also be handing off a true problem to avoid accountability on their own part.

   Leaders must decide if they can they adjust their calendars to adequately discuss the situation or if they need to discuss it in the near future. Note that asking to wait until later to discuss requires creating an authentic commitment and desire to truly hear what the other person has to say. You might say, "I am really sorry, but I don't have time right now to really listen to your concern. Can we set up 15 or 30 minutes to talk about it?" Leaders must not let this commitment slip and must follow up as soon as they can.

2. **Listen mindfully:** In mindful listening, a person listens to understand what the other person is saying. The listener avoids immediate replies and tries not to show judgment. Mindful listening takes practice; it is not intuitive.

3. **Manage the electronics:** It has been said that after a person looks at a text or an e-mail, it takes 16 seconds for an individual to return concentration back to a conversation. Because ignoring their electronics can be challenging for many leaders, they may need to take such drastic steps as not bringing their devices to meetings. When a person engaged in a conversation looks at an electronic device, the other party is very likely to feel less valued (Rath 2015).

4. **Paraphrase back:** Spirited conversations often mean that individuals feel they have not been heard. Paraphrasing what has been said is one of the best ways leaders can show that they have heard accurately. It is advisable to avoid such wording as "I understand how you feel" or "I know exactly how you feel." Because everyone has unique histories and experiences, these types of statements often cause speakers to disengage. More helpful statements in these settings might be, "It sounds as if you feel [name the emotion—frustrated, let-down, angry, etc.]." Naming what a person thinks the other party is feeling is a safe approach, because the listener can be corrected if the assumption is wrong.

5. **Establish an acceptable outcome:** During conflict, it is helpful for leaders to identify what the other party sees as an acceptable outcome. Not all conflict needs to be solved. Sometimes, individuals just need to vent. This approach has multiple associated gains. First, the other person has to articulate the outcome being sought.

Second, it establishes accountability for the other person to work toward a positive outcome. And finally, it allows the leader to delve into the why and what of the other party's desired outcome. By creating a moment that allows this conversation to evolve, the leader can use a series of repeated whys to delve into the underlying reason. Sometimes, the other person may not have even identified the acceptable outcome themselves, and this can be liberating for the conversation and for a positive outcome.

The other person or persons, if they feel the leader really heard them, will almost always give the leader time to process and look into their concern. This is a great opportunity to establish a pattern of accountability. The leader is accountable to investigate and find more information. The other party is accountable for further considering a position and can be held accountable to meet with the leader in the near future. Most situations are not emergencies and can be postponed a couple of days.

6. **Follow up:** This can be as simple as an e-mail saying, "Thank you for meeting with me. I will give some time and thought to your concerns. I look forward to our upcoming meeting." Following up is an opportunity for leaders to value the input of others, to share that they truly want to hear others' thoughts, and to reaffirm what each party is being held accountable to accomplish.

7. **Create a common message:** Leaders can ask the other person what the individual would tell someone if asked about the conversation that just took place. This simple act helps leaders script the message that others will hear, ensures that everyone is parting with a common understanding, and establishes lines of accountability. Settling on a common message works especially well in conflicts over delivery of care.

PITFALLS TO AVOID IN CONFLICT

E-mail and Texting

E-mail messages and texts are poor forms of dialogue. They work best for monologues and orders. In an e-mail and text, the tone is lost, nonverbal cues are missed, and real-time exchange is not possible. All texts and e-mails can be forwarded as well, so mistakes can live on for a long time. If leaders sense controversy or the potential of misinterpretation, they should ideally meet in person. Meeting can be a winning situation, and leaders often gain such unanticipated benefits as rapport and appreciation.

Recently a CMO was put in charge of the clinical response of a large integrated health system. She had personally only visited a few of the geographical locations, but over the following months, she saw neighboring systems develop challenges with disruptive physicians. Looking back, she shared that, over six months' time, she had not had one disruptive physician. She attributed this good outcome to her approach and the support of her team. With any text, e-mail, or rumor, she had called the individual physician and either spoke with the person on the phone or in person. In the conversation, she acknowledged that she did not know the right answer and did not have all the information supporting the team's decision. She asked for the person's thoughts and then listened quietly to understand, not to reply or to judge. This commitment to honoring relationships and humanness accelerated her acceptance in the organization and the success of her team and its systematic approach.

Arrogance

Seldom is there one truth, and in most cases, the conflict we deal with is very complex. We need to move away from the idea of winning. The establishment of acceptable outcomes is pivotal, and by maintaining this viewpoint, we can encourage win–win situations.

Aiming for outcomes acceptable to all parties also gives the conversation a constructive tone, avoids a personal focus, and creates room for compromise. Two great phrases to help support humility are "I do not know the right answer—I am open to your thoughts," and "You may be right; we will have to see. For now, are you able to give the option I have proposed a try, and then we can reconvene to see if it is working?"

USING A DASHBOARD TO IMPROVE THE VALUE OF CONFLICT

Healthcare leaders find using a dashboard in their efforts to mine and use conflict in their organization can help ensure that they put their efforts to the best use and avoid easy pitfalls. A dashboard, a tool that focuses on process metrics, is about process management and experiential learning. With each tactic in exhibit 10.1, leaders can choose one or two areas to commit to developing. Perhaps leaders could identify meetings where they could focus intently on listening to understand and avoid replying with judgment. Users could use this dashboard in various ways. They may simply just show check marks to indicate, "Yes, I tried this," or fill out in advance,

Exhibit 10.1 Dashboard

	Mindful Listening	Assumption of Good Intent	Mining for Conflict	Determining Desired Outcome	Sculpting the Message	Assigning Accountability
Week 1						
Week 2						
Week 3						
Week 4						
Week 5						
Week 6						

indicating "Staff meeting, Tuesday." They may also simply indicate how their tactic worked ("Friday: Listened quietly when Steve met me in the hallway to vent his frustration with EMRs") or even give themselves a score or grade. It typically takes six weeks to establish a routine. At the end of the six weeks, leaders can determine how these approaches may have been helpful.

EXERCISES TO DEVELOP KEY SKILLS

Here are a few exercises that leaders can practice to improve their ability to mine for conflict, to accept it as a normal part of an organization's growth, and to transform it into personal or organizational improvement.

Mindful Breathing

Mindful breathing requires ongoing practice. Otherwise, this calming technique will not be available or remembered in a stressful situation.

1. Each morning or evening, find a quiet place. Close your eyes. Count to a number silently as you slowly inhale through your nose. Sitting up straight will allow you to take a deep breath. Most leaders using this skill find the number they count to while inhaling is between four and eight. Once you have reached full inhalation, pause. Then exhale slowly through your mouth counting silently to yourself. Once you have fully exhaled, pause and repeat.
2. Repeat this cycle ten times.
3. Try to find the same numbers every time. When your mind wanders, try to visualize the numbers in your brain and stay on track.

4. By doing this exercise that only takes four minutes a day, you will gain mindful-breathing skills and reduce your stress levels, better control your reaction to stress and fatigue, and enhance your ability to work through conflict.

Investing in Colleagues

1. Each day, review your calendar and identify one or two meetings containing a difficult challenge.
2. Write one or two things that are positive or valuable about the person involved in the meeting.
3. Before the meeting, review these thoughts. At the beginning of the meeting, when you first have contact with this person, think about those positives.
4. Most leaders who have engaged in this experience find the interaction to be markedly improved from the past.

Assumption of Good Intent

The more leaders assume the other party has good intentions, the greater the impact of this tactic. In reviewing the calendar, identify a meeting with an individual who may be particularly challenging. Regardless of the subject to be discussed, actively assume the other person's intent is good. Then try to look at it from this individual's perspective.

Mindful Listening

1. Choose a trusted partner, and ask the person to help you practice mindful listening. Explain that for one or two minutes, they will answer a question you ask them. Your

goal will be to fully listen to understand, to not reply, and to avoid judgment. When the partner has finished answering, this individual will ask you the same question and will listen to understand, to not reply, and to avoid judgment.

2.   Choose an open-ended question for this exercise. A favorite when leaders are engaging healthcare workers is "Tell me what in your current job gives you fulfillment and why."

3.   After both of you have finished, discuss which felt better, to listen or to be heard? And how often does that happen to your partner, or does this person listen like that to others?

CONCLUSION

Conflict is prevalent in the roles that all leaders play, and the more sensitive leaders become to developing conflict and the more they respectfully mine for it, the more successful they become as servant leaders. And as a result, the more engaged others feel. Physicians develop as leaders from the moment they are accepted to medical school, but unfortunately, they are seldom taught conflict-mining skills. Their greatest gap may be the ability to manage conflict and communication. Despite these shortcomings in physicians' training, healthcare leaders need expertise in conflict management to ensure higher levels of physician engagement.

REFERENCES

Greenleaf, R. 2018. "A Novice's Journey: The Servant-Leader Is Human." Center for Servant Leadership. Published March 12. www.greenleaf.org/novices-journey-servant-leader-human.

Lapakko, D. 2007. "Communication Is 93% Nonverbal: An Urban Legend Proliferates." *Communication and Theater Association of Minnesota Journal* 34: 7–19.

Lencioni, P. M. 2012. *The Advantage: Why Organizational Health Trumps Everything Else in Business*. San Francisco: Jossey-Bass.

Levine, R., K. Shore, J. Lubalin, S. Garfinkel, M. Hurtado, and K. Carman. 2012. "Comparing Physicians and Patient Perceptions of Quality in Ambulatory Care." *Journal for Quality in Health Care* 24 (4): 348–56.

Mathews, M., M. Seguin, N. Chowdhury, and R. T. Card. 2012. "A Qualitative Study of Factors Influencing Different Generations of Newfoundland and Saskatchewan Trained Physicians to Leave a Work Location." *Human Resources for Health*. Published July 25. www.ncbi.nlm.nih.gov/pmc/articles/PMC3464152/.

Rath, T. 2015. *Are You Fully Charged? The 3 Keys to Energizing Your Work and Life*. Arlington, VA: Silicon Guild.

CHAPTER 11

Gender Issues

Kathleen L. Forbes

Women are half of all medical school entrants in the United States. They are a third of the profession and growing. Despite this, and evidence that they provide higher quality care than male physicians in some instances, their experiences as doctors are much different on average than their male counterparts, and not in a good way. They earn significantly less doing the same kind of work, often tens of thousands of dollars less.
—Timothy Hoff, "The Challenges of Being a Female Doctor," 2019

BY UNDERSTANDING THE INDIVIDUAL and work characteristics and the unique perspectives and obligations of female physicians, hospital administrators, practice leaders, managers, and colleagues can better encourage physician engagement in their organizations. Giving physicians a true voice at the table; proper respect for their title and expertise, irrespective of gender; and an appreciation for the demands on the lives of all medical providers will help encourage participation. Fair compensation, flexible models of employment, and leadership development that identifies with women physicians closes the deal.

LET'S REVIEW THE DATA

Although a large majority (80 percent) of the healthcare workforce is female (Lanka 2018), there is an imbalance of women in healthcare leadership roles. This imbalance becomes more pronounced the higher up on the leadership ladder one goes, and it points to enduring systemic issues. In fact, the American College of Healthcare Executives cited that "women comprise only 11% of healthcare CEOs in the U.S." (Henkel 2016). Even more significant, women healthcare consumers make 80 percent of all buying and usage decisions in healthcare (Stone et al. 2019), and 50.5 percent of first-year medical school students are women, as detailed by the American Association of Medical Colleges (Boyle 2019).

As the face of medicine continues to evolve, there is a significant presence of female physicians in the workforce. Currently, 36 percent of the nation's professionally active physicians are women. A survey by Athenahealth indicates that 60 percent of physicians younger than 35 are women, while just 40 percent are men. Even in the next age bracket (35 to 44 years of age), women predominate, making up 51.5 percent of this group (Johnson 2018).

Breaking down the healthcare leadership representation, the data shows that women make up 3 percent of healthcare CEOs in the United States, 6 percent of department chairs, 9 percent of division chiefs, and 3 percent are chief medical officers (Lanka 2018). While women can be found in medical director roles in clinics and in frontline leadership roles, they are less often found in higher-level leadership roles. To truly have a voice with leadership and be part of the solution is what is meaningful and engaging to female physicians.

"In academic healthcare," says Jennifer Hunt, MD, a board-certified pathologist in Little Rock, Arkansas, "with each academic rank jump, we lose approximately 10 percent of the women. Only 20 percent [of department chairs] are held by women [and] specialties like surgery have less than five percent female chairs. The number is similarly low at the Dean level." Dr. Hunt, a Fellow of the College of American Pathologists and chair of Department of Pathology and Laboratory Services at the University of Arkansas for Medical Sciences, adds, "There has been a slow increase, but nowhere close to where it should be for the demographics of practicing physicians. We continue to have a significant gap" (Weber 2019).

The good news is that academic healthcare medicine recognizes these statistics and is focusing on four approaches:

1. Standardize awards and broaden promotion opportunities; systematizing these processes can reduce the gender gap.
2. Balance recognition for accomplishments in the field. Research efforts are male dominated and often receive more recognition than do education and service efforts, which tend to be female dominated.
3. Involve male colleagues in efforts to improve gender diversity in leadership.
4. Create academic opportunities for development and sponsorship.

An additional factor that contributes to the challenge of female physician engagement is professional burnout. Among physicians, professional burnout is higher for women than it is for men. Shannon (2017) reported on two surveys conducted by Athenahealth and noted that of 1,029 practicing physicians, "women under 45, in particular, were significantly more likely to report burnout than men." The study also concluded that men produced 30 to 40 percent more work relative value units (RVUs) than women did, but it identified a difference in the approach of productivity for men and women. Men perform work with RVUs attached, and women will attend events like family care meetings and counseling activities with patients—tasks that do not produce RVU credit. Women are often viewed as calm, caring, and empathetic. That expectation leads to burnout among women physicians because they strive for perfection that doesn't exist. They may find themselves in a conflict between productivity challenges and patients' expectations of emotional support. These conflicting priorities can lead to professional burn-out, which diminishes their desire to engage in leadership activities.

In many aspects of their personal lives, women physicians' experiences diverge from men's. Hoff (2019) points to some troubling differences:

> Compared to male physicians, women physicians are more likely to get divorced. Working longer hours for them means higher chances for divorce, whereas for male doctors, working longer actually decreases divorce risk.
>
> Women physicians may experience negative psychological states like depression and burnout more than their male counterparts. More of them compared to male doctors may engage in thoughts of suicide. They experience work–family conflict to a larger degree than men do, in part because they take on more of the home and parental duties. They have greater chances of being harassed at work and are often less likely to be promoted or move into leadership positions. They marry other doctors at a higher rate than their male colleagues, and in such dual career cases, are more likely to sacrifice aspects of their medical careers, work less, and earn less money.

CAREER DECISION CHALLENGES DURING TRAINING

One of the biggest challenges that women face as healthcare professionals is the timing of their undergraduate medical education (medical school) and residency training. During this time, many physicians are considering parenthood; an estimated 40 percent of physicians plan to have children during their graduate medical education training (Hingle et al. 2018). The impact of childbearing during a residency program weighs heavily on women and may influence the timing and learning investment of their training and, ultimately, their career choices. There is significant pressure around this issue, and some view pregnancy during training as the "mommy track," with negative connotations by peers, supervisors, and attending physicians—including, surprisingly, other women.

An additional challenge is that regardless of it being a more modern era, women are still categorized as the primary caregivers of their family units (Weber 2019). Some people doubt that women can be both caregiver and professional effectively, and others question women's ability to balance both. Some women also have these doubts about themselves. The 2016 Academic Medicine Study noted that a woman's pregnancy during graduate medical education training is more likely to alter her career plans than would a partner's pregnancy for their male counterparts. Women may also lose research productivity, have altered call schedules, and, ultimately, complete their professional training later than their male colleagues do (Blair et al. 2016). Additionally, a 2018 *JAMA* study found just 8 of 15 residency-sponsoring institutions affiliated with 12 prominent US-based medical schools offer paid childbearing or family-leave provisions for residents (Magudia et al. 2018). The American College of Physicians (ACP) reports—more alarmingly—that only 28.9 percent of physician employment contracts provide comprehensive maternity coverage. However, an unpaid leave results in an average loss of $10,000 in income, a loss that discourages women physicians from planning a pregnancy (Weber 2019). These physicians then must make tough choices as they seek a work–life balance.

So, what do gender-related differences mean to societal expectations, financial and other organizational support, and the choice of specialty? The length of a residency program, call demands, the ability to complete a pregnancy during training, and, ultimately, a person's practice options will all determine a physician's specialty. All these factors not only influence the choice of a specialty but also affect the level of engagement of female physicians. By understanding female physicians' struggles to have both a successful clinical practice and a meaningful work–life balance to raise a family, health-care leaders can gain insight into how to improve these physicians' engagement.

CHALLENGES WITH SELECTING A PROFESSIONAL PRACTICE

Given all the issues just reviewed, female physicians deliberate on many aspects of their practice when deciding on a professional pathway. The following items may be considered:

- **Hours available for a professional career:** The length of the workday and workweek can be a real concern for most professionals. For example, some physicians may desire to work less than full-time. This preference can be challenging to an organization or a practice that wants a full-time provider both for patient hours and for call coverage. A creative model that has demonstrated success is *role sharing*. Through this approach, two physicians are hired to share one full-time role, thereby reducing both their patient-care time commitment and call-coverage responsibility. There are several examples of this approach, and all of them can lead to a rewarding work–life balance.

- **How a professional practice fits into family life:** Family responsibilities are a very real consideration for any physician. Unfairly or not, these burdens can weigh more heavily on women, for a variety of reasons. A study found that "40% of women physicians go part-time or leave medicine altogether within six years of completing their residencies" (Paturel 2019). The primary reason? Family. Some 77.5 percent of the female physicians who either left clinical practice completely or changed their employment to part-time status specify family as the primary determinant. Among physicians with children, 31 percent of women and 5 percent of men worked part-time (Jagannathan 2019). Herein lies the greatest opportunity not only to improve engagement with female physicians, but also to help reform professional practice expectations and design. Organizations can prevent burnout and the exodus of female physicians by supporting their work–life balance with more flexible opportunities for practice.

- **Time available and opportunities for leadership roles:** When professionals decrease their number of working hours, they will naturally have fewer hours available for leadership activities. This disadvantage also applies to areas of specialization. For example, fewer female physicians who desire to have a family elect more competitive and more time-consuming specialties than do male physicians. These areas include the historically male-dominated areas of neurosurgery, plastic surgery, and orthopedics (Weber 2019). A contemporary restructuring of training programs and professional practice time expectations will help promote a change for future physicians as they select residency programs and areas of specialization.

- **Time available for additional activities:** Finally, physicians burdened with outside responsibilities or in-house duties unrelated to leadership may miss out on other opportunities for professional development and fulfillment. They could, for example, lose out on elected or appointed committee memberships, department chairs, medical staff officer positions, and participation in clinical improvement efforts. For example, if a woman physician is assigned routine support activities such as patient relations, she may lack the time to push for membership on a decision-making committee.

IMPLICIT GENDER BIAS

Beginning in medical school, female physicians in training quickly begin to experience barriers that their male classmates seldom face. This disparity creates significant impact on women's academic and clinical careers. In a 2017 survey, 41 percent of women physicians said they had experienced gender bias, in contrast to 6 percent of their male counterparts. In fact, "female physicians regularly operate in less welcoming and supportive environments, which compromises their authority, promotes marginalization, and overshadows relationships with colleagues and patients" (Weber 2019).

The survey shows that women experience profound microaggressions on a daily basis. The most notable example is the tendency to call male physicians "Doctor" and then to refer to female physicians by their first names. Disparities like these can erode the credibility of, and people's respect for, the women at the table and can lead female physicians to feel disengaged. Surprisingly, anecdotal evidence suggests that it was still common in 2020 for patients and others to refer to women in healthcare as "nurses," and men as "doctors." Consistency by leaders in how they address all professionals, particularly women, is one small way to help break down these prejudices.

DEVELOPING FEMALE PHYSICIANS' LEADERSHIP AND ENGAGEMENT

One way to engage female physicians is to encourage their participation as leaders or champions. Ensuring that their voices are heard and showing that their opinions matter can both be rewarding and mitigate physician burnout. With the aftershocks of the COVID-19 pandemic, many organizations are focused on volume recovery, regaining patient trust, reinforcing safe clinical practices, and ensuring an adequate supply of personal protective equipment. And now it is time to return our focus on delivering healthcare services. Because of the challenges brought on by the pandemic, some aspects of women's leadership may not get the attention needed. Ammerman and Groysberg (2020) write, "As we've watched the coronavirus crisis unfold, we see many of the barriers that stymie women's careers and lead companies to underutilize and lose their female talent become magnified."

Now is not the time to postpone leadership inclusion efforts. Clearly, now is the time to put compassion, humility, and teamwork to their best use. And these qualities are often found in female physicians. According to an article from McKinsey, gender-diverse executive teams are 21 percent more likely to see above-average profitability (Berlin et al. 2020). There is a strategic value in having multiple voices, perspectives, and skills at the leadership table during a crisis and in postcrisis recovery.

Organizations can support female physicians' engagement and leadership in multiple ways. Leaders should consider which approaches would work best in their organization.

Formal Programs and Training

Healthcare organizations can offer formal programs and training for physician leader development. The caveat here is to help bring the programs to the physician through remote learning and flexibility of training. Additionally, organizations should support programs especially designed to offer skills and knowledge to female physicians.

Informal Training and Coaching or Mentoring Opportunities

In her book *Presence*, Amy Cuddy highlights some techniques that female leaders can use to level the playing field. She discusses the need to be aware of key body language so that the women can "take up more space" and appear confident and present in the conversation. In addition, Cuddy encourages women to learn the art of speaking up to be part of the conversation (Cuddy 2015).

Style of communication is also important. People's conflicting perceptions of assertiveness and aggressiveness are always a consideration. Implicit biases and stereotyping may cause a woman with one style and approach to be viewed as aggressive while a male with the same style and approach may be viewed as assertive. The same disparity holds with listening opportunities. A woman may be viewed as timid or passive when she is listening quietly, whereas a similarly quiet man may be viewed as pensive or observant. Being aware of these differences can help leaders mitigate the stereotypes (Roter et al. 2002).

Pay inequities may still exist between female and male physicians. Lagasse (2020) reports that "in nonsurgical specialty practices with 90% male representation, female physicians earn as much as $91,000 less per year than their male peers." And Finnegan (2020) notes that "male physicians starting their careers are paid an average of $36,600 more than their female colleagues." Some key reasons cited are that women generally do not spend as many hours working and that they generally select primary care specialties, which are lower paid. Yet Finnegan (2020) reports though that "60% of the gap in starting salary primarily [could be explained by] by differences in specialty and hours spent in patient care. However, they couldn't entirely explain the salary differences." Moreover, organizations need to be much more cognizant of gender pay differences. And coaching and guiding female physicians on when and how to address pay and benefit issues is highly effective.

Many professional societies, including the ACP, American Association for Physician Leadership, and American Academy of Family Physicians, promote the development and deployment of comprehensive leadership training, which includes the art of negotiation and career guidance inclusive of early career physicians and physicians-in-training. Many cite the need to have specific topics related to women in medicine and leadership given the challenges of family commitments (Butkus et al. 2018).

TEN SUGGESTIONS FOR HEALTHCARE ORGANIZATIONS TO ENGAGE FEMALE PHYSICIANS

1. Mitigate and Ultimately Eliminate Implicit Gender Bias

The ACP highly encourages implicit bias training for all organizations that provide undergraduate or graduate medical education and that employ physicians. The American Medical Association supports a threefold approach:

- Stop penalizing physicians who work fewer hours; offer a balanced compensation plan and support. Recognize work–life balance.
- Provide universal access to paid medical and family leave.
- Expand paid leave to more than six weeks.

2. Across the Gender Spectrum, Be Equally Respectful of All Physicians

Healthcare leaders should avoid covert discrimination and be cognizant of what Dr. Hunt coins as the "fallacy of familiarity." For example, some leaders tend to use first names when introducing female physicians and the title "Doctor" when introducing male physicians. Dr. Hunt explains: "The person talking thinks that they are demonstrating rapport and friendship with the woman they are introducing, but in fact they are just invalidating them as experts and specialists. When that happens day after day, the time [females] spent in training and their level of expertise feels diminished" (Weber 2019).

3. Support Programs for Leadership Development and Negotiation

Organizations can offer leadership training to physicians, recognizing the need to make the training easily accessible for them, given the multiple demands on the physicians' schedules and their desire for work–life balance. Training can be directed to cover issues that all genders experience and gender-specific challenges and growth opportunities. To ensure successful engagement of physicians through these programs, organizations must offer programmatic support, recognition of completion, and the opportunity to put the newly learned skills to good use.

4. Improve Visibility of Female Physicians in Leadership Roles

Women can be at a disadvantage in hiring processes because of recruiters' or interviewers' subconscious biases. People on search committees consider confidence important but fail to recognize the quieter demonstrations of confidence that women often employ. For this reason, leaders should make certain that search committees and hiring managers are aware of how implicit biases cause them to misread candidates in favor of men over women.

5. Examine Compensation Practices

Compensation needs to be fair and equitable. The healthcare organization should review compensation annually for each individual and give its physicians the opportunity for professional review and growth opportunities. In addition, the organization should regularly review its compensation models so that those compensation review practices are standardized, up-to-date, and equitable. Review of compensation should have physician representation of all genders.

6. Provide for Mentorship and Role Models

To encourage the participation of female physicians, assign them leadership roles and ensure access to executive opportunities. Doing so paves the way for women's voices to be heard, acknowledged, and valued. According to Deborah Shilan, MD, a medical management consultant based in Florida, "Female physicians are still underrepresented in positions of power, especially at the most senior levels." She goes on to say, "We need to eliminate those double standards that penalize women for traits and behaviors that are rewarded in men, like assertiveness, daring, risk-taking, and bravery. Yes, we need to 'lean in,' but we also need to push back" (Johnson 2018).

7. Encourage Meaningful Leadership Roles for Women

Giving female physicians a role that goes beyond simply directing a clinic but that gives them a voice at the table will support their engagement. If they are not engaged, physicians may choose a factory-shift mindset (simply putting in their hours at work) and may overemphasize the "life" part of their work–life balance. In addition, since the onset of the COVID-19 pandemic, many professionals are working more hours from home and taking care of children, who are also at home. Of course, this trend was happening before the pandemic, as physicians would work at home on their new EHR responsibilities. This arrangement has placed a greater burden on working women than it does on men. An organization can help its leaders and physicians, both women and men, support their family needs and work in a way that suits their schedules while still providing their expertise to the organization. There are many ways to be creative in these endeavors.

8. Don't Rule Out Physician Parents for the Duration of Their Careers

When their children are young, some physician parents are likely to prioritize work around their children's schedules. But children grow up. Since the bulk of childrearing still falls on women's shoulders, leadership should keep in mind that time changes parents' priorities. The leaders should continue the conversation throughout a physician's career. Over time, as family priorities and dynamics evolve, leadership opportunities may become of greater interest to a physician.

9. Look Beyond Volunteers

Some anecdotal observations suggest that men are more likely to raise their hands for special projects and committees (common in a crisis or pandemic situation) even when they may not be the most qualified for the task. Women tend to be more deliberate and not immediately volunteer. To counter this difference, organizations in crisis must be sure to get input from various parties and actively engage and seek leadership not just from the hand-raisers but from those qualified to think and act wisely in a crisis.

10. Nominate More Women

Many women will not volunteer themselves as a candidate for key leadership roles, but if nominated by others, they are more likely to consider a leadership opportunity. Organizations can and should reach out to women in their ranks and nominate them for key roles.

CONCLUSION

As healthcare continues to evolve, there is increasing awareness of the importance of cultivating and supporting female physician engagement. Patrice A. Harris, MD, former president of the AMA, notes the increasing numbers of women in medicine: "Women now make up 34.7% of the U.S. physician workforce, compared to just 5% as recently as 1970. More women than men are now entering medical school, and already half of all U.S. medical school students—and graduates—are women" (Harris 2019). Given this change in physician demographics, healthcare leaders and organizations must find ways to help women feel valued and essential in driving healthcare services and meeting the needs of patients.

REFERENCES

Ammerman, C., and B. Groysberg. 2020. "Why the Crisis Is Putting Companies at Risk of Losing Female Talent." *Harvard Business Review*. Published May 5. https://hbr.org/2020/05/why-the-crisis-is-putting-companies-at-risk-of-losing-female-talent.

Berlin, G., L. Darino, R. Groh, and P. Kumar. 2020. "Women in Healthcare: Moving from the Front Lines to the Top Rung." McKinsey & Company. Published August 25. www.mckinsey.com/industries/healthcare-systems-and-services/our-insights/women-in-healthcare-moving-from-the-front-lines-to-the-top-rung.

Blair, J. E., A. P. Mayer, S. L. Caubet, S. M. Norby, M. I. O'Connor, and S. N. Hayes. 2016. "Pregnancy and Parental Leave During Graduate Medical Education." *Academic Medicine* 91 (7): 972–78.

Boyle, P. 2019. "More Women Than Men Are Enrolled in Medical School." Association of American Medical Colleges. Published December 9. www.aamc.org/news-insights/more-women-men-are-enrolled-medical-school.

Butkus, R., J. Serchen, D. V. Moyer, S. S. Bornstein, and S. Thompson Hingle. 2018. "Achieving Gender Equity in Physician Compensation and Career Advancement: A Position Paper of the American College of Physicians." *Annals of Internal Medicine* 168 (10): 721–23.

Cuddy, A. R. 2015. *Presence: Bringing Your Boldest Self to Your Biggest Challenges*. New York: Little, Brown and Company.

Finnegan, J. 2020. "Gender Gap Averages More Than $36K for Physicians Starting Their Careers, New Study Finds." *Fierce Healthcare*. Published January 23. www.fiercehealthcare.com/practices/gender-gap-averages-more-than-36k-for-physicians-starting-their-careers-new-study-finds.

Harris, P. A. 2019. "Women in Medicine Are Trailblazers, Advocates and Leaders." *American Medical Association*. Published September 16. www.ama-assn.org/about/leadership/women-medicine-are-trailblazers-advocates-and-leaders.

Henkel, G. 2016. "Does U.S. Healthcare Need More Diverse Leadership?" *The Hospitalist*. Published June. www.the-hospitalist.org/hospitalist/article/121639/does-us-healthcare-need-more-diverse-leadership.

Hingle, S. T., G. C. Kane, R. Butkus, J. Serchen, and S. S. Bornstein. 2018. "Achieving Gender Equity in Physician Compensation and Career Advancement." *Annals of Internal Medicine* 169 (8): 591.

Hoff, T. 2019. "The Challenges of Being a Female Doctor." *Medical Economics*. Published July 9. www.medicaleconomics.com/view/challenges-being-female-doctor.

Jagannathan, M. 2019. "Too Many Female Doctors Go Part-Time or Stop Working—Why That's a Big Problem." MarketWatch. Published August 7. www.marketwatch.com/story/too-many-female-doctors-go-part-time-or-stop-working-and-thats-bad-for-patients-2019-08-06.

Johnson, M. 2018. "A Majority of Younger Physicians Are Female." Athenahealth. Published February 14. www.athenahealth.com/knowledge-hub/practice-management/healthcare-future-female.

Lagasse, J. 2020. "Physician Practices with More Female Doctors Have Smallest Gender Pay Gaps." *Healthcare Finance News*.

Published July 31. www.healthcarefinancenews.com/news/ physician-practices-more-female-doctors-have-smallest-gender-pay-gaps.

Lanka, V. 2018. "Women Make Up Just 3% of Health Care CEOs. Here Are 4 Ways to Fix That 'Woefully Inadequate' Number." Advisory Board Daily Briefing. Published October 25. www. advisory.com/daily-briefing/2018/10/25/gender-gap.

Magudia, K., A. Bick, J. Cohen, T. S. C. Ng, D. Weinstein, C. Mangurian, and R. Jagsi. 2018. "Childbearing and Family Leave Policies for Resident Physicians at Top Training Institutions." *JAMA* 320 (22): 2372–74.

Paturel, A. 2019. "Why Women Leave Medicine." Association of American Medical Colleges. Published October 1. www.aamc. org/news-insights/why-women-leave-medicine.

Roter, D. L., J. A. Hall, and Y. Aoki. 2002. "Physician Gender Effects in Medical Communication." *JAMA* 288 (6): 756–64.

Shannon, D. 2017. "The Way the System Works Against Women Doctors." Athenahealth. Published July 7. www.athenahealth. com/knowledge-hub/practice-management/way-system-works-against-women-doctors.

Stone, T., B. Miller, E. Southerlan, and A. Raun. 2019. "Women in Healthcare Leadership 2019." Oliver Wyman. Published January 7. www.oliverwyman.com/content/dam/oliver-wyman/ v2/publications/2019/January/WiHC/Women-In-Healthcare-Leadership-Report-FINAL.pdf.

Weber, S. 2019. "The Systemic Barriers Preventing Physician Workforce Equality." *Physicians Practice*. Published December 2. www.physicianspractice.com/view/systemic-barriers-preventing-physician-workforce-equality.

CHAPTER 12

Cognitive Diversity

Raúl Zambrano

Cognitive diversity is the inclusion of people who have different ways of thinking, different viewpoints and different skill sets in a team or business group. Many of these same companies have already realized the benefits of encouraging diversity in age, gender and ethnicity for years but are perhaps new to the idea of cognitive diversity.
—Janine Schindler, "The Benefits of Cognitive Diversity," 2018

THE UNITED STATES continues to grapple with issues of racial, cultural, and gender diversity and economic fairness in society—issues that we as a nation should indeed be grappling with. Another, less apparent aspect of diversity, often overlooked in the healthcare field, is cognitive diversity. Although a discussion of the cultural, political, and economic changes needed to improve racial and gender equality is critically important to healthcare, the topic lies outside the scope of this book. This chapter will consider one aspect of diversity—cognitive diversity—that also must be embraced if organizations are to successfully engage all their physicians.

Malcolm Forbes reportedly once said, "Diversity [is] the art of thinking independently together." The words embody the concept of cognitive diversity well. This idea has concrete benefits, and companies that place a priority on diversity have outperformed those that don't (Tulshyan 2015). The real question is how cognitive diversity applies to physician leadership (Henry 2019). The following discussion will explore how solutions to larger societal problems can guide healthcare leaders' approach to cognitive diversity and how they can use this diversity to an advantage in managing many challenges that face healthcare today. Physician engagement and physician leadership are critical challenges today; the job of physician leaders is one of the hardest jobs in healthcare: As Martin Luther King Jr., once said, "A genuine leader is not a searcher for consensus but a molder of consensus" (King 1968).

THE CHALLENGE

In the United States, one in every six dollars goes to healthcare (CMS 2019); by 2027, healthcare expenditures are projected to rise to one in every five dollars (Sisko et al. 2019). In an effort to control costs and improve the quality of patient care, the market and legislation are moving away from fee-for-service models and toward value-based care, a paradigm shift of epic proportions. Healthcare leadership in the United States is at a watershed moment.

In the current model of healthcare leadership, those at the helm are homogenous in gender, race, and background. Henkel (2016) reports that in the period between 2011 and 2013, hospitals saw the percentage of minority patients seen in hospitals grow from 29 to 31 percent, while underrepresented racial and ethnic minorities (UREMs) in C-suite positions remained flat, at 14 percent. By 2043, more than half of the US population will comprise racial and ethnic minorities (Henkel 2016). Providers, ethnically, are predominantly white (56.2%), Asian (17.1%), Hispanic (5.8%), African American (5.0%), multiple-race non-Hispanic (1.0%), unknown (13.7%), other (0.8%), American Indian or Alaska Native (0.3%), and Native Hawaiian (0.1%) (AAMC 2020). In the US population, all racial and ethnic minorities are underrepresented in the physician world, and the same pattern is seen in gender and many of the other classic diversity characteristics.

Most health systems today are facing unprecedented pressures in financial matters, delivery of services, and cultural issues. Providers who, before the COVID-19 pandemic, were already suffering from high rates of burnout are now being asked to do more with less on the front lines. Physician leaders are being asked to lead, inspire, and marshal these caregivers. This leadership mission is particularly daunting when one considers that many physician leaders are given significant responsibility with no direct authority. Moreover, in the era of mergers and acquisitions, many physician groups and hospital systems have pieced together federations of providers with poor channels of communication, and physician leaders are rarely given the required education and other support to enter their new roles. Under these circumstances, physician leaders need to understand cognitive diversity and its challenges and embrace its strengths to face the changing environment. The literature has consistently demonstrated that strong physician leadership with engaged providers produces significantly better patient outcomes, financial growth, and retention among the physician workforce than does disengaged leadership and clinicians.

Although the unique culture and characteristics of providers haven't been the source of suffering and societal inequality that UREMs experience, we can apply some of the racial-diversity approaches we have learned to improve cognitive diversity in healthcare.

PROVIDERS AS UREMs

In the growing field of healthcare, providers increasingly have a diverse set of characteristics and behavior patterns, including attributes and attitudes mirrored in the history of traditional diversity groups. The following attributes and attitudes, among others, contribute strongly to the cognitive diversity that we see among providers:

- Degree (MD, DO, DNP, NP, PA, CNE, etc.)
- Specialty (surgical, medical)
- Practice setting (independent, employed, inpatient, outpatient)

- Educational pedigree (foreign medical graduate)
- Patient population (pediatric, adult, geriatric)
- Role (leader, provider)

Understanding these characteristics is key to engaging and leading physicians in today's healthcare delivery systems. The term *systems* is used to encompass outpatient and inpatient care, primary and specialty care, and employed and independent providers. It reflects that all care is now integrated over multiple platforms and providers and is embedded in complex logistical structures.

An Association of American Medical Colleges (AAMC) study projects a shortage of up to 139,000 physicians by 2033 (Boyle 2020). This shortage has been consistently predicted since the beginning of the twenty-first century and has led to significant burnout among MD and DO providers and the growth of advanced practice professionals (APPs) in the delivery of healthcare since around 2010. Providers are always being asked to do more with less and, evidently, with decreasing autonomy—as greater than 50 percent of the workforce is now in employment arrangements rather than in private practice. These pressures have now created conflict about healthcare professionals' degrees. Distinctions are made in the medical literature, hospital medical staffs, and employed groups. With each degree group feeling marginalized to some extent and hostile toward the others, the result has been much frustration and little resolution.

Ironically, even the categorization of degrees has further subdivision in terms of a provider's specialty. Although no situation is ever "always" or "never," some groups have things in common—particularly groups that have endured long and stressful experiences together. These generalizations are the basis for generational demographics (baby boomers and Generations X, Y, and Z) and the usefulness of various types of personality indicators. Different generations and different medical specialties (surgeons, gastroenterologists, etc.) have clear preferences in communication style, medium, and content, and these variations are similar to cultural preferences seen in UREMs. Effective physician leaders should be aware of these preferences in terms of how they facilitate settings, communicating with various groups, and achieving buy-in to goals and expectations.

Physicians' practice settings affect their perspective on healthcare systems, much as the neighborhood where one lives affects one's perception of, and trust for, leaders and authority in general. Whether employed or independent, whether practicing in an acute care hospital or an ambulatory setting, in all these settings the clear distinction is the likelihood of distrust with settings outside their own. Some of this distrust is well founded, and some of it is not. The doubts reflect a lack of trust in the intentions of the government, payers, and healthcare delivery systems. For example, UREM people's lack of trust in healthcare authority is understandable, considering the literature that documents healthcare disparities based on race and socioeconomic status, as evidenced in the literature of healthcare disparities (see Smedley et al. 2003; Soto, Martin, and Gong 2013).

Another issue of note pertains to physician leaders. Often seen as pawns of the system, they sometimes feel caught in the middle between two sparring factions. Ironically, even if physician leaders still practice, they may be viewed as outsiders by the people they lead and the administration that hired them. At times, the people the physician leaders oversee view them as puppets, and the administration views them as individuals who cannot understand the "no money, no mission" mantra. Many physician leaders live in the narrow space between these two conflicting groups, juggling quality versus the cost of care. They must learn to take their experiences on both sides of the fence and build consensus.

THE PATIENTS

The US Census predicts that white people will constitute less than 50 percent of the US population by 2045 (Frey 2018). The literature has shown that the role of cultural competency and provider–patient communication directly affects quality outcomes (Brach and Fraser

2002). However, given the shifting demographics of race in the United States, we can make a strong case for the economic benefit of considering the wide diversity of the American population in healthcare strategic planning. The consumers of healthcare will no longer be predominantly white, and the approach to advertising and to growing the market share will have to consider the context of the culture at large. Cost-effectiveness also increases as communication effectiveness and engagement of the patient increase, leading to improved compliance. Simply put, patients enjoy better outcomes when they trust the provider and understand and embrace the reason for a treatment.

THE PROVIDERS

This chapter does not directly address the recruitment and retention of UREM providers other than to comment that although US demographics are changing quickly, the demographics of the providers are not keeping pace. Given the demographic shifts previously discussed, this discrepancy between the homogeneity of providers and the diversity of their patients must ultimately be ameliorated if a healthcare organization is to capture market share. People feel more comfortable with, and are more willing to secure the services of, physicians whom they identify with culturally. Healthcare leaders would be wise to explore and adopt much more aggressive means to enlarge their UREM provider ranks.

MANAGEMENT OF PHYSICIANS

Those who are experienced in managing physicians suggest some of the most important practices:

- Managers and other leaders should avoid giving physicians a direct order without an explanation.

- A democratic or laissez-faire approach is the best in all but emergent circumstances.
- Physicians need and want help with accountability and setting boundaries and goals.
- Physicians with good data and a mission are unstoppable forces for good.

All of these principles acknowledge that cognitive diversity is one key to engagement and performance. The reasoning behind the advice to avoid giving physicians a direct order without an explanation is that even if the message is a verifiable fact, their first answer will usually be no. Every provider has been trained to analyze the data independently, process it, and then render an opinion on it. Physicians may agree with anyone in the final analysis, but they want to follow a process. Furthermore, the training of physicians is grounded in differential diagnosis. This simply means that challenging assumptions to synthesize the best possible answer for patients is a common routine. In treating patients, physicians prize cognitive diversity, but when it comes to dealing with each other and the systems that employ them, physicians rarely employ cognitive diversity.

Given how strongly physicians prize cognitive diversity, it should be no surprise that they work best in either a democratic or a laissez-faire environment. In both these systems, individual contributions are molded together to produce a better product than any single individual can produce alone. The challenge for physician leaders is knowing how to facilitate this sort of collaboration. They need to realize that their job as leaders is not to provide the solutions but to clearly lay out the rules of engagement for the conversation, track the time, ensure that everyone can contribute, and be the tiebreaker or referee who helps resolve any conflict in the group. In this collaborative system, engagement is guaranteed and physicians will consistently outperform expectations. Physicians strongly dislike working in a group when decisions have already been made or when they feel their contributions are not heard or considered. When there is no strong enforcement of the rules for a working group and no push to reach consensus, physicians feel less engaged. They may believe that their efforts produced nothing—a sentiment that can disengage anyone who, like so many physicians, wants to see immediate results.

In the end, a healthcare organization that respects providers' need for cognitive independence and cognitive diversity in approaching problems is responding to two defining features of the vast majority of physicians:

1. Most if not all physicians will put the patients and the quality of their care first.
2. Physicians need data and will follow the Socratic method to a fault.

Ironically, these two characteristics are so strong among physicians that they will frequently put themselves at a disadvantage to follow these maxims. By understanding these maxims and appreciating cognitive diversity, healthcare leaders can create an almost-universal motivation that can be used to drive results. With these two characteristics as a backdrop, leaders can better manage many of the smaller differences physicians spend so much time on. However, details are critical, and although the differences are small, if they are not managed well, they can become catastrophic.

TRUST

Trust is earned slowly but can be lost quickly. At the core of the many challenges physician leaders face is a distrust with other leaders of healthcare systems and the government. Stephen Covey (1995, 243) states, "Trust is the glue of life. It's the most essential ingredient in effective communication. It's the foundational principle that holds all relationships," and this observation holds true for physicians. The distrust that exists among providers today is magnified many times over in the distrust that UREM patients have in the healthcare they receive. UREM people's distrust comes from disparities in care, for example, the Tuskegee Airmen syphilis experiment, the widespread use of Henrietta Lacks's cancer cells without her knowledge or permission, and clear discrepancies in morbidity and mortality seen during the COVID-19 pandemic and in other health outcomes.

In providers, the distrust with healthcare systems and the government comes from a long history of these institutions' asking providers to do more with less and decreasing reimbursement for services rendered. Like many other people, a number of physicians have an inherent distrust of any leadership other than their own, and healthcare leaders have to acknowledge this doubt and be honest and direct with providers. There is a popular belief that because providers would be upset by the truth, healthcare leaders should be less than fully transparent and apologize later. Physicians are not ignorant, however, and if a leader is not forthright with them, they will quickly lose trust in the leader. By telling the truth from the outset, leaders gain respect and trust. Although the message may not be pleasant, the physicians recognize when they are told the truth.

Constant communication that occasionally reiterates important information, and that does so in a medium well suited for providers, is the best way to keep them informed. Most physicians have little time for administrative duties or extra meetings but appreciate having information constantly provided to them in formats they can quickly assimilate. In approaching the issue of trust, to quote Covey again, leaders must "seek first to understand" (Covey 2004). This first step requires appreciating all the aspects of diversity among physicians.

COMMUNICATION

When choosing a form of communication, healthcare leaders must consider generational dynamics, the providers' specialties, and message content. By 2021, there were five generations in the provider workforce: the Silent Generation (born 1928–1945), baby boomers (1946–1964), Generation X (1965–1980), millennials (or Generation Y, 1982–1996), and Generation Z (1997–2012). Leaders need to consider how they will communicate with, motivate, and otherwise interact with each group. Although each person's response to a communication style is unique, this section will use some generalities in the interest of showing which types of communication work best for different people.

The Silent Generation and baby boomers predominantly favor face-to-face interactions and discussions; both groups of people will use e-mail and text but are not likely to use these as primary information sources. Leadership should consider the generations who are quickly disappearing in hospital physician lounges. Generation X is the middle child and bridges the Silent Generation and the baby boomers on the one hand and the millennials and Generation Z on the other. Generation X is selective about the communication medium. For things like routine notifications, e-mail and texting is preferred; for social interaction and serious discussion, this group wants to go face-to-face. Millennials prefer most of their routine messaging through such digital platforms as Instagram and Snapchat, but the literature is beginning to show that for career discussions and mentoring, they favor face-to-face interaction (USC Marshall School of Business 2013). Generation Z is growing up in the era of Facetime and Zoom, and the early literature hints at a slight preference for video interaction and crowdsourcing for problem-solving interactions—more so than shown for millennials—but for career matters, Generation Z also prefers face-to-face interactions.

In summary, for routine communication, talking directly to the Silent Generation and boomer colleagues is likely to be more effective. In interactions with Generations X, Y, and Z, leaders may find that e-mail, text, and social media are more effective. Interestingly, all groups prefer face-to-face communication when discussing career progression and when problem-solving.

Once a platform has been chosen, the providers' specialty will dictate how this messaging is shaped. Only the larger nomenclature of surgery and medicine will be explored in this chapter, but one can easily see how individual specialties and employment status (employed, independent) could also affect the messaging. Although no observations can cover all members of a group—there will always be exceptions—the discussions in this section will, for simplicity's sake, use some generalizations.

Surgeons typically do not want fluff. They want messages to be direct and to the point, and should an action item be required, they want it to be highlighted up front. Most surgeons do not want bad news sandwiched between good news. Because they prefer messages to arrive before or after their surgery time, leaders should schedule face-to-face meetings for early morning or late evening.

Providers in general medicine, on the other hand, value discussion and the niceties of social interactions. When communicating with them, leaders should keep in mind that these providers value process and a clear explanation of the rationale behind a decision. During a meeting, they enjoy some social interaction before getting down to business and prefer their meetings either during the lunch hour or after office hours.

Although it should be obvious, messaging for independent providers and employed providers needs to be looked at separately. Traditionally, independent providers have significant distrust for the institutions they serve. For these providers, receiving messages that focus on institutional or employed-provider goals can be off-putting. The independent providers want to know what directly affects them and their businesses.

This discussion of communications styles is not meant to be exhaustive. But it gives the readers some preliminary ideas on how leaders should examine the groups they interact with and shape the medium and style of their messaging to allow for effective communication and secure buy-in from their intended audience.

MEETINGS

As mentioned earlier, because of the fierce independence of providers and their natural inclination toward cognitive diversity, democratic and laissez-faire approaches can be highly effective in mobilizing providers and accomplishing tasks. Note the word *can* in the previous sentence. Democracy and laissez-faire processes only work well when they are correctly facilitated. As eloquently depicted by Patrick Lencioni in *Death by Meeting*, when the facilitation is not done well, meetings are viewed as a painful waste of all the participants' time (Lencioni 2004). A bad meeting lacks a clear agenda with goals, does not structure participation to be productive, and has no expectation that decisions will be made and acted on.

One example of how to manage meetings involves the optimization of multiple surgical projects. The process of effectively communicating the issues surrounding this project and driving results would apply to other issues that healthcare leaders face.

As most readers know, many meetings are poorly attended and accomplish little. This failure is not due to any individual but is caused by increased demand for production and a work pace that is quicker than the monthly or bimonthly meetings can manage. The way that healthcare leaders can change this culture is simple in theory but requires tremendous groundwork in implementation. On the front end, leaders must establish agendas with clearly defined goals. And most important, leadership should research all items and resolve any conflicts they can before the meeting so that the committee can make decisions after discussion.

In the surgical optimization example, the leadership could, before the meeting, establish the importance of utilization rates and physicians' understanding of them. Traditionally, a rate of 80 to 85 percent utilization is used in high-functioning operating rooms, and a rate as low as 30 to 40 percent is tolerated in less-than-optimal situations. Before engaging with a surgical committee, the leaders must hold discussions with the nursing staff, the sterile processing group, scheduling staff, and the C-suite to see what can be delivered and what an acceptable range would be to all parties. Then, the leadership would review the current utilization by provider for at least the last six months if the review includes the fourth quarter or for a year if it does not. The data must be validated and reviewed before it is presented to the providers. The leadership should also think about the mindset of the committee members, and should it expect resistant, or occasionally even recalcitrant, groups of individuals be present, the leaders must develop a plan beforehand to address their concerns.

Armed with this information, leadership can hold face-to-face meetings with the groups involved to discuss the issues and make a decision. The leaders can facilitate these meetings by making sure the groups understand the goals of the meeting, what topics must be discussed, and, in the surgery block time example, what percentage would constitute an acceptable utilization rate to maintain a surgeon's block time. Another point to make certain is that a majority vote at the end will determine this utilization rate.

During the meetings, leaders will then manage the discussions so that all present can voice their opinions. Meeting facilitators should ensure that quiet participants are asked to engage and that dominating members are appropriately controlled. The leaders should also remember that physicians as a group will rely on the data and the Socratic method. Many times, the first meetings are poorly attended. But when people learn that a clear decision has been made at these meetings and that it is being implemented, subsequent meetings will draw larger crowds and more active discussion as the group begins to realize the meetings bring concrete actions and results.

This example should demonstrate how choosing the platform for delivery (face-to-face), the style (direct and data driven), and the message (a decision will be made) can lead to improved engagement and leadership (see exhibit 12.1). This process will also address a common problem in getting engagement from providers—their general feeling of powerlessness. In today's healthcare environment, UREMs and providers share another challenge—the feeling that they often cannot affect their own outcomes. UREMs' sense of powerlessness

Exhibit 12.1 Three Simple but Powerful Ways to Improve Physician Engagement

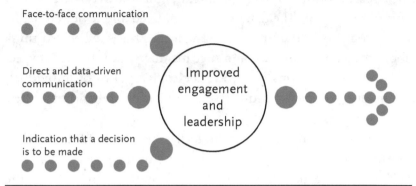

often does have an actual basis, but for providers, this perception is completely incorrect. Most hospital bylaws clearly stipulate that the medical staff has significant control over the working conditions in the hospital and anything that concerns patient quality. Patients can become allies in applying pressure to hospitals and hospital systems in improving quality and working conditions. Physicians rank third among the professions most trusted in the United States, and patients listen to what they have to say (Herleth 2020). Teaching providers that they, in fact, can have an effect is a tremendous tool in promoting engagement and trust.

BURNOUT

Although burnout among physicians has improved between 2015 and 2020, self-reported rates of burnout among physicians still range from 40 to 50 percent (Berg 2020). The approach to this issue has been divided along two lines: the symptoms and the cause. For many healthcare systems, the quick and easy solution is to offer more pay and fewer work hours, and multiple programs have shown that this approach can improve the problem for a short time

(Patel et al. 2019). However, the treatment of symptoms does not get at the root cause of the problem. Physicians, by definition, are highly resilient individuals, given that they have undergone the crucible of applying to and attending medical school and have survived medical training. Although there can be burnout during training, its rate is lower, between 15 and 41 percent, depending on specialty (Rodrigues et al. 2018). The root cause for the burnout and the differences in its rates may be that physicians feel isolated as their input and buy-in to the constantly changing initiatives of the profession has led to feelings of a lack of control. Also, the current focus on treating the symptoms of burnout ignores the fact that providers are a diverse group—considering their generational dynamics, gender, specialty, race, and employment status—and thus the solution for each group might be different. Given the diversity among the providers, and similarly, that resolving the diversity issues facing our country will depend on the group in question, their location, and the particular issue, the solutions are going to be varied and complex.

CONCLUSION

Journalist H. L. Mencken (1920, 126) says that "there is always a well-known solution to every human problem—neat, plausible, and wrong." In managing physicians, many leaders follow Mencken's adage and aim for a simple and direct solution to leading and problem solving with providers. If the current results of healthcare—high costs and poor quality—in the United States are any indicator, many leaders are wrong in this approach. It is time to approach the issues from a new direction. Given that white people will make up less than 50 percent of the US population in the coming years, on the simplest level, healthcare leaders need to appreciate and adapt to the diversity of the patients being treated to maintain their organization's market share and to provide efficient and cost-effective care. In managing and working with the providers of care, leaders will have to acknowledge the diversity in this workforce to best meet the increasing demand for healthcare services and the need to reduce healthcare costs. No longer will the simple solution of raising providers' pay be a panacea for the stress and lack of engagement that providers feel and the mistrust the public has for many aspects of healthcare. The diversity, both classic and cognitive, will need to be addressed to effectively lead and engage providers.

Psychologist Herbert Gerjuoy, who is quoted by Alvin Toffler in his classic *Future Shock*, says, "Tomorrow's illiterate will not be the man who can't read; he will be the man who has not learned how to learn" (Toffler 1971, 414). It is time that physician leaders embrace not only the diversity in the patient populations they treat but also the value of cognitive diversity in working with and leading their providers. As Bill Leaver, CEO and president of Iowa Health System, is quoted as saying, "Physicians go where they are welcomed, remain where they are respected, and grow where they are nurtured" (Lochmann 2016).

REFERENCES

Association of American Medical Colleges (AAMC). 2020. "Diversity in Medicine: Facts and Figures 2019." Accessed October 20. www.aamc.org/data-reports/workforce/interactive-data/figure-18-percentage-all-active-physicians-race/ethnicity-2018.

Berg, S. 2020. "Physician Burnout: Which Medical Specialties Feel the Most Stress." American Medical Association. Published January 21. www.ama-assn.org/practice-management/physician-health/physician-burnout-which-medical-specialties-feel-most-stress.

Boyle, P. 2020. "US Physician Shortage Growing." Association of American Medical Colleges. Published June 26. www.aamc.org/news-insights/us-physician-shortage-growing.

Brach, C., and I. Fraser. 2002. "Reducing Disparities Through Culturally Competent Health Care: An Analysis of the Business Case." *Quality Management in Healthcare* 10 (4): 15–28.

Centers for Medicare & Medicaid Services (CMS). 2019. "Medicare Trustees Report Shows Hospital Insurance Fund Will Deplete in 7 Years." Published April 22. www.cms.gov/newsroom/ press-releases/medicare-trustees-report-shows-hospital-insurance-trust-fund-will-deplete-7-years.

Covey, S. R. 2004. *The 7 Habits of Highly Effective People: Restoring the Character Ethic.* New York: Free Press.

Covey, S. R., A. R. Merrill, and R. R. Merrill. 1995. *First Things First.* New York: Free Press.

Frey, W. 2018. "The US Will Become 'Minority White' in 2045, Census Projects." Brookings Institution. Published March 14. www.brookings.edu/blog/the-avenue/2018/03/14/the-us-will-become-minority-white-in-2045-census-projects.

Henkel, G. 2016. "Does US Healthcare Need More Diverse Leadership?" *The Hospitalist.* Published June. www.the-hospitalist. org/hospitalist/article/121639/does-us-healthcare-need-more-diverse-leadership.

Henry, T. A. 2019. "Employed Physicians Now Exceed Those Who Own Their Practice." American Medical Association. Published May 10. www.ama-assn.org/about/research/employed-physicians-now-exceed-those-who-own-their-practices.

Herleth, A. 2020. "For the 18th Year in a Row, Nurses Are the Most Trusted Profession, According to Gallup." Advisory Board. Published January 10. www.advisory.com/daily-briefing/2020/ 01/10/nurse-trusted.

King, M. L., Jr. 1968. "Remaining Awake Through a Great Revolution." In *A Knock at Midnight: Inspiration from the Great*

Sermons of Reverend Martin Luther King, Jr. 205–24. New York: Warner Books.

Lencioni, P. 2004. *Death by Meeting: A Leadership Fable—About Solving the Most Painful Problem in Business.* San Francisco: Jossey-Bass.

Lochmann, D. B. 2016. "Physicians Go Where They Are Welcomed." *Psychiatry & Behavioral Sciences Communicator* (KU School of Medicine–Wichita). Published June. https://wichita.kumc.edu/Documents/wichita/psychiatry/KUCommunicatorJune2016web.pdf.

Mencken, H. L. 1920. *Prejudices: Second Series.* New York: A. A. Knopf.

Patel, R. S., S. Sekhri, N. N. Bhimanadham, S. Imran, and S. Hossain. 2019. "A Review on Strategies to Manage Physician Burnout." *Cureus.* Published June 3. www.ncbi.nlm.nih.gov/pmc/articles/PMC6682395.

Rodrigues, H., R. Cobucci, A. Oliveira, J. V. Cabral, L. Medeiros, K. Gurgel, T. Souza, and A. K. Gonçalves. 2018. "Burnout Syndrome Among Medical Residents: A Systematic Review and Meta-Analysis." *PLoS One.* Published November 12. https://journals.plos.org/plosone/article?id=10.1371/journal.pone.0206840.

Schindler, J. 2018. "The Benefits of Cognitive Diversity." *Forbes Coaches Council* (blog). Published November 26. www.forbes.com/sites/forbescoachescouncil/2018/11/26/the-benefits-of-cognitive-diversity/.

Sisko, A. M., S. P. Keehan, J. A. Piosal, G. A. Cuckler, S. D. Smith, K. E. Rennie, and J. C. Hardesty. 2019. "National Health Expenditure Projections, 2018–27: Economic and Demographic Trends Drive Spending and Enrollment Growth." *Health*

Affairs. Published February 20. www.healthaffairs.org/doi/abs/10.1377/hlthaff.2018.05499.

Smedley, B. D., A. Y. Stith, and A. R. Nelson (eds.). 2003. *Unequal Treatment: Confronting Racial and Ethnic Disparities in Health Care*. Washington, DC: National Academies Press.

Soto, G. J., G. S. Martin, and M. N. Gong. 2013. "Healthcare Disparities in Critical Illness." *Critical Care Medicine* 41 (12): 2784–93.

Toffler, A. 1971. *Future Shock*. New York: Bantam Books.

Tulshyan, R. 2015. "Racially Diverse Companies Outperform Industry Norms by 35%." *Forbes*. Published January 30. www.forbes.com/sites/ruchikatulshyan/2015/01/30/racially-diverse-companies-outperform-industry-norms-by-30/.

University of Southern California (USC) Marshall School of Business. 2013. "Surprise! Millennials Prefer Face-to-Face Not Facebook." Published October 14. www.marshall.usc.edu/news/surprise-millennials-prefer-face-face-not-facebook.

CHAPTER 13

Physician Flourishing:
Moving Past Burnout

Katherine A. Meese and Andrew N. Garman

Flourishing physicians deliver the highest quality patient care.
It is time to help our healers flourish.
—Jordyn Heather Feingold, "Toward a Positive Medicine:
Healing Our Healers, from Burnout to Flourishing," 2016

AN OIL REFINERY is a massive, expensive, and high-pressure system. If there is even a slight malfunction or weakness in the system, the refinery can explode and people are likely to die. Hundreds of millions of dollars in damages can occur in a matter of minutes. Therefore, oil companies know that they must have routine maintenance and scheduled downtime for these systems.

Surprisingly, the healthcare industry has failed to draw the same conclusions. The providers are the most important producers of healthcare, yet they are rarely given scheduled downtime and routine maintenance. They often receive poorer treatment than that given to an oil refinery, despite being highly trained and, more important, human. As a result, physicians are placed in high-pressure environments and expected to ignore their own well-being. That is, this is the expectation, until they explode, or people die, or millions of dollars are lost. And even then, many healthcare organizations continue to function as they always have.

The healthcare industry makes two fundamental errors in its approaches to providers. First, it treats providers like machines designed to maximize outputs, instead of like human beings. Second, the industry fails to give providers the same level of care and treatment that a machine would typically get.

Physician burnout has gained attention in recent years, with healthcare systems working to identify and reduce sources of burnout. For physicians, delivering the best possible care to a patient is the ultimate goal. There is a long road between excellent and "not dead." In similar fashion, just "not burned out" should not be the goal. The goal should be a state of flourishing.

WHAT DOES FLOURISHING MEAN?

Martin Seligman, PhD, a pioneer in positive psychology, proposes a model for well-being and flourishing called PERMA, for the five elements of flourishing described earlier in the book: positive emotion, engagement, relationships, meaning, and accomplishment (Seligman 2012). He suggests that these elements that lead to flourishing for an individual are pursued for their own sake, not as a means to an end (exhibit 13.1).

Exhibit 13.1 Seligman's PERMA Model of Well-Being

Positive emotion	Feelings of happiness, gratitude, hope
Engagement	Being fully absorbed in the moment, being in flow
Relationships	Connection to others
Meaning	Being part of something bigger than the self
Accomplishment	Achievement, success, mastery

Source: Adapted from Seligman (2012).

POSITIVE EMOTION

Positive emotion is the way that many people might characterize happiness. This element involves positive feelings such as optimism or hope. Positive emotions may be experienced through a range of activities such as eating a delicious meal, enjoying a good view or sunset, reflecting on happy memories from the past, or seeing a patient celebrate after being cured from an illness. People's own disposition might limit the degree or frequency to which they may feel these positive emotions. Some people may have a naturally cheery or optimistic disposition and therefore frequently feel positive, whereas those with a more analytical or pessimistic nature may experience these feelings less often. Fortunately, positive emotion is only one component of flourishing and is not the only means to get there.

ENGAGEMENT

Engagement can be understood as the state of becoming lost or immersed in one's activity. It is a sense that time slows down or becomes irrelevant, and a person is so engrossed in an activity that self-awareness diminishes in the moment. As described in an earlier chapter, engagement has also been called achieving a state of flow or being in flow (Csikszentmihalyi 1990). A surgeon may experience a state of flow while operating, going for a long run, playing the violin, or engaging in a hobby. People can even experience flow during unlikely tasks like mowing the lawn. In healthcare, some circumstances may interfere with a physician's ability to be fully engaged in a task or to achieve a state of flow. These conditions may include alert fatigue (desensitization to alerts because of frequent exposure to them) from the electronic health records (EHRs) and frequent interruptions.

RELATIONSHIPS

One cannot flourish without relationships. As John Donne explains in his "Meditation VII," in *Devotions upon Emergent Occasions* (1624), "No man is an island, entire of itself." Loneliness and social isolation can wreak havoc on a person's sense of well-being. Relationships may exist at work, at home, in the community, and, ideally, a combination of all these. Historically, a physician's relationships with patients and teams could contribute to a sense of well-being. For this reason, there has been concern that several features of the way care is currently delivered hinder the pursuit of meaningful relationships. First, as their margins are squeezed by reforms, healthcare organizations are generally trying to do more with less. These efforts can lead to production pressures, which give physicians less time to spend with each patient. Less time means less opportunity to get to know the patient or to enjoy a friendly conversation about something outside of the acute issue at hand. Organizations trying to reduce costs may also require longer working hours from their physicians, leaving these professionals with less time to pursue and invest in meaningful relationships outside work. Second, documentation requirements associated with EHRs have increased to the point where physicians now report spending more time with the EHR than with their patients during a given workday (Arndt et al. 2017).

MEANING

Seeking meaning generally means feeling that one is part of something larger than oneself. A sense of meaning may be achieved through a person's work, faith, family, or community. Generally, a sense of meaning is what draws people to work in healthcare. Those in this field often describe the desire to help others as a calling and passion. Physicians often feel a deep sense of meaning in helping their patients and in fighting against the effects of disease, but administrative burdens can weaken or even break the link between a physician's work and the higher purpose of serving others. You can hear the loss of this link whenever a physician says something like, "I thought I was going into medicine to help people, but instead . . ." Feeling stripped of the meaning of caring for patients not only can threaten well-being but can also lead to moral distress or moral injury. The PERMA model provides a helpful framework for understanding the various components of flourishing. Less clear is the boundary between individual and organizational responsibility to promote well-being and flourishing in healthcare. Clearly, many of these objectives (engagement, meaning, etc.) must be pursued by the individual. A healthcare organization can do little about a person's predisposition for positive emotion or lack thereof, or how a physician manages relationships or hobbies outside work.

ACCOMPLISHMENT

Accomplishment or achievement may be pursued for its own end, outside of any other motivation. Success may also be pursued for its own enjoyment, rather than as a means to other ends such as more money or a promotion. For example, a surgeon may seek to perfect a technique for no other reason than the satisfaction of mastering it. For some, the drive and desire for achievement can sometimes outweigh the drive for other elements of well-being.

That said, organizational leaders do have a responsibility to create an environment that maximizes the likelihood that its members will flourish and be well at work. Despite all the talk of work–life balance, the reality is that people live at work. People's work selves are no different from their home selves. Therefore, well-being must be pursued not only in life but also at work.

Organizations can create environments for their physicians to flourish in a number of ways, including thoughtful work design to consider the human impact in all decisions. Individual-, team-, and organizational-level strategies can help optimize the work environment to help physicians flourish.

INDIVIDUAL-LEVEL INTERVENTIONS

Work Design

One of the most important steps in creating a work environment where physicians can flourish is through work design. Specific job elements and characteristics must be present for effective work design (Hackman and Oldham 1980). It must require a variety of skills, clearly identify the task or tasks needed, demonstrate the significance of the work, afford the person autonomy, and allow for feedback (Hackman and Oldham 1980). Other components of work design are not sufficient to motivate an employee but are likely to cause major dissatisfaction if they are not designed well (Herzberg 2003). Thus, these factors also need careful attention so as not to create job dissatisfaction and disengagement. These include administrative policies, supervision, compensation, and working conditions. Leaders must pay careful attention to thoughtfully designing jobs that help physicians flourish at work. A list of job design characteristics and barriers are listed in exhibit 13.2.

Exhibit 13.2 Elements to Include in the Design of Physicians' Work

Element and Descriptions	Barriers to Success
Skill variety: The job requires physicians to use their many talents and skills.	Because healthcare is becoming increasingly specialized, physicians may have less variety in their daily work.
Task identity: The job requires finishing a task from beginning to end.	Subspecialization and care responsibilities shifting to advanced practice providers (APPs) may reduce a physician's ability to see a task (e.g., a case) from beginning to end.
Task significance: The task has an impact on others.	As physicians spend more time documenting in the EHR, they may feel that their daily tasks are less meaningful.

(continued)

Element and Descriptions	Barriers to Success
Autonomy: Physicians have a high degree of freedom and discretion over how the work is carried out.	Transitioning from private practice to employed models and the growing responsibilities of APPs may lead to diminished autonomy.
Feedback: Direct information about the quality of performance is readily available.	Communication is often focused on errors, near misses, and improvement, with little positive feedback for good performance.
Administrative policies: Policies governing work and conduct provide adequate flexibility and discretion.	Malpractice avoidance and extensive documentation requirements may generate strict policies that cannot always accommodate nuanced situations, and the defensive postures can place an excessive administrative burden on the physician.
Supervision: Supervision is skilled and supportive.	Especially in academic centers, department leaders may be chosen for their success in securing grant funding or conducting research, not for their leadership skills. Physicians may also be supervised by nonclinical leaders who do not fully grasp the nuances of physicians' work.
Compensation: Compensation for work or services is perceived as adequate and fair.	Reduced reimbursements and thinning hospital margins mean compensation may decrease over time despite a physician's increased skills, experience, and competence. Income is reduced by heavy burdens of medical school debt.
Working conditions: Adequate attention is paid to physical environment factors (e.g., lighting, ventilation, ergonomics) and the limits of personal stamina (e.g., working hours, the ability to take breaks to eat and drink).	Some specialties require intense involvement over long periods (e.g., long surgical cases, overbooking of patients); these extended periods may make it difficult for physicians to take regular breaks.

Support and Encourage Job Crafting

"Nobody cares about your job more than you do." This is a common refrain among managers and mentors alike, yet the advice is easily forgotten in the quest for well-being at work. Healthcare leaders and managers need to actively encourage physicians to engage in *job crafting* (Wrzesniewski and Dutton 2001), and they need to be receptive to changes in work design. In crafting a job, a person identifies which features of the work can better align with the individual's strengths and interests. If given the opportunity, physicians often have an abundance of suggestions for how to make adjustments to improve their jobs. Empowering them to make these changes can give physicians a greater sense of autonomy and improve their satisfaction at work.

Additionally, job crafting may involve opportunities to either change the demands of one's work or increase the resources to meet those demands (Tims and Bakker 2010). These changes can pertain to the overarching work, to individual tasks, or to the social component of one's work.

Changes to the work itself should start with the physicians' assessment of which components of their work they find the most enjoyable, energizing, meaningful, or engaging and which are the most depleting. They should not assume that what is the least enjoyable to them will be the same for others. For example, one physician in a group may enjoy doing telemedicine visits because it reduces commute time and gives the physician more time with family. A colleague may dislike telemedicine because in-person interaction with patients is a part of the job that brings this physician the most enjoyment and meaning. Both these physicians could potentially do more of the work they enjoy by trading tasks with each other.

Another way to job craft is to change the scope of a job by adding, reducing, or expanding tasks. For example, a physician who is beginning to find clinic visits monotonous may enjoy the variety offered by working on a task force on process improvement across several units, even though doing so represents additional work.

Alternatively, physicians who are starting to experience burnout may be able to restore their enjoyment of the work by reducing their hours or negotiating for more support such as a scribe or an advanced practice provider (APP). A physician may find that teaching residents and fellows renews their excitement for their specialty.

Supporting the Second Victim

Several stressors at work affect physicians and can diminish their well-being. First, unfortunately, terrible things happen to patients in the healthcare setting. Providers must often witness brutal, gruesome, heart-wrenching tragedy—sometimes multiple times a day. Despite a push for increased empathy among healthcare providers in recent years, this same empathy can make the constant exposure to the suffering of others extraordinarily taxing on the providers. This exposure can cause what is known as a *second victim effect* (Wu 2000). The first victim is obviously the patient, but the second victim is the physician. Physicians' direct exposure to the trauma, or their inability to mitigate its damage, can cause psychological harm to the physician.

Next, there is the issue of moral distress or moral injury. Moral distress can be defined as the feeling that one cannot do the right thing or that one is unsure of the right thing to do. When rigid hospital policies fail to allow for the morally right response in a nuanced situation, moral distress can occur. Not only can moral distress upend physicians' sense of meaning or purpose in their work, but it can also give them the opposite feeling—that they are doing more harm than good. When a provider makes a judgment call that causes harm for the patient, the physician is morally distressed. For example, when ventilators or beds must be rationed in the middle of a pandemic, or when the patient must choose between affording some medication and paying rent, the provider can feel moral distress.

Healthcare leaders must proactively seek to support physicians who are experiencing second-victim effects or moral distress. The presence and availability of counseling and mental health resources and peer support programs can be effective in beginning to support healthcare workers exposed to, or involved in, the trauma of others. Ideally, these support systems should take a proactive approach and reach out to the physician after a distressing event (whether it was an error that harmed the patient or was a complex trauma) to offer support and check in on the provider's well-being.

TEAM-LEVEL INTERVENTIONS

In addition to individual-level interventions, health organizations should seek out opportunities to improve the team environment in which the physicians work. Healthcare services are increasingly delivered by teams comprising different types of professionals. That means, by default, that tending to the well-being of all team members is likely an important part of improving physician well-being. Physicians cannot function in healthy teams unless the well-being of nurses, APPs, administrators, and other members of the care team has also been supported.

There is some evidence that burnout is contagious and that healthcare professionals often model the behavior of others (Bakker, Le Blanc, and Schaufeli 2005; Jung et al. 2020). Consequently, when one or more members of a team are burned out, their exhausted state is likely to affect the well-being of other team members as well. For example, one aspect of burnout is depersonalization. People experiencing depersonalization are less likely to show empathy and compassion for their teammates. Additionally, a 2019 study found that residents experiencing burnout showed increasing signs of racial bias toward patients (Dyrbye et al. 2019). Burned-out team members may also demonstrate similar antagonistic patterns toward their coworkers, creating an uncivil or hostile environment.

An additional focus is on microaggressions. The concept of microaggression, originally studied in the context of racism and discrimination, is that small acts of incivility can be very damaging over time and erode one's well-being. These acts may include rude or degrading comments, slights or insults, or nonverbal acts like eye-rolling. This concept has been applied more broadly to microaggressions between ages, genders, and professional statuses in healthcare teams (Molina et al. 2020). All these forms of microaggression may reduce the team's ability to create a climate of civility and may erode physician well-being.

Create an Environment Where Healthy Relationships Can Form

How can the team environment be optimized to ensure that physicians and other team members can flourish? First, the team needs the conditions that create a foundation for forming healthy and meaningful working relationships.

Decades of research have reinforced the finding that social cohesion is significantly associated with improved team performance and outcomes (Evans and Dion 1991). Sharing a meal and celebrating team successes together can build connections and relational fibers across gaps between professional groups. People also need consistent, civil interactions over time and need to practice working together to form cohesive teams. Consistent, frequent interactions with team members are especially challenging for physicians working in large organizations or covering multiple services or locations. The consistency is also challenging with a constant flux of rotating students, residents, and fellows from various disciplines. When it's possible, leaders should facilitate stable teams so that people have an opportunity to get to know one another and develop good working relationships.

Additionally, norms of civil and respectful behavior must be reinforced. Overt hostility, aggressive behavior, microaggressions, and discrimination cannot be tolerated. These behaviors, committed by anyone on the team, need to be addressed and corrected. When the organization is selecting people for promotion and roles of leadership, the degree to which they foster and support an environment of civility should be a significant element of the promotion criteria.

Reduce Sources of Unproductive Conflict

Although conflict is inevitable, it isn't all bad. Conflict that allows different viewpoints and ideas to be heard can be productive, and important for patient safety. However, sources of unproductive conflict should be minimized. Two potential sources of conflict and stress particularly affect physicians.

Role Ambiguity

Role ambiguity exists when one is unclear about one's responsibilities and authority at work or what one must do to fulfill the role. Such lack of clarity is associated with occupational stress, anxiety, burnout, depression, and physical illness. Role ambiguity can also lead to dissatisfaction with work tasks, coworkers, supervision, and the job overall; low commitment to the job and to the organization; high turnover intention; absenteeism; decreased performance; and increased tension (Örtqvist and Wincent 2006).

In the quest for expanded access to care and reduced costs, healthcare organizations have tried to expand the scope of practice for such APPs as nurse practitioners, physician assistants, and certified registered nurse anesthetists. In many environments, these APPs are practicing nearly autonomously, and some do not require the oversight of a physician. These changes confuse the traditional boundaries of responsibility between the physicians and nurses. What once was a clearer hierarchy now involves more shared responsibility and decision-making. This overlap of accountability can create confusion and conflict, as both parties may not know where the APP's duties end and the physician's begin. Organizations should carefully evaluate how each member of the team can make the greatest contribution to the delivery of excellent care, and they should clearly define roles to reduce confusion, missed handoffs, and unproductive conflict.

Role Conflict

Roles become conflicted when employees receive incompatible directives about how they fit into the team or organization (Örtqvist and Wincent 2006). Role conflict can occur when an employee has multiple supervisors who may have conflicting goals or inconsistent standards and expectations. Like role ambiguity, role conflict is also associated with negative outcomes such as emotional exhaustion, job dissatisfaction, low organizational commitment, poor job performance, and turnover intentions (Örtqvist and Wincent 2006). The reporting structures of many healthcare teams create a ripe environment for role conflict. For example, a large medical center's operating room may have a surgeon, an anesthesiologist, a nurse, a scrub tech, a certified registered nurse anesthetist, a medical student, a nursing student, and a resident. These eight people may each report to different direct supervisors, each of whom probably has different styles, performance expectations, directives, and goals. Reporting hierarchies may not converge until they get to the C-suite or CEO position, many levels beyond where the work is being produced. When possible, reporting hierarchies should be streamlined and aligned to reduce the number of bosses simultaneously (and differently) managing the efforts of one team.

Institutionalize the Practice of Microempathy

Finally, just as individuals need peer-support programs, teams should routinely check in on the well-being of team members. Just as microaggressions erode well-being by slowly chipping away at a person's well-being, multiple exposures to trauma, patient aggression, or difficult cases can do the same. A team can counteract these effects by practicing microempathy. With this practice, members of the team do small acts of kindness for one another and build into the day some routine check-ins. It might be as simple as asking, "Before we go home today, are you doing okay?" during a shift change. There is no way a leader or single team member can be aware of all the many ways a person may have experienced stress or psychological harm during a shift. When people only check in with one another sporadically, when something "big" happens, they miss an opportunity to catch smaller damage that can amass over time if unaddressed.

The Circle Up model (Rock et al. 2020) suggests a daily debriefing huddle and discussing the following questions to improve team members' well-being:

- "What are your reactions to today?"
- "What helped your team work well together?"
- "How could our work be 1 percent better?"
- "How did the shift affect you personally?"

These approaches are likely to be most effective when the team has created an environment of trust and safety.

ORGANIZATION-LEVEL INTERVENTIONS

Individual- and team-level interventions, while important, inevitably take place in the context of an organization, whose culture, policies, and norms will influence their success. Although every health system we are aware of defines its mission in relation to improving health, the focus of that mission, if defined at all, typically involves patients or communities, and not the system's own employees directly. Since people on average spend a third of their life at work, it stands to reason that what happens there—what they eat, how active they are, their sense of accomplishment, and the quality of their relationships—will account for at least a third of their health outcomes. In other words, if a health system is serious about improving health, the quality of work itself needs to be an important component of its strategy.

The idea of a quadruple aim for health systems—adding care for the care providers to the triple aim of improving population health, patient experience of care, and lowering cost—has slowly been gaining more attention in the literature (Bodenheimer and Sinsky 2014). Organizational practice guidelines have begun to emerge, but core measures of clinician well-being are not yet widely recognized. Consequently, meaningful, outcomes-based comparisons across organizations are limited.

Early efforts to characterize organizational best practices have identified several important components. Some of the most important initial steps involve formal recognition of well-being as a corporate priority and the systematic measurement of physician well-being (Shanafelt and Noseworthy 2017). The National Academy of Medicine has made available a summary of practical guidance on approaches organizations can use, including a review of validated physician well-being measures (Dyrbye et al. 2018). With metrics in place, the next critical step is to create accountability for the results. For this purpose, organizations would ideally identify or appoint a "chief well-being officer," someone who is part of the executive leadership team (Shanafelt et al. 2019). With both metrics and accountability in place, organizations would next pursue a true culture of well-being. They would invest directly in maintaining and improving physician well-being and would consider key operational decisions as much for their potential impact on well-being as they are for their potential financial impact (Shanafelt, Goh, and Sinsky 2017).

POLICY-LEVEL CONSIDERATIONS

While healthcare leaders' primary responsibility is to their organization, they must also advocate for those they serve and lead. Additionally, leaders must be aware of how policy decisions beyond their walls may affect the flourishing and well-being of their physicians.

Many policy decisions collectively send the message that physicians are becoming less valued in the eyes of society. At the heart of this message is a refrain to physicians: "We don't care about you or what you do." First, physician compensation has been steadily decreasing in an effort to manage healthcare costs (Tu and Ginsburg 2006). Average physician fees fell 25 percent between 1995 and 2006, during which time their average working hours fell approximately 7 percent (Staiger, Auerbach, and Buerhaus 2010). As a result, many physicians believe that they will be paid less in the future for their services, despite gaining additional skills and years of experience. In the United States, 60 percent of residents have medical school debt burdens of more than $100,000, and 40 percent have accrued more than $200,000 in medical school debt (Chesanow 2016). The real and opportunity costs of becoming a physician in the United States are high. Given the rigor of medical training, medical students are rarely able to work while in medical school to offset expenses, unlike their nursing counterparts. To devalue their training and expertise once they have made the personal investment in more than a decade of training at considerable cost to themselves is a great disservice.

Second, various nursing associations have made a national push for increased autonomy of nurses who are APPs. These efforts have been characterized by changes in scope-of-practice laws, the reduction of physician oversight, and a push toward doctorate-level nurses. This trend sends the collective message that the additional training, rigorous residency, and education obtained by a physician is no longer necessary. Specifically, the policies regarding expanded scope of practice need to be carefully evaluated. Often, the research undergirding these decisions to expand the scope for APPs has been funded and commissioned by professional nursing associations and has failed to control for important characteristics such as organizational and environmental factors (Lewis et al. 2014). The arguments often center around expanding access and reducing costs—important considerations—but rarely on optimizing quality.

Further signifying the devaluation of physicians, the Centers for Medicare & Medicaid Services announced its proposed reimbursement rates for the next year during the height of the coronavirus pandemic in 2020. Emergency medicine, critical care medicine, and anesthesiology—specialties whose practitioners are at high risk for contracting COVID-19 and which were critical to the response—would receive a 6 to 8 percent cut. APPs, by contrast, would get an 8 percent raise (CMS 2020). The message could not be clearer: The value of the sacrifices and risks of a physician's work is diminishing. This collective message, reinforced repeatedly through policy, is also affecting the morale and well-being of physicians.

Leaders must acknowledge these policy-level forces that may damage the well-being of their physicians. People at the top must actively advocate for policies that prioritize the safety of patients and must appropriately value physicians for their training and expertise. Healthcare organizations should also have a role in working with professional associations and lawmakers to advocate for such policies. If leaders focus only on the dynamics within their organization's walls, they miss an opportunity to influence the industry trends that can also erode physician well-being.

CONCLUSION

Many opportunities exist to create an environment in which physicians can flourish. Various approaches have been outlined in this chapter, as well as traps to avoid. The key takeaway is that physicians must be treated as humans to be supported, not as machines to be optimized.

REFERENCES

Arndt, B. G., J. W. Beasley, M. D. Watkinson, J. L. Temte, W.-J. Tuan, C. A. Sinsky, and V. J. Gilchrist. 2017. "Tethered to the EHR: Primary Care Physician Workload Assessment Using EHR Event Log Data and Time-Motion Observations." *Annals of Family Medicine* 15 (5): 419–26.

Bakker, A. B., P. M. Le Blanc, and W. B. Schaufeli. 2005. "Burnout Contagion Among Intensive Care Nurses." *Journal of Advanced Nursing* 51 (3): 276–87.

Bodenheimer, T., and C. Sinsky. 2014. "From Triple to Quadruple Aim: Care of the Patient Requires Care of the Provider." *Annals of Family Medicine* 12 (6): 573–76.

Centers for Medicare & Medicaid Services (CMS). 2020. "Medicare Program; CY 2021 Payment Policies Under the Physician Fee Schedule and Other Changes to Part B Payment Policies." *Federal Register*. Published August 17. www.govinfo.gov/content/pkg/FR-2020-08-17/pdf/2020-17127.pdf.

Chesanow, N. 2016. "Residents Salary & Debt Report 2016." *Medscape*. Published July 20. www.medscape.com/features/slideshow/public/residents-salary-and-debt-report-2016.

Csikszentmihalyi, M. 1990. *Flow: The Psychology of Optimal Experience*. New York: Harper & Row.

Donne, J. 1624. *Devotions upon Emergent Occasions*. London: Stationers' Company.

Dyrbye, L., J. Herrin, C. P. West, N. M. Wittlin, J. F. Dovidio, R. Hardeman, S. E. Burke, S. Phelan, I. N. Onyeador, B. Cunningham, and M. van Ryn. 2019. "Association of Racial Bias with Burnout Among Resident Physicians." *JAMA Network Open* 2 (7): e197457–e197457.

Dyrbye, L. N., D. Meyers, J. Ripp, N. Dalal, S. B. Bird, and S. Sen. 2018. "A Pragmatic Approach for Organizations to Measure Health Care Professional Well-Being." National Academy of Medicine. Published October 1. https://doi.org/10.31478/201810b.

Evans, C. R., and K. L. Dion. 1991. "Group Cohesion and Performance: A Meta-Analysis." *Small Group Research* 22 (2): 175–86.

Feingold, J. H. 2016. "Toward a Positive Medicine: Healing Our Healers, from Burnout to Flourishing." University of Pennsylvania capstone project. Published August 1. https://repository.upenn.edu/cgi/viewcontent.cgi?article=1110&context=mapp_capstone.

Hackman, J. R., and G. R. Oldham. 1980. *Work Redesign*. Reading, MA: Addison-Wesley.

Herzberg, F. 2003. "One More Time: How Do You Motivate Employees?" *Harvard Business Review Press*. Published January. https://hbr.org/2003/01/one-more-time-how-do-you-motivate-employees.

Jung, H., E. Seo, E. Han, M. D. Henderson, and E. A. Patall. 2020. "Prosocial Modeling: A Meta-Analytic Review and Synthesis." *Psychological Bulletin* 146 (8): 635–63.

Lewis, S. R., A. Nicholson, A. F. Smith, and P. Alderson. 2014. *Physician Anaesthetists Versus Non-Physician Providers of Anaesthesia for Surgical Patients*. New York: John Wiley & Sons.

Molina, M. F., A. I. Landry, A. N. Chary, and S. Burnett-Bowie. 2020. "Addressing the Elephant in the Room: Microaggressions in Medicine." *Annals of Emergency Medicine* 76 (4): 387–91.

Örtqvist, D., and J. Wincent. 2006. "Prominent Consequences of Role Stress: A Meta-Analytic Review." *International Journal of Stress Management* 13 (4): 399–422.

Rock, L. K., J. W. Rudolph, M. K. Fey, D. Szyld, R. Gardner, R. D. Minehart, J. Shapiro, and C. Roussin. 2020. "'Circle Up': Workflow Adaptation and Psychological Support Via Briefing, Debriefing, and Peer Support." *NEJM Catalyst*. Published September 22. https://catalyst.nejm.org/doi/full/10.1056/CAT.20.0240.

Seligman, M. E. 2012. *Flourish: A Visionary New Understanding of Happiness and Well-Being*. New York: Simon and Schuster.

Shanafelt, T., and J. H. Noseworthy. 2017. "Executive Leadership and Physician Well-Being: Nine Organizational Strategies to Promote Engagement and Reduce Burnout." *Mayo Clinic Proceedings* 92 (1): 129–46.

Shanafelt, T., J. Goh, and C. Sinsky. 2017. "The Business Case for Investing in Physician Well-Being." *JAMA Internal Medicine* 177 (12): 1826–32.

Shanafelt, T., M. Trockel, J. Ripp, M. Murphy, C. Sandborg, and B. Bohman. 2019. "Building a Program on Well-Being: Key Design Considerations to Meet the Unique Needs of Each Organization." *Academic Medicine* 94 (2): 156–61.

Staiger, D. O., D. I. Auerbach, and P. I. Buerhaus. 2010. "Trends in the Work Hours of Physicians in the United States." *JAMA* 303 (8): 747–53.

Tims, M., and A. B. Bakker. 2010. "Job Crafting: Towards a New Model of Individual Job Redesign." *South Africa Journal of Industrial Psychology* 36 (2): 1–9.

Tu, H. T., and P. B. Ginsburg. 2006. "Losing Ground: Physician Income, 1995–2003." *Tracking Report* 15 (June): 1–8.

Wrzesniewski, A., and J. E. Dutton. 2001. "Crafting a Job: Revisioning Employees as Active Crafters of Their Work." *Academy of Management Review* 26 (2): 179–201.

Wu, A. W. 2000. "Medical Error: The Second Victim. The Doctor Who Makes the Mistake Needs Help Too." Editorial. *British Medical Journal* 320 (7237): 726–27.

CHAPTER 14

Getting to "Us" from "We Versus They"

Robert Dean

The relationship between those who administrate care and those who deliver care has never been more strained because at a very basic level, both groups don't understand or trust one another.
—Sachin H. Jain, "Physicians and Healthcare Administrators: Friends or Foes?" 2016

MANY PEOPLE WORKING in healthcare do so with an altruistic motivation to help others and make society better. To this end, they often go through years of education and training. They work in complex organizational environments with multiple processes and interactions with various departments and people. Physicians doing clinical work have both the joys and the burdens of caring for others. In their respective roles, physicians have responsibilities that require knowledge and training to optimize the quality, effectiveness, and safety of the care they provide. They often provide emotional support to those they are caring for and their families. Physicians increasingly work in teams with other highly motivated individuals to do and achieve more.

Given the rigors and joys of healthcare, it seems that anyone choosing this field as a career would be fully engaged in the work. Unfortunately, physicians are often not engaged; their engagement can be quite low in some organizations. Many factors can cause physicians to disengage. A major cause is an organizational culture that is punitive or that does not recognize staff performance. Culture reflects how organizations treat both customers and staff. When an organization makes customer satisfaction a top priority, the experience and satisfaction of employees is usually a high priority as well.

When physicians work in organizations whose patient care processes regularly have problems, they become less engaged, especially when they believe that management is unable or unwilling to fix the problems. This typically causes physicians to fall behind on their daily schedules, which then negatively affects both patients and staff and, over the longer term, becomes wearing and also engenders resentment.

If staff members do not understand organizational strategy, values, or goals, their engagement also eventually erodes as they lose a sense of purpose in their work. One key to strong engagement is the ability to see how one's work contributes to the overall success of an organization. Top-down approaches that exclude physician input and involvement clearly contribute to physician disengagement.

WHY FINANCIAL INCENTIVES ARE NOT ENOUGH

Earlier chapters have referred to various definitions of engagement from the literature and have pointed out that engagement is a multidimensional concept difficult to pigeonhole. While there is no single, established definition of physician engagement, most definitions include the following factors. Among the more important are individual enthusiasm for the work being done, self-motivation, a sense that the organizations cares for individuals, and a feeling of enablement. Other factors include active participation, innovation, and a sense of organizational altruism. Finally, some physicians point to voluntary participation in performance improvement and quality initiatives as being major contributors to deep engagement.

Many of the factors that help improve engagement are grounded in the physician experience in the organization or the work setting.

Later in this chapter, we will dive deeper into some of these factors that improve the physician experience and hence engagement.

Some experts believe engagement can be improved with financial components. Although financial reward can sometimes improve engagement with physicians, organizations should not rely on financial incentives as a primary way to increase engagement. Lagarde, Huicho, and Papanicolas (2019) describe the shortcomings of financial rewards: "The evidence of their impact on quality of care is lackluster. Although they have been found to increase adherence to quality of care processes, their overall effects are mixed and, when positive, small." Emphasizing financial gain without first improving the overall experience usually results in failure to achieve either. If the relationship with physicians is strictly transactional then a true partnership is difficult to achieve. Any benefit beyond financial is not sustained once the economic relationship ends. If the motivation is primarily economic, the physician will not remain engaged in the organization once the transactional contract has ended. True physician engagement is about far more than money.

PHYSICIANS AS BENEFICIARIES

Interestingly, the primary beneficiaries of physician engagement are physicians themselves. Engaged physicians are happier and healthier both physically and behaviorally in their professional and personal lives. They have greater resilience and are less susceptible to burnout. They find more meaning and joy in their work.

To develop strategies to improve physician engagement, healthcare leaders must understand that the primary benefits of engagement go to the physicians themselves. Too often the motivation of organizations to improve physician engagement is to improve patient experience and care. While this mission is laudable, good patient care comes from engaged physicians whose health and well-being are in good shape. Good care will not happen unless physicians first benefit from engagement. Therefore, the goals and key performance

Exhibit 14.1 The Flow of Physician Engagement

Physician altruism → Physician feelings of worth → Physician resilience → Physician satisfaction with work and life → Physician self-motivation → High physician engagment → Enhanced patient quality and safety

metrics of engagement improvement strategies should begin with physicians. Engaged physicians will participate in and lead efforts to improve patient care because of their improved self-motivation and altruism. Exhibit 14.1 shows how this flow progresses.

Engaged physicians are more likely than unengaged ones are to collaborate with others to identify and correct process problems in patient care. Communication with patients and coworkers improves, as does physicians' interest in, and support of, organizational initiatives. Engagement often engenders a willingness to go an extra step in helping patients and teammates. Physicians will invest more time and effort in improving the environment and experience of patient care. It becomes an ongoing cycle: Improved physician engagement leads to improved patient experience and care, which in turn leads to further physician engagement.

The salutary effects of improved physician engagement go beyond caregivers and patients. With the complexity of the healthcare industry and its many challenges, the industry must improve quality, safety, and cost of care. Affordable care is out of reach for many. If the industry is to successfully implement serious meaningful reform of care delivery and develop payment models that encourage and reward these reforms, healthcare organizations will need significant physician participation and leadership. Engaged physicians with seats at the table are essential to the innovation and implementation of new ideas that can transform the current environment. Healthcare reforms require energy, motivation, and clinical and operational expertise. Only engaged physicians working with other involved stakeholders in healthcare will be up to the challenge.

WHAT CREATES ENGAGEMENT?

As discussed throughout the book, healthcare organizations and their leaders have many ways to improve physician engagement. The following sections will examine six useful approaches and how to include them in the organization: inclusion, respect, efficiency, communication, data, and trust. Without all six of these elements, meaningful physician work experience is threatened (exhibit 14.2).

Inclusion

To improve engagement, healthcare leaders will want to include physicians in the discussion of organizational goals, strategy, and operations. Without meaningful inclusion and input into these organizational concerns, physicians will not take other engagement efforts seriously. When physicians are included in, and can contribute

Exhibit 14.2 Six Elements of Engagement

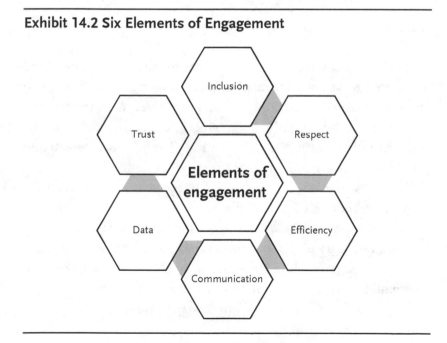

to, decision-making, they will develop ownership and commitment to the healthcare system's achievement and success. The organization will also benefit greatly by utilizing physicians' knowledge and experience in developing strategy and operational processes. Admittedly, organizations cannot include all physicians in all important corporate efforts. For this reason, a sound physician governance structure that allows for beneficial two-way communication is necessary.

Respect

Respect needs to be part of the culture for all stakeholders, including patients, physicians, executives, and clinical and nonclinical staff. When there is respect for all, the common and differing needs of individuals and stakeholder groups are recognized. Respect helps create a more courteous and civil work environment. It is key in decreasing disruptive behavior and workplace violence.

Efficiency

An efficient operational environment is one of the most overlooked and underrated means of creating physician engagement. Well-designed and well-executed care pathways and procedures make the best use of everyone's time and skills. Besides increasing productivity, quality, and safety, they instill confidence in the working environment and team dynamics as well as in organizational leadership.

Operational efficiency is a powerful engagement tool because it involves other drivers of engagement. Physicians need to be included in the development of care pathways and operational procedures. Data is a necessary part of measuring operational efficiency (process measures) and results (outcome measures). And organizations must communicate regularly on what the data is showing, what a team has identified as opportunities for improvement, and how individuals and teams are performing.

As much as efficiency can increase engagement, operational inefficiency can even more dramatically disengage physicians. Routine delays and mistakes because of a poorly designed process can quickly cause cynicism, blaming, and burnout. The effects are especially strong when staff members are not engaged in improvement efforts and their input is not solicited or heard.

Communication

Ongoing two-way communication is essential to physician engagement. Leadership needs to communicate its strategy, values, and organizational goals. Leaders should be sure that there are forums to share and analyze data and best practices and opportunities for improvement. Physicians also need to convey their ideas and feedback on strategy, operations, and their working experience. Communication on both sides needs to be transparent and not based on hidden agendas.

The COVID-19 pandemic has shown the importance of the bidirectional flow of information between leadership and physicians in dynamic working environments. Enhanced communication efforts and techniques increased engagement and partnership in healthcare delivery organizations to help all members of the organizations address and overcome many of the challenges the pandemic has brought. Although some of these efforts may be scaled back as the pandemic recedes, many will remain in place because of the improvements in engagement they have achieved.

Data

Many efforts related to increasing physician engagement rely on data. These efforts need data to develop, monitor, and improve processes and outcomes. Data can validate people's observations and make results transparent. Frequent and transparent data on processes being monitored ensures accountability and builds trust between stakeholders.

Data on efficiency requires a healthcare organization's investment and commitment. The organization should invest in a data system with multiple inputs, sound methodologies, and cohort benchmarking. With such a system, staff can analyze and present the data to physicians, quality staff, and leadership. Physicians must also set aside time from clinical duties to review the data and meet with leadership to discuss successes, opportunities, and accountability. Combined with well-executed methods for process improvement, data can drive organizational excellence and help create a rewarding clinical environment for patients and physicians.

Organizations face a learning curve in becoming data-driven. Nearly all stakeholders have initial skepticism about the credibility and veracity of data, especially if it does not show high performance. People will criticize the attribution, metric definitions, and the significance and timeliness of the data. The skepticism and critiques are opportunities to engage physicians in the improvement, acceptance, and use of the data for ongoing improvement. Getting physicians onboard with the use of data can take several months, but the time is well spent and is part of the overall investment that organizations need to make in data.

Trust

Developing trust in an organization is one of the harder tasks. Leaders build it one day and one challenge at a time, often over years. Unfortunately, trust can be also be compromised or lost much faster than it takes to build it.

Trust comes last on the list of prerequisites for engagement because it is the product of the preceding five. Including physicians in the development of strategy, operational plans, and performance improvement is one brick in the road to trust. So is respect for one another and collaboration on efficient operations. And as described, efficient operations management builds physicians' confidence in the competence of the leaders responsible for those processes.

The use of data can provide a sense of trust in metrics, whether they are for clinical outcomes or operational processes. Data can identify success and challenges; it drives accountability and action to improve. When all parties—physicians and administrators—are held to performance metrics, organizations can create equitable working environments to help drive trust, engagement, and performance. The data must be used transparently and objectively to ensure trust, and organizations must steer clear of using subjective data to bolster arguments.

Finally, constant and transparent communication that celebrates successes and addresses challenges is also essential to building trust. Unremitting two-way communication that is open and honest, and a willingness to discuss difficult issues candidly, are hallmarks of highly successful organizations. And nothing erodes trust like the "slow no" that keeps everyone hanging for answers. Only when all stakeholders are willing and able to have these discussions can the foundation for trust be built.

CONSIDERATIONS FOR AN ORGANIZATIONAL ENGAGEMENT STRUCTURE

Laying the foundation for the success factors just described requires building a structure and processes that stakeholders can participate in. If form follows function, then six structural elements underlie physician engagement (exhibit 14.3).

The Clinical Leadership Structure

At the core of any engagement structure is competent, altruistic, and representative clinical leadership. Rank-and-file physicians need mechanisms to convey the challenges of patient care they face, and

Exhibit 14.3 Engagement Structure and Governance

the physician leaders with whom they are communicating must be respected clinicians themselves. The physician leaders need to understand process improvement and business management and have keen negotiation skills. Developing a physician leadership pipeline can help create and replenish the cadre of leaders needed to sustain the engagement culture. Education, mentoring, and experience are keys to developing these leaders. Organizations should also include physicians in their process improvement efforts and in strategy development and clinical operations management.

Physician leadership helps organizations encourage the use and acceptance of data in daily patient care and operations. Some physicians can also be data champions, conveying the importance of linking clinical practice to data. Likewise, physicians can add their voice and leadership to information technology and electronic health records (EHRs) to improve their functionality and acceptance and to ensure that these tools fit the care model and are not simply an instrument for management.

A critical component of engagement structure is the inclusion of the patient voice and community needs. These voices help direct the focus and efforts of the engagement structure. Patient and family advisory councils and community representatives in strategy development, operational oversight, and quality programs can provide the voice of the customer. Without the perspectives of these customers, many initiatives will fail.

Engagement Starts at the Beginning

Consultants are often used to help organizations improve physician engagement. The question they usually address at the start is why physicians are not already highly engaged in careers in which they have invested so much time and education. The consultants often find that the physicians' work experience is not what they had hoped for and that they thus feel disengaged from their organizations.

The head of an employed medical group in the Midwest described the problem: "We recruit the best physicians we can find to join our group and describe the great features of our practice, our community, and their future with us. Then once they arrive, it seems that they get here, see the EHR, see their office or procedural area, and we turn them loose. Then we act surprised three months later when they are frustrated navigating the system and not knowing how to make it better." What follows their initial disengagement is often a loss in productivity, lower quality of care, and negative provider and patient experiences. The negative effects are costly to the physician, the patients, and the organizations. In today's competitive and mobile job market, retaining the best talent is far less disruptive than is constantly having to recruit replacements. Not only is turnover disruptive, but it is also quite costly. National estimates on the cost of turnover are $90,000 for registered nurses, $250,000 for advanced practice providers (APPs), and $500,000 to $1.5 million for physicians, depending on specialty.

Besides cost, implementing strategy and operational excellence are nearly impossible without engaged staff and physicians. From a customer's perspective, the clinical physicians are the brand. The more these physicians know and own the strategy, the better they can represent it.

Onboarding New Physicians

A growing number of organizations are understanding the benefit of formalized onboarding of new physicians. Much more than traditional orientation, contemporary onboarding creates familiarity with organizational culture, exposure to the leaders, and a deeper understanding of mission. New physicians are introduced to the strategy, values, and goals of the organization. Perhaps most important, the formal onboarding process explains in detail how physicians are evaluated on quality, performance improvement, and performance management (exhibit 14.4).

The onboarding program is delivered by the healthcare organization. All clinicians go through the program, whether they are physicians, APPs, or other healthcare staff, and they gain

Exhibit 14.4 Engagement Begins at the Beginning: Onboarding

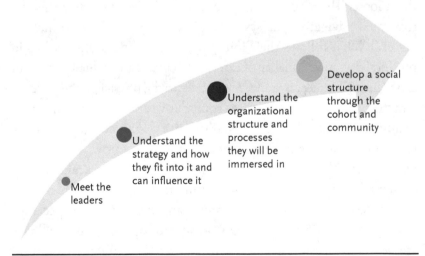

Develop a social structure through the cohort and community

Understand the organizational structure and processes they will be immersed in

Understand the strategy and how they fit into it and can influence it

Meet the leaders

much understanding and a good social structure through the onboarding process.

In addition, new physicians receive training in resilience skills and are helped to identify early signs of burnout. The programs ensure that they know how to identify patient safety issues and raise awareness of them at the system level. Additional information they receive includes an introduction to accreditation, how they can participate in physician committees, and how they can better adapt to their new environment.

Onboarding also helps new physicians create professional and personal networks. The more progressive programs include information on introducing their families to community education, religious, and recreational resources. Highly effective healthcare organizations understand that without successful integration into the community, many families may be unhappy in a new environment. Ultimately, family unhappiness can clearly create further turnover.

Finally, including a formalized mentoring program in onboarding efforts can help pull together the various areas addressed and add a human touch for new physicians. Mentoring programs give new physicians the chance to ask questions and clarify what they have heard about organizational values, culture, and staff issues. They have someone to ask about the community and its resources and someone who can be a newfound friend. The other benefit is that mentor selection helps identify those with the skills and interest to be future physician leaders in the organization.

The results of onboarding programs are quite good (Kee 2020). For organizations with formal nurse residency programs for first-year nurses, the turnover rate is 9 percent, while those without a program have a turnover rate of 18 percent (Vizient 2018). According to national averages, 29 percent of newly appointed physicians will have left for new positions elsewhere in the first three years. Studies suggest that six-month onboarding programs or longer ones have reduced three-year turnover by 50 to 75 percent (Vizient 2021). Given the multiple negative impacts of turnover, the development of structured and formalized onboarding of new physicians is worth the investment.

Different Ways of Thinking

Communication between physicians and administrators can often feel strained and seem to be missing the mark. One healthcare leader remarked, "Well, one side proposes a solution, and the other side says it won't work. And the entire approach to the problem is just so different for the two parties." Often unrealized is that physicians and administrators typically approach problems differently. Physicians are trained in depreciative thinking designed to create and rule out a differential diagnosis. They use data to confirm or rule out a potential diagnosis. If the input does not fit the course of the disease, exclude it as a possible diagnosis. In a meeting regarding strategy or operations, physicians may likely use the same approach when given a proposed solution. And with only an incomplete understanding of the variables, physicians may quickly dismiss the solution. How often have healthcare leaders sat in meetings where physicians say, "That will never work"?

Executives, in contrast, are trained in appreciative thinking. Such a thinking process runs along the lines of "Given what we have, how can we make this work?" They look at taking advantage of the assets they have to achieve the desired results and consider whether they need to add to those assets. One CEO described it this way: "It works like this. If one piece doesn't fit, I have to determine if I can change it to make it work." Stoller (2009) summarizes it well: "Because of the strong reflex for deficit-based thinking, physician-leaders must learn to switch nimbly between different reasoning and thinking processes—one that is 'deficit-based,' narrowly focused, and well-adapted for clinical practice and another that is more divergent or 'appreciative' for thinking about organizational or system issues and challenges."

Both depreciative and appreciative types of thinking have benefits, given the environment they are applied in. Either approach can lead to failure if it is applied without the other. The best executives and physicians can modulate between the two models and create a 360-degree view of the problem and solutions. An awareness of the differences in thinking can help the parties move past them in creating solutions. Onboarding can be a great forum to discuss these different approaches and to help physicians learn to balance the two for administrative and clinical success.

Leadership Development

Many organizations have invested in physician leadership development. Organizations support increasing numbers of physician leaders, understanding the need to have these leaders at the table to improve efficiency, communication, and the use of data. Physician leaders should be involved in strategy and operational model development, and this requires a skill set different from a clinical one. Despite the common refrain that "every physician is a leader" at both the microsystem and the team level, clinical leadership has a bearing on physician engagement and burnout. Bohmer (2013) writes, "CEOs may resist investing in developing clinical leadership and decentralizing control or may believe the process will be too slow to address current pressures. But the need is evident, the tasks are clear, and the skills are at hand—data orientation, the relentless pursuit of excellence, and a habit of inquiry are all second nature to physicians. Ultimately, investment in such leaders will be essential to achieving the goals of health care reform."

Shanafelt and colleagues (2015) showed that for every one-point increase in the leadership rating of physician department leaders, there was a corresponding 3 percent decrease in the burnout rates in the departments. Effective physician leadership decreases burnout and improves the working experience.

Consider physicians and how they serve as leaders in daily clinical practice. Many in society contend that physicians are given, and need to live up to, leadership status because of their selection, education, and training. The thinking is that in any clinical environment, physicians are the natural and designated leaders. Whether this premise is accurate or not, it does justify helping physicians use or develop their leadership skills so that they are more effective in team and leader roles in their daily work. Training that increases emotional intelligence and self-awareness is useful in any setting. Basic training in quality and performance improvement can benefit patients and care teams. After this preliminary training, candidates can be evaluated for further leadership education in light of their desire, aptitude, and potential.

A more merit-based approach to developing future organizational leaders begins with candidates who show interest, aptitude, potential for skill development, and other personal attributes. Those who are accepted into leadership programs then receive leadership education that includes basic management instruction, including techniques for quality and performance management. Personal development skills such as enhancing emotional intelligence should also be incorporated into leadership education programs.

The education program should be supplemented with an experiential component to help cement the learning into practice. Direct experience helps physicians learn how to apply their training and work in administrative teams. Experiential learning combined with mentoring and coaching can accelerate and round out leadership development.

The final step is deployment into a leadership role. Depending on the immediate needs of the organization, physician leaders may be assigned as department directors or medical directors. Opportunities may also exist in service-line leadership or organizational committees. In any case, the organization needs to deploy its physician leaders intentionally and thoughtfully to keep them engaged. The time and effort that physicians put into their leadership development should be rewarded with opportunities to put those skills into practice.

Engagement as a Priority

Efforts to improve physician engagement require continuous effort. There are no magic bullets for sustained engagement. To improve physicians' working experience and consequently improve their engagement, organizations must take both bottom-up and top-down approaches. Many of the levers to drive experience and engagement need to be built into strategic plans and then budgeted and operationalized. For example, organizations can create process improvement teams, aim to become data-enabled learning organizations, and develop leadership development programs.

Like any other improvement project, these efforts must establish a baseline and then continuously measure physician engagement. The efforts should be made at both the organizational and the unit levels. Baseline data shows which units and pain points need to be addressed first. Measurement of physician engagement can increasingly be integrated with other surveys, such as safety and general culture surveys. Combining these surveys not only decreases survey fatigue by the staff but also often shows correlation between the data sets. In turn, survey data can be combined with clinical quality and productivity data to give a holistic view of the interrelationships between experience, engagement, and safety and quality.

With reliable data, organizations can begin to set priorities. A small test of a change in a single unit can provide feedback and insight into the intervention before leadership decides to broaden the effort to multiple units of the entire organization. Understanding workflow and the cultural differences between units that are tested at a smaller scale can save effort and credibility before the launch of systemwide efforts.

Using focus groups to provide feedback on worker experiences and engagement are early steps in building inclusion and respect. Once that input has been obtained, staff should be included in solution and process design sessions. For example, unit-based data boards allow for daily visual data management to show leading indicator progress that ties to longer term, lagging data points. Communication needs to be authentic and transparent about the data and should clarify group findings. Leadership should spell out its processes for learning about physicians' experiences and for other forms of engagement with physicians. Leaders should also reinforce their commitment to these processes. Celebrating small wins and acknowledging challenges and failures as part of communication also helps build trust. These combined efforts can build a virtual cycle that can improve engagement and, with time, the organizational culture.

CONCLUSION

Improving physician engagement requires sustained and systemic efforts in multiple areas. It is not an easy process. Yet engagement is important not only for its own sake but also to improve the lives of the caregivers and to improve patient care. The investment in time, money, and leadership is large. Fortunately, the return on those efforts is even larger when they are done right. Physician engagement is a continuous journey that never ends but is well worth embarking on.

REFERENCES

Bohmer, R. M. J. 2013. "Leading Clinicians and Clinicians Leading." *New England Journal of Medicine* 368 (16): 1468–70.

Jain, S. H. 2016. "Physicians and Healthcare Administrators: Friends or Foes?" *Forbes.* Published June 29. www.forbes.com/sites/sachinjain/2016/06/29/physicians-and-health-care-administrators-friend-or-foe/.

Kee, L. 2020. "Clinician Onboarding: The On-Ramp to Engagement, Alignment, and Cost Savings." Vizient. Published November 17. https://newsroom.vizientinc.com/clinician-onboarding-on-ramp-to-engagement-alignment-and-cost-savings.htm?blog/clinical.

Lagarde, M., L. Huicho, and I. Papanicolas. 2019. "Motivating Provision of High Quality Care: It Is Not All About the Money."

British Medical Journal. Published September 23. www.bmj.com/content/366/bmj.l5210.full.pdf.

Shanafelt, T. D., G. Gorringe, R. Menaker, K. A. Storz, D. Reeves, S. J. Buskirk, J. A. Sloan, and S. J. Swensen. 2015. "Impact of Organizational Leadership on Physician Burnout and Satisfaction." *Mayo Clinic Proceedings* 90 (4): 432–40.

Stoller, J. K. 2009. "Developing Physician-Leaders: A Call to Action." *Journal of General Internal Medicine* 24 (7): 876–78.

Vizient. 2021. "Physician and Advanced Practice Provider Onboarding Program." Accessed February 15. www.vizientinc.com/our-solutions/clinical-solutions/health-care-onboarding-solution.

———. 2018. "Equipping Nurses to Improve Care Delivery." Published March 18. www.vizientinc.com/-/media/Documents/SitecorePublishingDocuments/Public/VizientNursingBrochure_EquippingNursesToImproveCareDelivery.pdf.

Conclusion: Summing Up the Experts' Knowledge

Carson F. Dye

Why is physician engagement so important? It creates more positive, stable relationships between health care organizations and their physicians. It also correlates with greater efficiency and productivity, improved patient care and safety, and lower operational costs.
—Katharine P. Redmond, "Steps to Improve Physician Engagement," 2020

AS WE HAVE SEEN throughout this book, physician engagement is a complex subject. Yet engagement is essential for organizations that aim to become—and remain—high-performing healthcare providers. Moreover, the post COVID-19 healthcare industry is going through some of the most monumental changes since the introduction of Medicare. Redesign of many structures, practices, and systems is already underway and will continue. And physicians must join in to play a role in shaping these future changes.

After an explanation of engagement, a literature review, and a description of engagement models in chapters 1 through 3, the remainder of the book provides substantial evidence of the benefits of increased physician engagement and leadership in an organization. While some of the content is theoretical, several key takeaways seem to be supported by all the authors. I will summarize these conclusions here.

UNDERSTANDING PHYSICIANS

"Well, they are all different." This statement about physicians may seem basic on its face, but unfortunately, many healthcare leaders tend to lump all physicians into a single category. Comments such as "they're greedy," "they don't care about anyone but themselves," "all they do is complain," "they just nitpick," "they are typical scientists—no personality," and so on, fail to serve any purpose. Organizations that do well with physician engagement and leadership recognize physicians' many different characteristics, including personality, age, practice, and stage of life. For example, in chapter 4, Douglas Spotts describes physicians as excellent clinicians. In Dr. Spotts's view, physicians are thorough (organized and conscientious), good listeners, direct and forthright, intellectually curious, cooperative, and emotionally intelligent. These are excellent criteria for all types of leadership roles.

GIVING PHYSICIANS A BIGGER ROLE

The vivid picture painted by Lisa Casey in chapter 5 is that of boats and paddles. Dr. Casey argues that we need more physician leaders in the boat and that they need larger paddles. Her paddle metaphor refers to the grip as the knowledge physicians need to better understand what is going on in healthcare and in their organization, the shaft as the driving factors creating change for healthcare, and, finally, the blade as the trust needed to get more and more physicians engaged and leading.

RECOGNIZING PHYSICIANS AS LEADERS

As I suggest in chapter 6, although nearly all physicians are already leaders, they may not fully realize it. What's more, many are certainly not fully developed as effective leaders. Much of the book's message is that healthcare leaders need to involve full-time clinicians to strengthen physicians' engagement.

ENSURING A LINE OF SIGHT AND PARTICIPATION

In chapter 7, Kalen Stanton summarizes his thesis on engagement:

> The art and science of engaging human beings—physicians in particular—in a meaningful dialogue or journey is ultimately to arrive at a twofold outcome:
>
> 1. A collective picture of a situation with shared meaning among the participants
> 2. A self-discovered conviction about the individual's role in, and accountability for, reaching a current or future state

In the literature on leadership, the term *line of sight* means an individual's view of how the person's work and effort tie to a larger vision or mission. Much as Mr. Stanton's story of the hunting villagers used imagery to emphasize a point, the story of three bricklayers in the Middle Ages can drive home a point about line of sight. One bricklayer was asked what he was doing, and he replied, "I am laying bricks and stones." The second, replied, "I am putting up a wall." When the third was asked, he replied, "I am building a great cathedral for the glory of God." For physicians to be highly engaged and serve as leaders, they must have this sort of line of sight.

UNDERSTANDING HOW PHYSICIANS FEEL ENGAGEMENT

In chapter 8, Harjot Singh presents a comprehensive review of the concept of *flow*, or a state of being where one feels so immersed in activities that one loses track of time. Dr. Singh shows how this concept applies to personal well-being and personal productivity and how it reduces the chance of burnout. He explains how organizations can increase opportunities for their physicians to feel flow and ultimately to become more engaged.

CONSIDERING COMPENSATION

In chapter 9, I provide a "compare and contrast" view of one of the more controversial issues of physician engagement—whether financial rewards are the primary driver of engagement. Although many readers might not necessarily change their minds after reading this chapter, they will have been exposed to a broader range of views on this subject.

MANAGING CONFLICT

Most people seek to avoid conflict, but in chapter 10, Jeremy Blanchard delves into the issue of mining for conflict, a concept popularized by Patrick Lencioni. Dr. Blanchard offers solid suggestions for exposing the conflict that may otherwise lie unexpressed in conversations as well as various ways to solve conflict.

PAYING STRICT ATTENTION TO DIVERSITY AND GENDER MATTERS

Kathleen Forbes (chapter 11) and Raúl Zambrano (chapter 12) provide wide-ranging discussion on issues that sit clearly at the forefront of not only healthcare but also all of society. With the greatly increasing diversity of physicians, in terms of both race and gender, say Drs. Forbes and Zambrano, healthcare leaders are working in a different world than that of a few years ago. These two chapters can help healthcare leaders understand how to embrace and take advantage of the benefits of this growing diversity.

HELPING PHYSICIANS FIND THEIR FLOW AND FLOURISH

Katherine Meese and Andrew Garman discuss the issue of flourishing (chapter 13). Building on the concepts introduced by Dr. Singh, they demonstrate how organizations need to address engagement from the perspective of helping physicians sense positive emotion, have meaningful relationships, find meaning in their work, and celebrate their accomplishments. Dr. Meese and Dr. Garman delve deeply into issues of work design, job crafting, supporting the second victim, team-level interventions, reducing sources of conflict, and institutionalizing the practice of microempathy.

ENDING ADMINISTRATIVE–PHYSICIAN COMPETITION

Finally, in chapter 14, Robert Dean addresses a key area that has historically harmed physician engagement—the age-old divisiveness between hospital administrators and the medical staff. Dr. Dean provides excellent suggestions on how to establish an engagement structure and governance configuration to make physician engagement more successful. His thoughts on physician onboarding as a unique way to enhance engagement provide useful practical guidance, as does his review of the key factors that must be present before engagement methods are tried.

Healthcare consultant Katharine P. Redmond, who was quoted in this chapter's epigraph, perhaps summarizes the importance of physician engagement the best: "Forward-looking health care organizations realize that physician engagement is key to their clinical and financial performance. At a time when physicians are feeling bombarded by economic and operational changes in health care seemingly beyond their control, and under greater personal pressure to heighten performance, ongoing organizational support and engagement can make a critical difference to their success" (Redmond 2020).

Although this first volume of the book provides some tactics for enhancing physician engagement, volume 2, *The Complete Guide to Enhanced Physician Engagement: Tools and Tactics for Success*, delves deeper into the issue. It offers many details and explicit suggestions on strategies to augment physician engagement. Readers looking to put into action the concepts they have just learned will find a wealth of information in volume 2.

REFERENCE

Redmond, K. P. 2020. "Steps to Improve Physician Engagement." *Physicians Practice*. Published March 24. www.physicianspractice.com/view/steps-improve-physician-engagement.

Index

Note: Italicized page locators refer to exhibits.

American Medical News: on physician leaders, 111
Ammerman, C., 212
Anchoring Physician Engagement in Vision and Values: Principles and Framework (Dickson), 28
Angood, P., 115, 123
Appreciation of others, 114
Appreciative inquiry, 74
Appreciative thinking: executives trained in, 276
Areas of Work/Life Survey, 147, 158
Arkowitz, H., 90
Arrogance: conflict and, 198–99; lack of, 114
Artificial intelligence: algorithms, 79; change management and, 70
Art of Possibility (Zander and Zander), 65
Assertiveness: implicit gender biases and, 213
Association of American Medical Colleges: physician shortage study, 226
Athenahealth: burnout and gender surveys, 206, 207
Atkinson, S., 98
Autonomy, 21, 57, 111, 123, 178; decrease in, 226; design of physicians' work and, *249*; job crafting and, 250; of nurses, 258
Autotelic experiences, 153
Availability: employee engagement and, 16
Awareness: action and, during flow, 150–51

Baby boomers, 226; adoption of social media and, 141; communication styles of, 232
Background information: the what in the paddle metaphor and, 95–96
Bacterial infections, 80
Baker, G. R., 91
Bangs, D., 54
Base salary, 173
Behavior: acceptable, conflict over, 187
Behavioral economics, 169

Being in the zone, 148–49
Being Mortal (Gawande), 80
Benefits, 173
"Benefits of Cognitive Diversity" (Schindler), 223
Best-practice alerts, 79
Birk, S., 115, 123
Black, C., 181
Blaming: operational inefficiency and, 269
Blanchard, Jeremy, 10, 286; insights on monetary compensation and physician engagement, 175
Board of trustees, 110
Boat metaphor. *See* Paddling a boat metaphor, engagement journey and
Body language: female leaders and, 213
Bohmer, R. M., 277
Bonuses, 172, 173, 175, 176
Boredom, 149, 150
Boundary setting: in management of physicians, 229
Brands, 141
Breathing: facing conflict and, 194; mindful, conflict management and, 200–201
Brenner, M., 20
Bricklayers story: line of sight and, 285
Briscoe, D., 32
Buckingham, Marcus, 16
Burger, J., 36
Burke, B. L., 90
Burnout, 2, 36, 84, 88, 160, 161, 163, 236–37, 244, 251; contagious nature of, 252; engaged physicians and lowered susceptibility to, 265; to engagement spectrum, 147, *147*; female physicians and, 207, 208; flow and reduced chance of, 155–56, 286; high potential for, 81–83; leadership and help with, 120; leadership development and decrease in, 277; onboarding and identifying signs of, 275; operational inefficiency and, 269; in organizations without physician engagement programs, 162; personal mismatch as root cause

of, 155, 178; physician disengagement
and, 33–34, 38–39; rates of, before
COVID-19 pandemic, 225; role
ambiguity and, 254; self-reported
rates of, among physicians, 236;
shortage of physicians and, 226;
spectrum from engagement to, 147,
147; types of, 155; work–life balance
and prevention of, 210–11
Byrnes, John, 32; insights on monetary
compensation and physician
engagement, 175–76

Camaraderie: providing for community
and, 118–20
Cancer, 80
Cancer screening: changes in, 70
Capitation, 173
Cardarelli, R., 34
Career guidance, 214
Care pathways: physicians and
development of, 268
Carsen, S., 115
Case studies: moving beyond engagement
to alignment, 78–80
Casey, Kevin: insights on monetary
compensation and physician
engagement, 178–79
Casey, Lisa M., 9, 284
Caucasians: projected percentage of, in
US population, 227, 237
Cechova, Dominika, 15
Centers for Medicare & Medicaid
Services: changes in reimbursement
rates, 258–59
Certified registered nurse anesthetists:
expanded scope of practice for, 254
"Challenges of Being a Female Doctor"
(Hoff), 205
Chambers, A., 19
Change: case for, 137, *138*, 139
Change management, 70–73; deepening
levels of physician engagement,
72–73; inviting physicians early to
the conversation, 71–72; physicians'
reluctance to change, 70
Cherf, J., 95, 96

Chief executive officers (CEOs): in
healthcare, percentage of women
among, 206
Chief medical officers, 108, 159, 160, 161;
evolving role of, 123; over-reliance
on, 88–89, 122–23; percentage of
women among, 206
Childbearing: residency program and
impact of, 208–9
Choice: in eight-factor model, 52, *53*, 54,
55–56
Chokshi, D. A., 100, 170
Choo, Michael: insights on monetary
compensation and physician
engagement, 179–80
Chronos, 153
Circle Up model, 256
Cleveland Clinic Foundation, 179
Clinical leadership: responsibilities of
organizational leadership *vs.*, *109*
Clinical leadership structure:
organizational engagement structure
and, 271–73, *272*
Clinical trials, 158
Coaching: female physician leader
development and, 213–14; leadership
development and, 278. *See also*
Mentoring
Coffman, Curt, 16
Cognitive diversity, 223–38
Cognitive diversity and healthcare
leadership: burnout and, 236–37;
challenges related to, 224–25;
communication and, 231–33;
management of physicians, 228–30;
meetings and, 234–36; patients
and, 227–28; providers as
underrepresented racial and ethnic
minorities, 225–27, 228; trust and,
230–31
Cognitive independence: providers' need
for, 230
Collaboration: physician leaders and, 229;
receptivity to, 76, *77*
Collaborative skills, 113
Colleagues: investing in, 201
Collegiality: physicians' lounge and, 118

Collins, Jim, 72
Commercial sources: physician
    engagement information and,
    cautionary note, 35
Commitment, 178, 179
Common messages: conflict management
    and, 197
Communication: at center of engagement
    program, 161; engagement and, 267,
    269; physician engagement and, 36;
    provider–patient, quality outcomes
    and, 227; skills, 113; transparent, 271,
    279; trust as essential in, 230
Communication styles: cognitive diversity
    and, 226, 231–33; gender biases,
    stereotyping, and, 213–14
Community: providing for camaraderie
    and, 118–20
Community benefit, postacute providers:
    engagement structure and
    governance and, 272
Community burnout, 155
Compacts: physician code of conduct vs.,
    102; sample language in, 103
Compassion: emotional intelligence and,
    68; female physicians and, 212
Compensation, 286; design, engaging
    physicians in, 180; design of
    physicians' work and, 249; physician,
    decrease in, 258; policies, 173;
    practices, fair and equitable, 216
Competencies: leadership, 75, 75, 114
Computers, 70
Concentration: flow and, 151–52
Conflict(s), 185–202, 287; about
    healthcare professionals' degrees,
    226; breeding, healthcare as perfect
    milieu for, 190; facing, concrete
    tactics for, 193–97; improving value
    of, using a dashboard for, 199–200;
    of leading with power, 188; meetings
    and resolution of, 234; mining
    for, benefits of, 191; mining for,
    how to do, 192–93, 286; mining
    for, key skills related to, 200–202;
    over delivery of care, 186; pitfalls
    to avoid in, 198–99; prevalence of,

185, 202; productive, welcoming,
    190; of professionalism, 186–88; of
    the story that never happened, 189;
    unproductive, reducing sources of,
    254–55
Conflict(s), tactics for the moment of
    truth, 195–97; choosing the right
    time and the right place, 195–96;
    create a common message, 197;
    establish an acceptable outcome,
    196–97; follow-up, 197; listening
    mindfully, 196; manage the
    electronics, 196; paraphrase back,
    196
Consolidation of healthcare organizations:
    inevitability of, 3–4
Consultants: physician engagement and,
    273
Consulting firms: literature on physician
    engagement provided by, 28, 34–39
Continuing medical education, 175
Continuing medical education
    department, 102
Contribution: in eight-factor model, 52,
    53, 54, 56
Control: flow and heightened sense of,
    152
Control burnout, 155
Cooper, B. B., 141
Cooperativeness: physicians and, 67–69
Cooperative skills, 113
Cooper-Thomas, H. D., 109
Copeland, L. R., 56
Cosgrove, T., 28, 123
Cost control: healthcare leadership and,
    224
Courage: in face of conflict, 191
Covey, Stephen, 121, 230, 231
COVID-19 pandemic, 1, 80; bidirectional
    flow of information essential during,
    269; burnout rates before, 225;
    Centers for Medicare & Medicaid
    Services reimbursement rate changes
    and, 259; female physicians and
    aftershocks of, 212; female physicians
    and work–life stresses during, 217;
    future changes in wake of, 283;

navigating, visual narrative and, 127; need for renewed physician engagement and, 32, 39; physicians feeling abandoned during, 2; redesign of healthcare industry due to, 8; servant leadership and, 192; underrepresented racial and ethnic minority patients and disparities in care during, 231; virtual healthcare management during, 90

Creativity: physicians and, 67–69

Credibility: implicit gender bias and, 212

Csikszentmihalyi, Mihaly, 148, 152, 153

Cuddy, Amy, 213

Cultural competency: quality outcomes and, 227

Culture of physicians: understanding, 120–22

Customer satisfaction: poor engagement and, 146; prioritizing, 264

Cynicism: operational inefficiency and, 269

Dashboards: improving value of conflict with, *199*, 199–200

Data: distinguished from learning map, 136; engagement and, *267*, 269–70; on imbalance of women in healthcare leadership roles, 206–7; operational efficiency and, 268; relevant and high-quality, 96; reliable, prioritizing engagement and, 279

Databases: of physician engagement information, 35

Data champions: physicians as, 272

Data-driven communication: improving physician engagement with, *236*

Data-enabled learning organizations, 279

Dean, Robert, 10, 287

Death by Meeting (Lencioni), 234

Deaths: medical errors as leading cause of, 2

Deci, E. L., 171

Decision makers: becoming acquainted with, 100

Decision making: unquestioned, physicians and, 107, 108

Dedication: defining, 55; in eight-factor model, 52, 53, *53*, 54, 55

Deficit-based thinking, 74

Delivery of healthcare. *See* Healthcare delivery

Democratic approach: in management of physicians, 229, 234

Denis, J.-L., 91

Department chairs: percentage of women among, 206

Dependability: as essence of trust, 99

Depersonalization: burnout and, 252

Depreciative thinking: physicians trained in, 276

Depression: female physicians and, 208; role ambiguity and, 254

Desirable behaviors: physicians and adoption of, 172

Desire for leadership, 111–12

Detsky, A. S., 181

Devotions upon Emergent Occasions (Donne), 246

Diagrams, 134

Dialogue, 127; distinguished from learning map, 136

Dickson, G., 32, 48

Differential diagnosis: physician training grounded in, 229, 276

DiLisi, Jeffrey, 46

Direct orders without explanation: avoiding, 228, 229

Discovery, 127; distinguished from learning map, 137

Discrimination, 252, 253

Disenfranchised physicians, 92–93, 104

Disengagement. *See* Physician disengagement

Disruptive behavior: respect and decrease in, 268

Distrust: with healthcare systems, providers and, 231; physicians' practice settings and, 227

Diversity, 286–87; cognitive, 223–38; description of, 223; racial, cultural, and gender, 223, 224

269–70; efficiency, *267*, 268–69; inclusion, *267*, 267–68; respect, *267*, 268; trust, *267*, 270–71

Engagement app, 142

Engagement at an individual level, 148–54; studies on, 148

Engagement plan: lack of, 158

Engagement programs: communication at center of, 161; disjointed nature of, 159

Engagement to alignment case study, 78–80

Epstein, D. J., 83

Ettinger, Walter H., 29, 139

Eudaemonic well-being, 154

Evidence: clear and concise, the what in the paddle metaphor and, 96–97

Evidence-based decision making, 89

Exceptional leadership competency model, *115*

Executives: trained in appreciative thinking, 276

Experiential learning: dashboards and, 199, *199*; leadership development and, 278

Extrinsic motivation: intrinsic motivation *vs.*, 171, *172*

Extrinsic motivators: balancing intrinsic motivators with, 181

Facetime, 232

Face-to-face communication, 103; crucial importance of, 98; improving physician engagement with, *236*; multigenerational workforce and, 232

Facts: illustrated in visual language, 128

Fairness burnout, 155

Falk, S., 96

"Fallacy of familiarity": being cognizant of, 215

Family life: how professional practice fits into, 210–11

Favoritism, 155

Feedback, 98; accepting, 76, *77*; design of physicians' work and, *249*; flow and, 151; focus groups and, 279

Fee-for-service model, 224

"Feelers" on teams: conflict and paying attention to, 192

Feingold, Jordyn Heather, 243

Female leadership representation: data on, 206

Female physician engagement, suggestions for, 214–18; be equally respectful of all physicians, 215; encourage meaningful leadership roles for women, 217; examine compensation practices, 216; improve visibility of female physicians in leadership roles, 216; include physician parents for duration of their careers, 217–18; look beyond volunteers, 218; mitigate/eliminate implicit gender bias, 214–15; nominate more women, 218; provide for mentorship and role models, 216–17; support programs for leadership development and negotiation, 215–16

Female physicians: career decision challenges during training and, 208–9; challenges with selecting a professional practice, 210–11; divorce and, 208; fitting professional practice into family life, 210–11; pay inequities and, 214; percentage of, in healthcare workforce, 206; role-sharing and, 210; time available for additional activities, 211; time available for leadership roles, 211; understanding unique perspectives and obligations of, 205

Female physicians' leadership and engagement, developing, 212–14; challenges related to pandemic and, 212; formal programs and training, 213; informal training and coaching or mentoring opportunities, 213–14

Finance knowledge: physician leaders and, 76, *77*

Financial aspects of physician engagement: ignoring, 157

Financial growth: strong physician leadership and, 225

General medicine providers:
communication style and, 233
Generational demographics: cognitive
diversity and, 226–27
Generational perspectives: conflict and,
187
Generation X, 226; adoption of social
media and, 141; communication
styles of, 232
Generation Y (millennials), 226;
communication styles of, 232; visual
movement and, 140–41
Generation Z, 226; communication styles
of, 232; visual movement and, 140
Gerjuoy, Herbert, 238
Giger, A., 36
Goals: clear, flow and, 151; purpose and, 98
Goldsmith, J., 47
Goleman, Daniel, 149
"Good Leaders Make Good Doctors"
(Khullar), 87
Good to Great (Collins), 72
Group reimbursement: individual pay
vs., 171
Groysberg, B., 212
Gunderman, R., 33

Haines, S. T., 109
Happiness: engagement *vs.*, 72; three
elements in, 20
Harris, Patrice A., 218
Harter, J., 146, 147
Harvard Medical School, 108
Haudan, J., 130
Hawthorne effect, 158
HCAHPS (Hospital Consumer
Assessment of Healthcare Providers
and Systems Survey), 168
Healthcare delivery: conflict over, 186;
provider shortages and, 226
Healthcare disparities, 227
Healthcare expenditures: healthcare
leadership and control of, 224
Healthcare industry: COVID-19
pandemic and redesign of, 8;
providers and fundamental errors
made by, 243–44

Healthcare initiatives: disenfranchised
physicians and, 92
Healthcare organizations: "three-legged
stool" and running of, 110–11
Healthcare professionals: physician
engagement and contributions of,
7–8
Healthcare setting: conflicts in, 190
Healthcare workforce: females as
percentage of, 206
Healthy relationships: optimizing team
environment for, 253–54
Hedgehog concept (Collins), 72–73, 73,
84; knowledge skill sets for physician
leaders and, 76; physician leadership
competencies and, 75
HEDIS (Healthcare Effectiveness Data
and Information Set) targets, 175
Henkel, G., 224
Henson, Lily: insights on monetary
compensation and physician
engagement, 174
"Herding cats" expression: disparaging
use of, 34
Herzberg, F., 180
High reliability: current state behaviors
on path to, 132, *133*, 134
Hino, R., 110
Hippocratic Oath, 172
Hiring: female physicians, subconscious
biases, and, 216
Hispanic providers, 224
Hoff, Timothy, 205, 208
Hogan, R., 112
Hospitalists, 119
Hostility, 253
"How to Prepare Physicians to Be
Leaders" (Quach), 87
HR Zone: on employee engagement,
146
Huicho, L., 265
Humility, 114; conflict management and,
199; female physicians and, 212
Humor: psychological safety and, 132
Hunt, Jennifer, 206, 215
Hunter, A., 47
Hurst, T., 36

Leadership behaviors: followers' engagement and, 110

Leadership development, 277–78; deployment into leadership role and, 278; supporting programs for, 215–16

Leadership performance: poor engagement and, 146

Leadership potential: characteristics tied to, 112

Leadership roles: encouraging, for female physicians, 217; improving visibility of female physicians in, 216; nominating more women for, 218

Leadership training: offering, 102

Leading with power: conflicts of, 188

Lean management: *gemba* in, 122

Learning maps, 135, 142; contrasted with other methods, 136–37

Learning roadmaps, 136

Leaver, Bill, 238

Lee, Janelle, 119

Lee, T. H., 28, 123

Legal, compliance, and regulatory aspects of healthcare: physician leaders and, 76, 77

Leiter, M. P., 147, 155

Lencioni, Patrick M., 185, 234, 286

Libby, Russel, 56

Lifelong learning: physicians and commitment to, 66

Likert five-point scale: physician engagement rating on, 50

Line of sight: in eight-factor model, 53, 53, 54, 57–58, 285

Listening: mindful, conflict management and, 196, 201–2

Listening skills: strong, 113; successful physicians and, 68, 68

Literature on physician engagement, 27–39; consulting and advisory firms, 34–39; examining, criteria for, 27–28; many views of physician engagement in, 30–39; multiple approaches to engagement, 32–33; organizational benefit, 32; overviews of, 28; physician engagement *vs.* physician control, 34; physicians'

personal benefit, 31; problems caused by physician disengagement, 33–34; traditional views of physician engagement in, 28–29

Liu, David, 87

Location of the workplace: physician variations and, 6

Loneliness, 246

Loyalty: physician ranks and, 29

Lubarsky, D. A., 170, 172

Luthans, F., 17

Macey, W. H., 17

MacKinney, A. Clinton, 46, 171

MacLeod, L., 99

Mahoney, Diana, 38

Malpractice suits, 119

Marginalization: of female physicians, 212

Market share: enlarged underrepresented racial and ethnic minority provider ranks and, 228

Markos, S., 15

Maslach, C., 147, 155

Maslach Burnout Inventory, 147, 158

Mastery, 178; flow and heightened sense of, 152

Maternity coverage: in physician employment contracts, 209

Matheson, D. S., 47

Mayo, 179

McKinsey: on gender-diverse executive teams, 213

McWilliams, Terry R.: insights on monetary compensation and physician engagement, 176–77

Meaning: happiness and, 20; in Seligman's PERMA model of well-being, 244, 244, 246–47

Meaningfulness, 20; employee engagement and, 16, 18, 19

Measles, 80

Medical and family leave: paid, 215

Medical education: focus on individualism in, 67–68

Medical errors: as leading cause of deaths in United States, 2; physicians and challenges related to, 119

Naysayers: mining for conflict and role of, 192

Negotiation: art of, 214; supporting programs for, 215–16

New Compact, A: Aligning Physician–Organization Expectations to Transform Patient Care (Kornacki), 103

"No money, no mission" mantra: physician leaders and, 227

Nonclinical leaders: understanding physician engagement and, 121

Nonverbal cues, 194

Noseworthy, J. H., 33, 47, 119, 120

Not Just for the Money (Frey), 167, 173

Nurse practitioners: expanded scope of practice for, 254; physician engagement and contributions of, 7

Nurse residency programs: onboarding programs and lower turnover in, 275

Nurses: doctorate-level, 258; physician engagement and contributions of, 7

Obbard, A., 21

Occupational therapists: physician engagement and contributions of, 7

Onboarding: new physicians, *274*, 274–75, 287; programs, developing, 104; understanding different ways of thinking and, 277

Ongoing involvement: in eight-factor model, *53, 53,* 54 57

Operational efficiency: engagement and, 268

Operations and facility management: engagement structure and governance and, *272*

Organizational altruism: as physician leadership competency, 75, *75*

Organizational best practices: components of, 257

Organizational care: two-factor model of physician engagement and, 46, *46,* 47, 52

Organizational decision making: involving clinicians in, 100

Organizational engagement structure, considerations for, 271–80; clinical leadership structure, 271–73, *272*; different ways of thinking, 276–77; engagement as a priority, 278–80; engagement starts at the beginning, 273–74; leadership development, 277–78; onboarding new physicians, *274,* 274–75

Organizational leadership: responsibilities of clinical leadership *vs., 109*

Organizational performance: physician engagement and, 32

Organization-level interventions: in support of flourishing physicians, 256–57

Orientations, 104

Paddling a boat metaphor, engagement journey and, 93–101, 284; blade, or trust in the paddle, 94, *94,* 99–101; building trust, 103–4; helping with the what, 102–3; helping with the why, 103; three parts of the paddle in, *94,* 94–95; the what, or grip in paddle, 94, *94,* 95–97; the why, or shaft in the paddle, 94, *94,* 97–99

Paid medical and family leave, 215

Paid time off, 175

Paller, Deborah, 37

Pandit, M., 110

Papanicolas, I., 265

Paranjpe, P., 95

Paraphrasing: conflict management and, 196

Pasteur, Louis, 185

Patient and family engagement advisers: engagement structure and governance and, *272,* 273

Patient care: physician communication skills and, 90; physician engagement in, 4; process, five essential steps in, 109; two-factor model of physician engagement and, 46, *46,* 47, 52

Patient compliance: improving, 90

Patients: diversity of, and homogeneity of their providers, 228

Patient safety: burnout and, 34; physician engagement and, 32
Patient satisfaction: burnout and, 34
Patient satisfaction scores: disenfranchised physicians and, 92
Pattern recognition: mining for conflict as form of, 192
Pay-for-performance programs, 169
Pay inequities: between female and male physicians, 214
Pearl, Robert, 55
Peer review: informal, physicians' lounge and, 119
Peer support: physicians and benefits of, 119; programs, need for, 255
PERMA model of well-being (Seligman), 154, *244*, 244–47; accomplishment, 154, 244, *244*, 247; engagement, 154, 244, *244*, 245; meaning, 154, 244, *244*, 246–47; positive emotions, 154, 244, *244*, 245; relationships, 154, 244, *244*, 246
Perreira, T. A., 33, 91
Personal control theory, 3
Personal rewards: employee engagement and, 18, *19*
Peterson, S. J., 17
Pew Research, 140
Pharmacists: physician engagement and contributions of, 7
Physical therapists: physician engagement and contributions of, 7
Physician alignment, 29
Physician assistants: expanded scope of practice for, 254; physician engagement and contributions of, 7
Physician code of conduct: compacts *vs.*, 102
Physician committees, 275
Physician disengagement: burnout and, 33–34, 38–39; causes of, 263–64; problems caused by, 33–34. *See also* Disenfranchised physicians
Physician engagement, 224; art and science of, 127, 285; change management and deepening

levels of, 72–73; conflict and, 185; in consolidated healthcare organizations, 3–4; as a continuous journey, 280; definitions of, 21; differentiated from alignment, 5, 29; employee engagement as a precursor to, 13–21; employee engagement *vs.*, 48; engagement structure and governance and, 271, *272*; flow of, *266*; flow opportunities, key question on, 162; importance of, summary statement, 287–88; improving, three powerful routes to, *236*; improving healthcare and, 1; increased physician leadership and, 124; intricacies and complications of, 4–5; involvement in decision making and, 118; lack of, over several decades past, 146; lack of precise definition for, 14–15, 27, 39, 45; measurement of, 279; observations about, 2; physician control *vs.*, 34; physician leadership as key component of, 6; physicians as beneficiaries of, 265–66; at the point of care, *49*; questions about, to ponder, 1; as strategic priority, key question on, 161–62; strong, possibility of, 6–7; tolerating a conclusion *vs.* embracing it, 7; as top strategic and tactical priority, 3; viewing from two perspectives, 50, *52. See also* Cognitive diversity and healthcare leadership; Literature on physician engagement; Monetary compensation and physician engagement
Physician engagement, mistakes to avoid, 156–61; ignoring the business case, 157; lumping all physicians together, 156–57; not having an engagement plan, 158; search for the perfect survey, 157–58; short-term approach, 158–60; systemic and personal hurdles to engagement, 160–61
Physician engagement models, 45–58; eight-factor model, 51–58, *53*; two-factor model, 45–51, *46*

Physician engagement programs: organizations without, 162

Physician governance structure: sound, 268

Physician leaders: developing, 74–76; encouraging trust in leadership abilities, 101; influence on 1, 115–16; insights on monetary compensation and physician engagement, 173–80; need for more, 88; physician engagement survey conducted with, 48–51, 61–62; physician engagement survey results, 62–63; progressive, 111; in stressful times, 80–81

Physician leadership: competencies, 75, 75; enhanced physician engagement and, 124; forms of, 108; as key component of engagement, 6; need for, in transitions of care, 79, 80

Physician mystique: ongoing existence of, 5

Physician parents: pursuing leadership opportunities with, 217–18

Physicians: captain-of-the-ship sensibility among, 14; characteristics of administrators *vs., 122*; as clear monetary assets to organizations, 156, 157; complex systems and navigational skills of, 91; conflict between administrators and, 190; cost of turnover for, 273; devaluation of, 258–59; developing into hedgehogs, 72–73, *73*; development of "range" and, 83; differences among, 6; employment relationship with healthcare systems, 111; excellent, evolving qualities of, 89–92; family responsibilities and, 210–11; giving a bigger role to, 284; good leadership and personality traits of, 101; as highly engaged individuals, 4, 48, 49; as the hub of the healthcare team, 88; involving in more decisions than mere input, 116–18, *117*; management of, 228–30; new, onboarding, *274*, 274–75, 287; pay inequities and, 214; personal

benefit of engagement, 31; projected shortage of, 226; ratings and reviews of, 92; real priorities for, universality of, 139; recognizing as leaders, 284–85; resilience of, 237; showing equal respect for, across gender spectrum, 215; successful, traits in, *68*, 68–69; at the table, advantages of, 77–78; trained in depreciative thinking, 276; underrepresented minorities in world of, 224; understanding, 284; understanding culture of, 120–22; unique challenges of, 119. *See also* Female physicians; Flourishing physicians

Physicians, understanding, 65–84; change management, 70–73; cooperativeness and creativity, 67–69; never-fail attitude, 67; tendency to question everything, 69–70; unique learning style, 65–66

"Physicians and Healthcare Administrators: Friends or Foes?" (Jain), 263

Physicians as leaders, 107–24; functions of leadership and, 107

Physicians becoming leaders, 110–14; competencies, 114, *115*; desire and, 111–12; innate attributes, 112–13; skilled behaviors, 113–14

Physician shortages: widespread nature of, 2

Physician's journey: conflict and, 193

Physicians' lounge, 118

Physicians Practice blog, 55

Physicians' training: example of, 66; shortcomings in, 202

Physician workforce, US: percentage of women in, 218

Pictures: in fabric of change, 128; watercooler process and, 134. *See also* Visualization

Pink, Daniel, 21, 57, 171, 175, 181

Point of care: physician engagement at, *49*

Policy decisions: in support of flourishing physicians, 257–59

Polio, 80

Pollyannas: mining for conflict and role of, 193

Population health, 91

Positive emotions: happiness and, 20, 245; in Seligman's PERMA model of well-being, 244, *244*, 245

Positive psychology, 148, 244

Practice settings: perspective on healthcare systems and, 227

Pregnancy: income loss and unpaid leave for, 209

Presence (Cuddy), 213

Press Ganey Associates, 35; on high workforce engagement, 92; physician engagement reports, 38–39; website of, 38

Preventive care metrics, 93

Preventive medicine, 69

Price-effect theory of economics, 173

Primary care physicians, 119

Process improvement teams: engagement structure and governance and, *272*

Process management: dashboards and, 199, *199*

Production pressures, 246

Productivity: flow and, 155; physician engagement and, 37

Professionalism: conflict of, 186–88

Professional networks: onboarding and, 275

Professional practice: female physicians and challenges with, 210–11

Profitability: gender-diverse executive teams and, 213

Project planning: physician leaders and, 76, *77*

Promotions: proactive team members and, 253–54

Providers: federations of, 225; homogeneity of, and diversity of their patients, 228; racial and ethnic makeup of, 224; as underrepresented racial and ethnic minorities, 225–27, 228. *See also* Advanced practice providers; Nurses; Physician assistants ; Physicians

Psychological well-being, 154

Purpose, 56, 178

Q12 survey (Gallup), 16–17

Quach, Steve, 87, 101, 108

Quadruple aim for health systems, 257

Quality metrics: disenfranchised physicians and, 93

Race: healthcare disparities based on, 227; shifting demographics of, in United States, 228. *See also* Underrepresented racial and ethnic minorities

Racial bias: burnout and, 252

Racism, 252

"Range": development of, 83

Reciprocity: in eight-factor model, 52, *53*, 54, 56–57

Redmond, Katharine P., 283

Regina Qu'Appelle Health Region (Saskatchewan): Practitioner Staff Affairs of, 28

Registered nurses: turnover costs for, 273

Reimbursement aspects of healthcare: physician compensation and, 168

Relatedness, 57

Relationships: in Seligman's PERMA model of well-being, 244, *244*, 246

Relative value units: compensation models based on, 172; conflicting priorities for female *vs.* male physicians and, 207–8

Remuneration: conflict over models of, 187

Reporting hierarchies: streamlining, 255

Residency: skills needed to make it through, 90

Resilience, 38, 82

Respect, 270; engagement and, *267*, 268; focus groups and, 279

Retention: strong physician leadership and, 225. *See also* Turnover

Reward burnout, 155

Rewards: in eight-factor model, 52, *53*, 54, 57

Rios, I. C., 67

Roadmap for Trust: Enhancing Physician Engagement (Kaissi), 28

Role ambiguity, 254–55

About the Editor

Carson F. Dye, FACHE, president and CEO of Exceptional Leadership LLC, is a seasoned consultant with more than 40 years of leadership and management experience. Over the past 20 years, he has conducted hundreds of leadership searches for healthcare organizations, helping to fill CEO, chief operating officer, chief financial officer, and physician executive roles in health systems, academic medical centers, universities, and freestanding hospitals.

Mr. Dye has provided clients with extensive counsel in succession planning, leadership assessment, CEO evaluation, coaching, and retreat facilitation. He is certified to use the Hogan Leadership Assessment tests for evaluation, coaching, and leadership development. He also has extensive experience working with physician leaders and has helped organizations establish physician leadership development programs.

Mr. Dye has served as an executive search consultant and partner with Witt/Kieffer, TMP Worldwide, and LAI/Lamalie Associates. Prior to these roles, he was partner and director of Findley Davies's healthcare consulting division in Toledo, Ohio. He has 20 years of experience in healthcare administration, serving in executive-level positions at St. Vincent Mercy Medical Center in Toledo, the Ohio State University Wexner Medical Center in Columbus, Clermont

Mercy Hospital in Cincinnati, and Cincinnati Children's Hospital Medical Center.

A regular faculty member for the American College of Healthcare Executives (ACHE) since 1987, Mr. Dye has presented workshops for 40 state and local hospital associations. He also teaches in the ACHE Board of Governors Examination preparation course. In addition, Mr. Dye is a faculty member of the Governance Institute and has held faculty appointments at the University of Alabama at Birmingham in its executive MHA program and at The Ohio State University in its Health Services Management program.

Mr. Dye has written ten previous books, all with Health Administration Press, including three James A. Hamilton Book of the Year Award winners: *The Healthcare Leader's Guide to Actions, Awareness, and Perception*; *Developing Physician Leaders for Successful Clinical Integration*; and *Leadership in Healthcare: Values at the Top*. Other notable titles include *Exceptional Leadership: 16 Critical Competencies for Healthcare Executives* and *Winning the Talent War: Ensuring Effective Leadership in Healthcare*. The Dye–Garman Leadership Competency Model, found in *Exceptional Leadership*, has been used by many healthcare organizations as a competency model for assessment, executive selection, development, and succession planning. Mr. Dye received his BA from Marietta College and his MBA from Xavier University.

About the Contributors

Jeremy Blanchard, MD, MMM, CPE, is the system chief medical officer (CMO) of North Mississippi Health Services. Dr. Blanchard has a wide breadth of experience as a physician executive in two previous health systems. He worked as a CMO and vice president of innovation for a national healthcare consultant group and was the head of player and family wellness for a professional football organization. Clinically, Dr. Blanchard served as an intensivist in both the US Army and in rural Washington. He led his US Army team to being recognized in APACHE Outcomes as the top intensive care unit (ICU) in the nation in cost and quality, compared with 137 other similar mixed surgical/medical adult ICUs. He completed his undergraduate studies at the University of Montana, his medical studies at the University of New Mexico, and his internship, residency in internal medicine, and fellowship in critical care in the US Army. He holds a master's degree in medical management from the University of Southern California's Marshall School of Business.

Lisa M. Casey, DO, is director and founder of the family medicine residency program at Mercy Health–St. Rita's Medical Center in Lima, Ohio. Dr. Casey has taught in family medicine residencies for more than 20 years and has held various leadership and administrative positions in the hospital organizations where she has been employed. She attended medical school at Ohio University Heritage College of Osteopathic Medicine.

Robert Dean, DO, MBA, is senior vice president of performance management for Vizient, Inc. Dr. Dean leads the Vizient member connections clinical, service line, and supply networks. These networks provide a forum for clinical leaders to engage in peer-to-peer learning, hear from national subject-matter experts, and build a national professional network. Dr. Dean is also the senior leader for Vizient's Clinical Workforce Solutions portfolio, which is composed of the Nurse Residency Program, Clinical Team Insights, and the Physician and APP Onboarding Program. Previously, Dr. Dean led the Vizient Transformation of Clinical Practice Initiative team and the Vizient Practice Transformation Network. His responsibilities included providing medical leadership and expertise across a range of clinical, advisory, and nursing projects as well as the development of interprofessional practice resources. A graduate of Grand Valley State University, Dr. Dean attended the College of Osteopathic Medicine and Surgery in Des Moines, Iowa. He completed his residency in anesthesia and critical care at the University of Chicago. He has an MBA degree from the University of Michigan in Ann Arbor.

Kathleen L. Forbes, MD, CPE, FAAFP, serves as the executive vice president of the academic group for Methodist Le Bonheur Healthcare, where she oversees the majority of operations for the health system. A board-certified physician executive and family physician and a graduate of Medical College of Ohio, Dr. Forbes holds a master's degree in healthcare management from the University of Texas at Dallas. She has more than 20 years of health system executive experience, including work with Premier Healthcare, OSF Healthcare System,

TriHealth, and the University of North Texas. Dr. Forbes also founded a primary care practice, where she provided leadership and clinical care for more than 11 years, serving in health system roles during that time.

Andrew N. Garman, PsyD, is a professor and the associate chair of external relations and development in the Department of Health Systems Management at Rush University in Chicago. Through his work with the nonprofit National Center for Healthcare Leadership, Dr. Garman helps healthcare organizations develop evidence-based approaches to leadership development aimed at supporting the organizations' current and long-term strategic objectives.

Katherine A. Meese, PhD, is an assistant professor in the Department of Health Services Administration at the University of Alabama at Birmingham (UAB) and serves as the director of wellness research at UAB Medicine. Dr. Meese has more than six years of industry experience, which encompasses work in ten countries, on four continents, and includes management for a large academic medical center. Her work has been published in *Anesthesia & Analgesia*, *Health Services Management Research*, *Journal of Health Administration Education*, and other journals. Dr. Meese's research interests include physician and healthcare providers' well-being and burnout, team performance, quality and safety, and delivery models that enhance organizational learning.

Harjot Singh, MD, FAPA, is a practicing physician turned healthcare leader turned leadership adviser at the consultancy he founded, HarjotSinghMD.com. He speaks and coaches and trains clients on leadership, engagement, burnout prevention, and communication. He is a faculty member for the American College of Healthcare Executives. Dr. Singh helps healthcare leaders consider the human side of things—where the performance breakthroughs happen. He is especially passionate about making sure the lengthy time that leaders spend in their workplaces is effective and productive, as well as enjoyable.

Douglas A. Spotts, MD, FAAFP, FCPP, is a family physician with more than 25 years of practice experience. Since 2018, he has served as vice president and chief health officer (CHO) of Meritus Health in Hagerstown, Maryland. His responsibilities as CHO include overseeing population, employee, and community health initiatives and the Meritus Family Medicine Residency he launched in 2019. Past leadership experience includes the positions of chief health information officer, chief medical information officer, and medical director for a skilled nursing facility. Dr. Spotts is a past president of both the Pennsylvania Academy of Family Physicians and the American Academy of Family Physicians Foundation. He received his medical degree from the Pennsylvania State University College of Medicine and is a Fellow of the American Academy of Family Physicians and a Fellow of the College of Physicians of Philadelphia.

Kalen Stanton, MBA, is the managing director for health transformation at Root Inc., a global management consultancy. He holds an MBA from Vanderbilt University and a bachelor's degree from Furman University. Mr. Stanton previously led health system and physician practice innovation partnerships at the Advisory Board and was the chief of staff for Southwind Health Partners. Mr. Kalen focuses on the intersection of strategy and culture activation with executive leaders across the clinical continuum of providers, plans, and other key industry stakeholders. He also plays a role in many international change efforts, at Root and at the not-for-profit organization Global Connections.

 **Raúl Zambrano, MD, MS, FACHE, FAAFP,** is senior consultant for The Greeley Company. Previously Dr. Zambrano served as a senior medical director for Oak Street Health in Indiana; a chief medical officer (CMO) for Lutheran Hospital in Fort Wayne, Indiana, and for Aurora Healthcare in Kenosha, Wisconsin; the deputy and interim CMO for VISN 7 (Veterans Administration Southeast Network) in Georgia; and the chief of staff at the West Texas Veterans Administration Health Care System. Dr. Zambrano received his bachelor's degree from Columbia University, his master of science in chemistry from the Massachusetts Institute of Technology, and his MD from the College of Physicians and Surgeons at Columbia University. Dr. Zambrano proudly served in the US Army Reserve from 2001 to 2012, with four deployments.